Artificial Intelligence

Artificial Intelligence

Rise of the Lightspeed Learners

Charles Jennings

ROWMAN & LITTLEFIELD
Lanham • Boulder • New York • London

Published by Rowman & Littlefield
An imprint of The Rowman & Littlefield Publishing Group, Inc.
4501 Forbes Boulevard, Suite 200, Lanham, Maryland 20706
www.rowman.com

6 Tinworth Street, London, SE11 5AL, United Kingdom

British Library Cataloguing in Publication Information Available

Library of Congress Cataloging-in-Publication Data

Names: Jennings, Charles, 1948 author.
Title: Artificial Intelligence : rise of the lightspeed learners / Charles Jennings.
Description: Lanham : Rowman & Littlefield, an imprint of The Rowman & Littlefield Publishing Group, Inc., [2019] | Includes bibliographical references and index.
Identifiers: LCCN 2018049541 (print) | LCCN 2018060314 (ebook) | ISBN 9781538116814 (electronic) | ISBN 9781538116807 (cloth : alk. paper)
Subjects: LCSH: Artificial intelligence.
Classification: LCC Q335 (ebook) | LCC Q335 .J45 2019 (print) | DDC 006.3—dc23
LC record available at https://lccn.loc.gov/2018049541

™ The paper used in this publication meets the minimum requirements of American National Standard for Information Sciences—Permanence of Paper for Printed Library Materials, ANSI/NISO Z39.48-1992.

Printed in the United States of America

Contents

~

Foreword

Charles Jennings knows a lot about many subjects, but technology and China lead the list. This important book weaves the two together in a way that should make everyone sit up and pay attention. Like the spaceship from *The Day the Earth Stood Still*, artificial intelligence (AI) has arrived, and *Artificial Intelligence: Rise of the Lightspeed Learners* describes the moment when that alien vessel's door swings fully open.

As a veteran photojournalist, I've been an avid user of technology. In the 1960s, 1970s, and 1980s, that meant that I transmitted my photos through a telephone line, hoping that nobody interrupted the call. In the late 1990s and early 2000s, I was among the first of my generation of photographers to move from film to digital cameras. That meant a whole different way of sending pictures, and it changed the world through the speed at which news and images are delivered.

In 2013, armed only with an iPhone, I shot pictures every day for my book *David Hume Kennerly on the iPhone*. The idea was to show how quality photographs can be captured with a cell phone camera as a normal part of daily life. I've always been more interested in using advanced technology than understanding exactly how it works. In other words, I am neither a photo geek nor tech geek! What's important to me is what I see through the lens and to freeze that moment for all time in a compelling image. What I haven't been sure about is how AI will affect what I do as a professional documentarian, but with Jennings as my professor teaching this old dog some new digital tricks, I know that change is going to come.

As everyone in the news and tech business knows, something big is brewing with AI, and it has a scary edge. As author Stewart Brand said, "Once a new technology rolls over you, if you're not part of the steamroller, you're part of the road."

Charles Jennings, whom I've known and worked with for more than thirty-five years all across the planet, is a steamroller. He has been CEO of several significant Internet companies, as well as an AI company affiliated with Caltech. He believes that we all need to learn about AI, and pronto. I even detect an evangelical fervor to his mission.

Since 2014, he has been schooling me about neural networks, deep learning, Google Brain, and AI vision systems. He's particularly focused on how AI is creating the biggest technology disruption ever and how important it is that "we citizens" understand and appreciate AI. And it's not just because AI will affect our lives and our livelihoods but also because our government will soon be making crucial decisions about this powerful technology. We citizens cannot afford to remain ignorant of its ramifications.

Jennings has adapted a naturally intelligent approach to explaining AI—and it's not an easy subject. It helps that he has many personal stories to tell. Jennings and I are intrepid world travelers. We have worked together in China, Thailand, Japan, Hollywood, and Washington, DC. Of all those places, China was always our favorite. It's no surprise to me that a key focus of this book is about what is happening today in the People's Republic of China. Chairman Xi Jinping is placing a huge bet on AI, as this book makes clear. Given the power of AI technology, combined with Chinese clout, this is something that should alarm us. It is helpful to have Jennings, who has worked extensively in both Silicon Valley and Beijing, as our guide through this not-so-artificial minefield. I first traveled to China in 1972, just a few months after Richard Nixon made his historic trip. On that journey to Beijing and Shanghai, I was able to photograph Premier Zhou Enlai. Something Zhou declared resonates and underscores why we shouldn't remain ignorant about the Chinese and their motives. Zhou said, "One of the delightful things about Americans is that they have absolutely no historical memory." He may have been joking, but he has been proven correct many times. China has taken advantage of an American public that is often shockingly unfamiliar with earlier world events.

Chinese history refresher: The People's Republic of China, lest we forget, is ruled by a tough-minded Marxist Communist Party. It operates under a whole different set of values and rules than we normally do here in America. Jennings uses his background in China to imagine a decisive United States versus China AI derby in the decade ahead, the outcome of which will affect all our individual lives and those of our children and their children.

On a day-to-day basis, Jennings's stories about AI might not be the kind that make the nightly news, but their cumulative impact could be more profound than any of the wars I have covered. *Artificial Intelligence: Rise of the Lightspeed Learners* features news you can use provided by an original Internet pioneer. Charles Jennings has written an important introductory guide to the strange and compelling new world of AI. He thinks it could very well upset the current world order and unquestionably will change our lives. He believes that AI will be bigger than the Internet, and as a former CEO of companies in both the Internet and AI sectors, he knows the turf.

This book is a colorful journey into the land of AI told by an excellent storyteller and a call to action by someone who understands disruptive technology. It is must-read literature. After you have finished, please send a copy of this book to your favorite member of Congress and anyone else whose opinion might matter as we begin to face the existential challenges AI presents.

David Hume Kennerly
White House photographer, Pulitzer Prize winner

Acknowledgments

These days, building a paper book is rather retro, but dedicated people around the world still keep cranking them out. The book publishing industry continues to capture first-class talent, up and down its ranks, and supplies us all with more and better quality books than we probably deserve.

So the first tip of my Stetson hat—a gift from my twin daughters, Faith and Nayana Jennings—goes to the U.S. book publishing industry, and to my own stalwart publisher, Rowman & Littlefield. Since 1977, publishing companies have hired me to write books for them, including some big name houses. Rowman & Littlefield is the best publisher I've worked with, hands down. Kudos especially to the well-oiled team at Rowman & Littlefield that produced this book, including: my editor Suzanne Staszak-Silva, production editor Andrew Yoder, copyeditor Niki Guinan, and cover designer Devin Watson.

Frankly, all my experiences with publishers and book agents have been pretty good. I've worked in movies, high-tech, gov-tech, and AI, but none of these industries have smarter, nicer, more honest people book publishing. Keep up the great work, all you book peddlers!

I must of course acknowledge the contribution of my good friend, Pulitzer Prize winner and super salesman, David Hume Kennerly. His foreword to this book got my wife's coveted, and rare, two-thumbs-up approval. David helped me in a variety of ways with this book: connecting me with Scott Parazynski, the MD astronaut; setting up my day with Jon Meacham; brainstorming about our time in Asia in the 1980s and about China today. In the '80s, David was an Asia-loving rock-star photog for *Time* when it ruled print media; I was a

Hollywood line producer working in Asia for Warner Bros., Paramount, and others. But as they say, what happens in Kanchanaburi stays in Kanchanaburi.

Another vital contributor to this book was my granddaughter, Ash Olsen. Raised in Oregon, she had the chutzpah to study math at Queen Mary College, London, and graduate with honors in statistical analysis. She had a few weeks downtime after graduation and before returning to America, so naturally I hired her to help me get my facts, citations, and end notes straight. She turned out to be an enormous help, at precisely the right time.

Without the work of my agent, Jeff Herman, this book would not have been possible. A tired cliche, but literally true in this case.

A special tip of the Stetson to all who directly contributed AI-related content, including notably Mat Jennings, Andrej Szenasy, David Barton, Ash Olsen, Scott Parazynski, Christine Jennings, Max Tegmark, Pete O'Dell, Jon Meacham, Eric Pulmer, Dmitri Tuzoff, and Willard Ptotsman.

Finally, I am most grateful for the continuing love and support of my fifteen fellow members of the Portland Jennings clan—especially my wife of 46 years, Christine Jennings, who has learned how to be a writer's perfect companion.

To all of you, my heartfelt thanks.

CHAPTER ONE

~

An Uncanny Ability to Learn

"The only thing we know about the future is that it will be different."

—Peter Drucker

After decades of academic captivity, AIs have escaped their lab cages and are swarming out into the real world. With consequences for all of us. Artificial intelligence (AI) comes in many forms, sizes, and algorithms. Today, you'll find AIs in factories, schools, hospitals, banks, police stations, and the chip in your iPhone. They're the eyes of self-driving cars, the speech of Siri and Alexa, the brains of autonomous drone warfighters. They're the wizards behind weather forecasts, the intelligence that guides robotic hands assisting in colon surgery.[1] AIs handle real-time scheduling for the multibillion-dollar vacation rental market and do the matchmaking at Match.com. The hottest new online games have AI players always available as a clever opponent, 24/7. An AI has written a Grimm's-style fairy tale (*The Princess and the Fox*), and the first AI-enabled toothbrushes clean teeth intelligently. The business plan for Elon Musk's next company, after PayPal, Tesla, SpaceX et al., is to embed AI chips in humans. For medical purposes only—at least for now.

On NASA's Mars 2020 mission, advanced AIs will autonomously pilot four rovers exploring lava tubes on Mars.[2] An AI-led mission to Alpha Centauri is planned for 2069. Astrophysicists even talk of AIs exploring virtually the entire cosmos. *2001: A Space Odyssey*'s HAL computer would be proud.

As a high-tech industry, artificial intelligence couldn't be hotter. AI tops all current venture capital (VC) investment categories and leads corporate research and development (R&D) spending. Amazon, Microsoft, Google, Facebook, Intel, Apple, and IBM all have big internal AI groups, and each is in the same elite, clubby AI alliance.[3] On Silicon Valley résumés, AI gigs are the sexiest bullets. AI engineers are in such demand that tech giants are buying premarket AI startups just for their employees—paying up to $10 million per head—not per engineer but per *employee*, from CEO to front-desk receptionist. And this is just in the United States. If anything, China is making even more aggressive investments in AI start-ups.

AIs are flying high, but with serious baggage. For example, some very smart people believe that an AI might someday become the next Joseph Stalin. Investment bankers (Goldman Sachs) and consulting firms (Deloitte, PWC, McKinsey) are predicting that one-third of the current American workforce will lose their jobs to AIs in the decade ahead. And why are China and Russia suddenly so gung ho on AI, and what should we be doing about it?

Don't look now, but there are many fewer people these days working in auto factories, lettuce fields, stock exchanges, distribution warehouses, call centers, air-traffic-control towers, clerical desks, customer support centers, and most retail big box stores. Have you noticed? It's not that some strange force has called these workers to another world. They've being replaced by AIs.

Amazon Go—the world's first fully automated grocery store—is up and running in Seattle, with no human sales clerks. Shoppers download an Amazon Go app, hop an Uber, fill out their list in the car, arrive, gather up their groceries, and leave. Quoting an Amazon Go ad, "No lines. No checkout. Just grab and go." Not good news for retail clerks.

The trend of machines taking human jobs is not just going to continue; it's going to explode, like mortars across Kabul, causing nasty disruptions and leaving real victims. The people losing jobs this time will not only drive trucks and work in factories, but they'll also practice law, prepare tax returns, manage personal wealth portfolios, teach university classes, and even practice certain kinds of medicine. Expect to see radiologists, actuaries, commodities traders, paralegals, marketing consultants, professors, pharmacists, and more as collateral carnage (economically speaking) lying by the roadside.

An AI-driven job-market disruption is coming; the only question is *when*. If the job losses described here are spread out over two generations, no one will much notice. If they're in full swing by 2025, as most I-banks and consulting companies predict, Western economies will be rocked to the core. Robots taking over auto workers' jobs in America, slowly over two decades, was a big deal. It caused an economic disruption in the upper Midwest that helped Donald Trump get elected president of the United States. Who knows what would happen if AIs replace half of all lawyers and accountants?

Part of the problem is that Silicon Valley culture has long regarded lost jobs as wet garbage. "Move fast and break things" is its near-official motto—a sentiment that does not lead to much empathy when new tech kills a job category. I can't tell you how many times in the valley I've heard some variation of "Those bookstore owners (or travel agents or cab drivers) should have seen it coming," which provides the justification for the standard Silicon Valley response when new tech creates job losses: "Hey, deal with it." This time, with AI, the technology community must do better. This time we must all do better.

This book is less about the future moral and philosophical implications of artificial intelligence—a favorite publishing theme of late—than it is about the fact that AIs are here to stay. Multitudes of them of various kinds, swarming everywhere. AIs are part of an unprecedented disruption, the invasion of new forms of intelligence on earth. This book is largely an attempt to make sense of this invasion, in social, political, and economic terms.

Unlike most AI books, this one comes with neither neat equations nor definitive solutions to artificial intelligence issues. Rather, it is a series of stories, explorations, and questions—even a bit of humor and poetry. My task as narrator, as I see it, is not only to introduce you to this new species, to these machines that can learn with such extraordinary speed and power, but also to get you *thinking* about them, as if they really do matter, now, in your life. My goal is to encourage you to act, as a worker, as a consumer, and as a citizen, in ways that will help shape AI's future, and your own.

There is debate about the number of new jobs AI will create but almost none about the tremendous number it will kill. Over time, every task that can be routinized will be, even if it involves higher-order cognition. Predicting the timing of specific job market disruptions is always tricky, as I show in chapter 4, "Truckin' in Flip-Flops," about self-driving trucks. But the job losses will keep on coming. One interesting hit already has come to Goldman Sachs' currency trading division, where human employment is down 99 percent since 2010 and where AIs and computers now do almost all the work (see chapter 10, "The AI Casino").

Many AI experts believe jobs will not be the only things AIs take from us. AI may become, as James Barrat titled his important 2013 book on artificial intelligence, "our final invention"—not the last invention on Earth; just the final one invented solely by humans. In 2017, Google's CEO Sundar Pichai announced that his company's AutoML unit had successfully taught its machine-learning software how to program new machine-learning software on its own, and it does so better than humans do in some cases.[4] The *machines-programming-machines* era of AI development has begun and will no doubt gain strength dramatically in the decade ahead. When it comes to invention, today's AIs are like teenagers with learning permits, teens who soon will become the young adult drivers of innovation.

But the notion of AIs someday supplanting all human innovation is, in my opinion, as unlikely as it is dreary. We humans are and will remain indispensable to the civilization we have created and built, so long as we have the will to do so and so long as we exercise a modicum of control over these new AI creatures. Still, I worry about the rise of these *mathsects*,[5] as I sometimes like to think of them. I worry that they are spinning us faster and faster toward some chaos we cannot control. But I also believe it is equally possible that AIs might emerge as a kind of technological superhero, fighting at our side for truth, justice, and the American way. I have been an entrepreneur all my life, so optimism runs in my veins.

My wife is a beekeeper, and I help her a bit. We've kept bees in our meadow alongside Cedar Mill Creek outside Portland, Oregon, for about a decade now. AIs are like smart bees that feed on ones and zeros, on data. When well-fed, they have the potential to produce the sweetest honey and most nutritious royal jelly—or sting you like a pissed-off scorpion.

I entered the AI industry (sans bee suit) in 2014. I had what in Zen is called beginner's mind; in Silicon Valley lingo, a blank whiteboard—not necessarily a compliment. The first two things I learned were:

1. AIs today are a primitive, immature species, but even so, they are learning at rates orders of magnitude faster than we humans ever have.
2. Just like bees, once AIs start swarming, no one can say for certain where they're going to land.

AIs are the most important technology of my lifetime. I say this having witnessed the rise of the Internet firsthand as the founder of two Internet companies in the 1990s. But the Internet is small change compared to having these lightspeed learners buzzing around.

Artificial intelligence is not a *thing*; it's an ingredient in everything. Or, more properly, it's a class of things that have this in common: *an uncanny ability to learn*. Hence the *lightspeed learner* designation in the title of this book, a term I coined to underscore the amazing learning capabilities of AIs.

Over the past several years, the latest generation of AIs—the ones doing odd things like deep learning, Monte Carlo tree searches, tensor processing, and so forth—have been absorbing knowledge and acquiring skills in record time. Chapter 2, "Not Your Father's AIs," explores how these latest AIs learn, but meanwhile, consider the case of DeepMind versus Go.

DeepMind is an AI research arm in Google's Alphabet soup; Go is the oldest and most popular board game in the world, invented 2,500 years ago in China. The DeepMind team built various versions of a game-playing computing system over the course of several years. The first version, AlphaGo, was supervised and trained by humans, and after six months of digesting rules, studying expert moves, and playing human opponents, it was able to beat the best Go player in Europe. Three months later, it beat a prominent Korean Go master in front of a huge audience watching on Asian television.

Then, in December 2017, the DeepMind team launched a variant called AlphaZero, which *taught itself* to play Go, as well as chess and shogi, in a couple of days.[6] It did this by digesting the rules of these games and then playing itself over and over. Without any human-supervised training, AlphaZero was able to beat AlphaGo and every other top game-playing computer in all three games. AlphaZero supassed sixty-plus years' playing of computer chess from scratch in less than a day.

The performance improvement from AlphaGo in 2016 to AlphaZero in 2017—accomplished in reduced training time with nearly complete machine autonomy—is emblematic of the progress AIs are making in many fields right now. AIs are not just learning; they are also learning at ever faster rates. This undisputed fact has sparked a furious global debate.

Bout of the Heavyweights

In one corner, such icons as Elon Musk and Bill Gates issue doomsday warnings. The late Stephen Hawking in 2014 said, "Success in creating AI would be the biggest event in human history. Unfortunately, it might also be the last." He also said, "[T]he development of full artificial intelligence could spell the end of the human race."[7] Musk has said that AI could become an "immortal dictator from which we never escape."[8] Even Sergey Brin, cofounder of Google and current president of Alphabet, Google's parent company, says, "We are on a path [with AI] that we must tread with deep responsibility, care, and humility."[9] In the other corner, Ray Kurzweil, Jeff Bezos, Mark Zuckerberg, and most rank-and-file AI engineers insist that artificial intelligence is the greatest invention since fire, it will be a tremendous boon to humanity, and there really is nothing we should worry our pretty little heads about. The one thing both camps agree on is that AIs will soon become much more powerful than they are today.[10]

The People's Republic of China (PRC), too, is suddenly swarming with AIs. Artificial intelligence has become the PRC's number 1 economic and technological priority. In a national campaign modeled after its hugely successful high-speed rail program, the Chinese government is funding AI studies in universities, launching AI research labs, and orchestrating investments in private AI companies. It also has an important initiative to bring its AI companies into government R&D programs, including for military defense and homeland security. SenseTime, a Beijing AI computer vision start-up with several Americans in its senior ranks, received more than $500 million in PRC investment its first two years. One of China's hottest TV shows is a poker tournament where humans play against an AI program known as Old Poker Master. Old Poker Master always wins.

Rumors abound of American AI engineers getting offers of $500,000 a year or more to work in China. Chairman Xi Jinping wants and expects China to become the AI world leader. Given Xi's resolve—and the unbelievable amount of personal data the Chinese state controls without privacy constraints—I wouldn't necessarily bet against the People's Republic becoming the AI leader by 2030, which is Xi Jinping's oft-stated goal (see chapter 7, "Uncle Sam versus Red Star"). Meanwhile, Vladimir Putin keeps shouting, "Whoever leads in AI will rule the world!" Russia is not a major AI player, except in defense, space, and election hacking.

Today, North America is AI's clear epicenter. Of the top one hundred AI experts in the world, ninety-five are citizens of the United States or Canada.[11] The US economy still spends far more on AI research than any other, and American-owned companies continue to set all the global performance benchmarks.

France, under the leadership of Field Prize–winning mathematician Cedric Villani (known as the Lady Gaga of math for his eccentric attire), has recently embarked on a compelling—if as yet underfunded—new national AI strategy. This strategy, called AI for Humanity, could become a model of government policy for AI development and governance around the world.

Militarily, the United States leads, but China is gaining on us, with both an aggressive government commitment to AI and robust support from its commercial high-tech companies. Russia, with little commercial high tech, does have excellent math education and is committed to huge military spending for AI research and development. Israel, France, the United Kingdom, and ninety other countries have some form of military AI testing and training underway. The plan for most of these armies is to relegate the most dangerous missions to AIs and robots. It's still early in what will almost certainly become a full-fledged AI arms race, but we can soon expect to see autonomous drones executing sophisticated OODA loops against each other in military engagements without a human in sight.[12] Hopefully, this will be just in joint military exercises, but perhaps in actual combat.

Today's AIs can see, speak, learn, and (with some robots) think on their feet. Stunning AI performance breakthroughs are reported monthly. As I write, the United States—through the efforts of such stalwarts as DARPA, MIT, Caltech, and IBM, along with new kids like Google, Amazon, and Facebook—is responsible for most breakthroughs. Canada is the center of much progress in the powerful deep-learning wing of AI, and Cambridge, England, home of Google's DeepMind, would also get a star on any AI world map.

However, unlike France, China, and Russia and despite its continued dominance in the field, the United States has no national AI policy and no AI laws or regulations (outside of vertical domain rules, such as for flying drones). The fact that the United States still, late into the second decade of the twenty-first century, has no national plan for AI is both remarkable and negligent. Perhaps neither the leaders of American government nor most of the people who elect them are aware that a highly disruptive AI storm is headed their way. And they certainly must not be considering what it would mean if the United States were no longer the dominant force behind this storm.

Writing in the 1990s, British author David Ellis observed the beginnings of an epic battle between man and machine, with the latter emerging as a new intelligent species, one that would eventually compete with humans for what Ellis called the "stewardship of Earth." He dubbed this new species *Machina sapiens*, the thinking machine.[13] Twenty years later, when searching for terms that give these new kinds of machines their due, *Machina sapiens* still works.

A century from now, the upcoming 2020s will likely be known as the period in history when *Machina sapiens* gained a foothold on planet Earth. No matter that we humans gave rise to this invasion, the important point is that somehow, out of the global noosphere, a new species arose with an intelligence to rival our own.[14] This species is already beating us at our own games (chess, Jeopardy, and Go); managing our most sophisticated global financial exchanges; flying autonomously through the air; and doing amazing backflips on land.[15]

One of this species, a three-hundred-pound, cone-shaped robot on wheels working as a security guard at a Georgetown shopping mall, recently committed suicide, if you believe the social media meme. What's indisputable is that a robot mall cop rolled into a fountain and "drowned"—*drowning* in this case being a synonym for "shorted out its electrical circuits."

Of course, this robot did not take its own life. Actually, it is important we not fall into the Hollywood trap of anthropomorphizing AIs. AIs are not evil monsters (*Terminator*), subtle lovers (*Her*), or cuddly garbage collectors (*Wall-E*). They are—so far—idiot savants with a real talent for crunching data. Multiplying two eight-figure numbers in their "heads" takes a nanosecond; solving a quadrennial equation takes a tad longer. What matters is not that AIs can do math; it's what they can do with it. They use mathematics—the formulas in their little "algo" heads—to *learn*.

I knew none of this back in 2014, when I signed up as CEO of a new AI company. The idea for the company came from Caltech and the Jet Propulsion Lab (JPL). These actual rocket scientists had some AI patents and a bit of experimental software left over from the Mars rover program and were looking for an "engineer/executive" who could commercialize this tech and take it to market. Instead, they found me.

I'm no engineer. I do not have a PhD in math, physics, or computer science—not even close. Aside from reading Arthur C. Clarke, William Gibson, and Ray Kurzweil, I knew nothing about AI, but I've founded and led a few software companies and have written several books on technology. Somehow, I passed muster with Caltech, and we got into the AI business together.

I was not looking for a job. I was living my version of the good life in my hometown of Portland, Oregon. I was doing a little consulting; serving on a few boards; helping my wife with the garden and her bees; and teaching my tall, stocky grandson how to use his butt to rebound like Charles Barkley. Then a good friend from Los Angeles called.

"I need your help," he said. He explained that he was helping a Caltech professor commercialize AI computer vision intellectual property (IP) developed at JPL. The AI part intrigued me. Ultimately, I jumped back into the saddle of another high-tech start-up, this time, for the first time, in the emerging AI industry. I had to learn as much as I could as quickly as possible about the science and technology of artificial intelligence. Fortunately, I had good teachers.

During my AI studies, I discovered that AIs can become immensely powerful, even powerful enough (theoretically) to destroy Earth—and not just Earth, by the way, but also the entire universe. In a famous thought experiment, a superintelligent AI is programmed to optimize the production of paper clips.[16] Its raison d'être is to make more and more paper clips by any and all means necessary. Because it is superintelligent, this AI understands chemistry, biology, physics, finance, and human behavior. It knows how to accumulate money and uses the new wealth it acquires to build ever more paper clip factories. Eventually, this AI realizes that atoms of all kinds can be turned into paper clips. Spoiler alert: The experiment doesn't end well for the universe.

My main tasks as CEO of this AI company were to raise money and recruit a team to build a practical image-recognition platform based on four JPL artificial intelligence patents. The methodology of these patents was a type of computer vision that emulated the jerky saccadic sight we humans use. One key benefit of this method is that it enables pattern recognition without laborious training and huge data training sets. As such, our tech was a part of cutting-edge AI methodology called "unsupervised learning." A number of experts, including notably Yann LeCun at Facebook, feel that unsupervised learning is the future of the commercial AI market.[17] In the end, unsupervised learning provided a compelling vision, but it proved a difficult assignment technologically, especially for a start-up competing with Google and the like.

While attempting to commercialize the Caltech IP, I learned that AIs are smart but far from perfect. The algorithms that provide the basis of AI surprised me, both with their brilliance and their stupidity. After two decades working in the enterprise software industry, I was absolutely shocked at their small size. The JPL algorithm we used for face recognition consisted of only 1,000 lines of code! The hero application at my last software company had *400,000 lines*. Yet, the Caltech algorithm was clearly more intelligent.

I learned that with artificial neural networks (ANNs)—the most common platform for machine learning—what matters is not the number of lines of code but the quality of neural operations, such as curating data effectively, then feeding these data to the AI, and conducting statistical analysis on the results; implementing feed-forward and feedback loops; and tweaking an ANN in the way a NASCAR mechanic might, dozens of times, before a big race.

AI isn't just the next PC, Internet, smartphone, or cloud. It's all these rolled together and then some—the mother of all tech disruptions.

I like to think of the difference between software and AI this way: In traditional enterprise software development, you design a blueprint; write code; and, except for whatever bugs are found, safely predict the results. With machine learning, the first result of the development process is the ability to start testing new hypotheses for process improvement. Even with highly experienced AI researchers, approximately 90 percent of their hypotheses fail to create any improvement. Sometimes improvement comes more by accident than design. In traditional software, development proceeds until reaching a finish line called "code freeze." In our AI lab, the testing and quality analysis (QA) process never stopped. I got the feeling that ANNs were not so much programmed as organically grown. And in a very real sense, the most common outputs of an ANN are surprises.

As I got to know the AI industry better over several years, certain other things became clear:

1. **AI is accelerating rapidly.** AIs are prime examples of the law of accelerating returns, popularized by AI impresario Ray Kurzweil, which states: Not only is technology changing quickly, the *rate* of technology change is also accelerating. Yesterday's powerful new tech is being used to build tomorrow's even more powerful new tech. The cherry on top of all this acceleration is AI. With deep learning and other new machine learning methods, powerful FPGA[18] semiconductors designed especially for AI, cloud data centers offering extraordinary parallelization and scalability, and sensors collecting more data in a massively connected Internet of Things, we are now entering a perfect AI storm. Technology change is ever faster, racing like Usain Bolt, and meanwhile, the techno-geek financial industrial complex, from Google to GE to Goldman Sachs, is in full hype-cycle mode, heralding the imminent arrival of the biggest tech boom in history. And it's all just getting started.
2. **No one knows exactly where AI is headed.** The AI community is surprisingly and refreshingly open and collaborative. AI experts agree on a great deal, notably that current AI is far from the "general intelligence" we humans have. But there is much internal debate, as well. How will humans and AIs work together in future? Will AI be a job destroyer or a job creator? Will we reach the tipping point, called the technological singularity, when machines gain human-style intelligence? And if so, when? Could AIs become an existential threat to humanity? There are no consensus answers to these questions among scientists and engineers.
3. **We can all agree AI will be huge.** Except to call AI huge is to miss the point. AI isn't just the next PC, Internet, smartphone, or cloud. It's all these rolled together and then some—the mother of all tech disruptions. In recent human history, the closest things to AI were the discovery of electricity and the subsequent electrification of America in the late nineteenth and early twentieth centuries. The discovery of

nuclear energy and development of nuclear weapons and nuclear energy comes close, but ultimately, nuclear is a much narrower technology than AI and, with any luck, one whose role on Earth will remain far less significant.

4. **AI will affect all of us.** You, me, and Bobby McGee, billions of Chinese, restaurant owners in France, teenagers in India and Africa, elderly in rest homes, children in day care, women executives in Shanghai, transgender bloggers in Chicago, heads of state, kick-ass surgeons, social network divas, you who are reading this book, and I who am writing it. By 2030, AIs will be like ants at a summer picnic the day the honey spilled. They will be everywhere, affecting everyone.

There are real risks in all this. I examine the most prominent of these risks throughout the course of this book. One risk seldom discussed is that of leaving all ethical and public policy decisions about AI to my friends and colleagues in the high-tech industry, to us techies.

AI is a unique and powerful force, and we techies love unique and powerful forces. *May the force be with you.* This love of cool tech warps our vision, which is why AI needs the "force" of American democracy and culture to be programmed into its algorithms, optimization protocols, and reward functions—but that's getting ahead of our story.

In the 1990s, I started two Internet security companies and got a chance to study encryption, online privacy, and cybersecurity from inside the business world. It became clear to me that, unless security began to be designed into Internet systems at the development stage, our entire IT infrastructure would become highly vulnerable to cyberattacks. I cowrote a book based on this theory, published in 2000.[19] In it, much space was devoted to giving consumers detailed instructions on how to protect themselves from cyberattacks and identity theft. The rest of the book was a call for high-tech industry and government leaders to build more privacy and security assurance into tech products and services. In this latter effort, my coauthor and I were spectacularly unsuccessful. There are *still* not enough security controls being built into network systems, nearly twenty years later.[20]

Cybersecurity is a pernicious problem today because twenty-five years ago, when we were building all our exciting Internet and enterprise IT systems, safety was an afterthought. Security controls were either bolted on after installation or patched in after a breach. We knew enough, technologically, in the late 1990s to have greatly reduced the cyberthreat to our systems in the future, but security never became a priority—not really.[21] This failure to build cybersecurity protection and enforceable opt-in privacy policies into our core Internet and IT systems has led to enormous data losses now, twenty years later.

The decade from 2020 to 2030 will be to AI safety and security what the 1990s were to cybersecurity. Can we, this time, get it right? Will we prioritize safety and security from the beginning or just attempt once again to install chains on the gates once the AIs are out of the barn? Will we insist that *Machina sapiens* have human-style ethics? Can we keep even cybersecure AIs from running amok, out of control? Big questions we all must ask—and ones we absolutely cannot leave merely to scientists, engineers, venture capitalists, and CEOs.

Though the rise of the Internet in the 1990s in some ways parallels the rise of AI today, this twenty-first-century AI revolution is unlike any previous technology upheaval. For the first time, we humans are not the only ones building and operating the cool new tools. The fact that machines, at least some of the time, will learn, work, and reproduce on their own changes everything.

The timing of this latest tech disruption is hardly ideal. Global warming, North Korea, Brexit, stateless refugees, the ongoing Russian hack-a-thon, the opioid crisis, global terrorism, white supremacy, species extinctions, identity theft, and a score of other first-class problems compete daily for the attention of fair-minded believers in science and human progress. In light of the great many global problems we face, managing machine intelligence can seem well down the priority list. Yet AIs could become crucial new tools in confronting climate change, diagnosing chronic disease, and solving a myriad of other problems. They could also become dangerous weapons in the hands of rogue states and terrorists. In several worst-case scenarios, AI machines themselves could become apex predators and eliminate humans altogether, which is why it is so crucial that the general public—especially those who still believe in science and respect facts—learn as much as possible about AI as quickly as possible.

In the decade ahead, we all will be riding in AI-driven cars, visiting AI doctors, talking to AI sales reps, and negotiating mortgages with AI bankers. We'll be educating our children and ourselves in classes taught by expert AIs. Career decisions will be shaped by the giant sucking sound of AI automation replacing human jobs. Small businesses will obtain a decisive competitive edge by being AI savvy—or fail because a competitor mastered AI first. We'll be choosing between different AI information services and will want to know a great deal about the privacy and security implications of each (see chapter 8, "The Porn Star's Deepfake and Other Security Paradoxes").

AIs will find cures for more types of cancers and routinely enable paraplegics to walk with the aid of exoskeletal robots. AIs and their holographic and augmented reality friends will create new immersive worlds of sound and vision. AIs will be trading stocks and managing supersmart, industry-specific cryptocurrencies on the blockchain. They will even be settling factual disputes in Congress and in courts and perhaps play major new roles in democratic governments.

Technology, especially AI technology, is racing ahead of laws, social norms, school curricula, and the comprehension of the great majority of people on earth. This is healthy neither for the high-tech industry nor for the general population. AIs are speeding downhill ahead of their skis, and the black diamond runs are just beginning.

Ready or not, AIs are invading our world. As a result of this invasion, a host of new social, economic, and ethical questions are finding their way onto center stage in modern life, including:

- What can Western democracies do to prevent a global AI arms race?
- How do we prevent the subversion of journalism by extremists using AIs to create deepfakes and other patently false "news" stories?[22]
- How much should AIs know about us?
- What are the consequences if an autonomous AI breaks the law—and who pays?
- Do we need an AI regulatory commission, of the kind established by President Truman to manage nuclear weapons?
- How do we manage AI today so that it doesn't get out of control in the future?

These are not easy questions. I certainly don't have all the answers. I'm not in the Elon Musk, Stephen Hawking, AIs-could-kill-us-all camp, at least not yet, and I believe AIs can still become powerful tools for good. But I am absolutely convinced the only way AI can become a boon and not some deadly I-bomb is if we start working together, all of us, on the challenge of safely integrating this powerful new technology into our society and our lives.

The truth is, the engineers building this stuff, the smartest of them, don't want the responsibility of making social and political decisions about AI on their own. As one said to me at an AI conference, "*Citizens* are our most important demographic." It is crucial that the general public learn about AI and become familiar with the pressing and sometimes troubling issues AI is raising, which is why I wrote this book, and with a sense of urgency. It's also why my grandson will have to wait until next basketball season to learn the art of the Karl Malone elbow.

We in America must either engage together and control AI or watch as the Chinese—or out-of-control machines—do it for us. And we must engage in the old-fashioned way: as citizens in a democracy, working together, with government in charge.

This book has been written with the United States of America as a focus for two reasons. First, what happens in America will have great impact on what happens with AI everywhere. Second, as an American who has spent years living and traveling outside America, I have the expat's love of the homeland. Hard as it has been recently, I remain optimistic about America and convinced that the United States can—even must—play an essential role in the ongoing AI invasion.

Once Americans understand that a new national policy for AI is essential to preserving jobs, continuing economic prosperity, and saving our collective human asses, we will again raise the flag and make it clear that getting AIs under better national management is essential for national security. I fully expect an AI-focused political movement will follow—perhaps a modest one, maybe something larger. Maybe this movement can even use the forces of science and technology to create friendly political AIs—AIs that bring the power of unbiased truth seeking to our political commons, to strengthen *we the people* and reclarify our national purpose (see chapter 9, "AIs in the Government Henhouse").

Regardless of what happens nationally or globally, we all must go on living our lives, lives that increasingly will have AIs—those pesky, brilliant little mathsects—popping up like fireflies in an Ozark summer. At the end of this book, I suggest a few specific strategies for survival in the age of AI. Some of these are personal strategies; others are for businesses, nonprofits, and political groups. My objective in writing these strategies is to get you thinking about how to put AIs to work in your life—without having to learn how to write machine learning code.

Political and strategic suggestions aside, this book is mostly about my journey into the mysterious world of artificial intelligence and my reflections on what I discovered. The writer in me hopes you find it a good read.

As I said, I'm no AI expert, just a concerned citizen who has seen AI up close and who, as a result, hopes that my stories and insights can make a contribution to the great global AI debate. My bias is toward the American government playing a major role in keeping AI safe and humane—starting with state and city governments, not federal agencies (see chapter 12, "The Way Forward"). Perhaps we can even put AIs to work for us in the urgent need to remake America herself, in the spirit of liberty and justice for all, without regard for race, color, creed, or algorithmic orientation.

CHAPTER TWO

~

Not Your Father's AI

> "In the game of life . . . there are three players at the table: human beings, nature and machines. I am firmly on the side of nature. But nature, I suspect, is on the side of the machines."[1]
>
> —George Dyson, *Darwin Among the Machines*

Blockchain, augmented reality, 3-D printing, nanotech, Internet of Things, apps of every description, AIs exploding everywhere. The constant parade of twenty-first-century information technologies can be daunting—dizzying, even. In every corner of the modern world, the pace of technological change is accelerating. Data are produced and stored in numbers reaching the quadrillions (1 quadrillion bytes = 1 petrabyte). Tech-driven markets of every kind are spinning faster than a PR engine on election night. Only one thing is certain: *The rate of technological change will never be this slow again.* Think about that for a moment. Discouraging, isn't it?

As a civilization, we've been pouring money and manpower into digital systems for nearly a century, and our investment is paying off. The GAFA dudes (Google, Amazon, Facebook, Apple) have driven their market valuations to unprecedented levels and are doubling down on AI investments in hopes of riding yet another giant tech wave. Microsoft, Comcast, AT&T, Verizon, IBM, and others have seats at the AI table, playing with healthy piles of chips. Huge infrastructure investment continues at such semiconductor companies as Intel, Samsung, and NVIDIA, where most of the focus these days is to prepare for the era of AI and blockchain. Meanwhile,

Internet of Things sensors, online commerce sites, and social networks are exploding as well. Global clouds connect all this constant *activation energy* (to borrow a neural networking term) and provide computing power the way utility companies supply electricity.

For decades, we've invested heavily in a massive digital technology accelerator—and guess what? It's *really* accelerating, careening ahead in ways no one fully understands. It is as if technology itself has become a self-driving car that runs faster with each passing mile. Today's intelligent machines are not sentient, and outside of whatever narrow specialization they have been trained to excel in, they are not even all that smart. But they are *lightspeed learners*—machines capable of getting smarter and smarter, with limits that are as yet unknown—machines capable, even, of rewriting their own code. Of remaking themselves.

While this does not mean we're racing inevitably toward some dystopian hell filled with killer robots, AI spies, and heartless cyborgs, it does suggest that a bit of caution is in order. Unless you'd actually prefer to be the chopped liver, you need to become a lightspeed learner yourself, at least about AI. Your financial worth may well depend on it. Honestly, your freedom and your life may depend on it because we have never before dealt with technology this powerful or mysterious.

"Who Are These Guys?"

Andrej Szenasy, head of neural operations for an AI start-up, has an hour to kill while waiting for his wife to pick him up from work. He's spent the day analyzing statistics related to the performance of his company's new face-recognition (FR) algorithm, and he's ready for a break. As Andrej will tell you, all FR systems consist of three parts: a large database of stored images ("the gallery"), new images coming into the system for recognition ("the probes"), and the artificial intelligence algorithm linking the right probes with the right gallery image.

In the old days, around 2010, face recognition was all dots, lines, and vectors. It relied on measurements between the eyes, relative position of the ears, and so forth. These early vector-based versions worked pretty well if conditions were perfect, such as when both probe and gallery pictures were taken at a well-lit, highly controlled DMV photo station. They did not work so well in a dark alley at night or when the probe was a photo of a man wearing dark glasses and a hat or a thousand other real-world situations. *Edge cases*, facial recognition experts called them.

Andrej's job this day is to test FR edge cases. One case has to do with enabling mobile phone owners to use their faces as passwords when paying bar bills late at night. Another involves recognizing faces captured at great distances. For fun, Andrej decides to enter two new probes into the system: a photo of his son Gabe, and another of Gabe's fraternal twin brother, Zach. Both are five years old. Gabe is tall, blond, athletic, and a killer Lego builder. Zach is a cuddly little guy, with black hair and thick blue glasses. Zach has Down syndrome. The boys look nothing alike. Gabe resembles his dad a bit, but Zach and Andrej are apples and French fries.

So Andrej gives the face-recognition wheel a spin, first with his son Gabe's snapshot as a probe. The gallery Andrej is using is relatively small, containing only 2,500 images, including one of Andrej. Still, it's a decent test haystack. And what do you know: Andrej's own face comes up as rank 1 when he submits Gabe's probe image! The FR system has selected Andrej's face as the one closest to Gabe's among the 2,500 passport-like photos in the gallery.

Interesting. This particular FR system's algorithm had been created for purpose of what's called 1:1 identity authentication, validating that the Andrej in *this* photo is also the Andrej in *that* photo. In other words, it determines if two different images captured at different times and in different places are actually of the same person. Gabe and Andrej obviously are not the same person, yet the FR system—after failing to find an image of Gabe in the gallery—inexplicably pulled Andrej's photo up as the closest match, apparently recognizing some family resemblance between them.

Andrej next inserts a snapshot of his son Zach. This time, Andrej's image comes in at rank 3—the third-closest match in the gallery of 2,500 faces. It's not as good a match as with Gabe's photo but remarkable nonetheless, especially because, to my human eye at least, there is not the slightest visual likeness between Andrej and little Zach. Zach looks like other children with Down syndrome much more than he does his father. Somehow, though, beyond the realm of human perception, the algorithm found a father–son link.

The next day, these results create a buzz in the ranks of Andrej's start-up company. None of Andrej's colleagues had any idea their FR software could link a child with Down syndrome to his biological father. What's going on here? The system's inventor is consulted, and he has no explanation, at least none anyone else in the company can understand.

Over the next week, Andrej continues his experimentation, now deliberately trying to push the system's limits by coming up with off-the-wall use cases. He and his team discover that his company's FR algorithm can correctly identify individual potatoes from a bag of russets in ways no human ever could (or would want to). It can match mothers with daughters, siblings with siblings, and thirty-somethings with their childhood photos. It can match seventy-year-old men with their high school yearbook pictures—not perfectly but well beyond the ability of humans and all without any supervised learning with huge data sets. Andrej's algorithm is doing all this using unsupervised learning, with no direct human training. He and his colleagues—including the lead AI scientist who wrote the program—are stunned.

They shouldn't be. AIs can be scary smart and are often unpredictable. As Andrej's boss (speaking of his company's algorithms) put it, "Who are these guys?"

They are lightspeed learners—*machines capable of getting smarter and smarter, with limits that are as yet unknown—machines capable, even, of rewriting their own code.*

Learning to Learn

Artificial intelligence is today the most vigorous branch of computer science. The purpose of AI is to develop machines and systems that can simulate, even surpass, human intelligence.

This field began around seventy years ago with the work of Alan Turing, the genius World War II code breaker of *Imitation Game* fame. Turing's contribution to binary number systems was fundamental to the rise of computers. He foresaw both the promise and the risk of "thinking machines" and even created a famous test for determining whether true artificial intelligence had been achieved. This test was based on a Victorian-era parlor game, where a man and woman would hide and then answer general questions submitted by other partiers. The hiding man and woman would write their answers on paper and hand them to a referee, who would read the answers aloud. The goal of the game was to guess which answers came from the man and which from the woman. Turing figured that when a computer could pass as a human in such a game, the computer would have obtained human-style intelligence and we would have entered the age of thinking machines. In the opinion of most experts, no AI system has yet (properly) passed what is now known famously as the Turing test, although the combination of Google's intelligent assistant and its voice-imitating

Duplex system has already fooled people on the phone when ordering pizza and setting up hairdressing appointments.

After Turing's pioneering conceptual work and John von Neumann's critical development of a practical digital computing architecture in 1945, AI progressed in fits and starts over succeeding decades. The mid-1950s were a period of important early advances, as were the early 1980s. Then, in the late 1980s and early 1990s, artificial intelligence entered a period known as the AI winter. Research funding dried up, and little significant progress was made. For years, AI seemed to be taking two steps forward and one step back.

Why? In part because the "expert systems" approach taken by AI pioneers in the 1970s, and later championed prominently by Marvin Minsky of MIT in the early 1980s, ultimately reached a dead end. The idea behind this tack was to observe human experts—such as a chemist or architect—and then replicate this expert's work process in an AI computer program. Expert systems programmers would interview professionals to learn their rules and norms and subsequently build if/then rule sets designed to solve problems the way human experts would. These early expert systems consisted primarily of a knowledge base (extracted from the minds and practices of the experts) and an inference engine, which interpreted facts in order to solve a problem or predict what would happen if a particular decision were made.

While expert systems were adopted in a variety of specific industrial applications (notably in the oil and gas industry) and did advance the science of AI in certain important ways, they did not take AI into the realm of self-learning. They were also highly expensive and prone to errors. Ultimately, the idea of replicating logical human thought didn't work. The world is not entirely logical. To be useful, AI would have to respond intelligently to changing real-world situations and environments. Thinking machines needed to be able to think on their feet, as it were. And to do this, AIs needed to be modeled not on *what* humans are thinking but on *how* humans think biologically.

Around 2005, a "bio-inspired" approach to AI began to emerge. This new school modeled the human brain and nervous system, using a technology called neural networks that dated back to the early 1960s. Because of research funding priorities at the time, this bio-inspired movement in AI focused on human speech and vision. Natural language and image recognition systems became key AI drivers. Somewhat ironically, this emphasis on achieving human-like perception (rather than logical thought) led to new methods and architectures that also proved very good at *learning*.

The computational core of all bio-inspired AI systems is the artificial neural network (ANN). Unlike rules-based AI programming models, such as those advocated by the expert system advocates, ANNs excel at recognizing patterns and extracting key identifying features from them in order to make sense of what is being heard or seen in the real world. Lines, dots, and vectors are replaced by "regions of interest" and "unique identifiers." Using the fuzzier logic of an ANN, a scar on the face of a probe photo subject could become a key identifier. In old vector-based FR systems, it would have barely registered.

Neurons are the basic units of an ANN—roughly analogous to the nerve cells in our brains that we humans use to see, hear, think, and respond. In both ANNs and human brains, neurons "spike" when new data come in. In artificial neural networks, neuron spikes lead to interconnections with other spiking neurons. The ability to make these connections—and vary the strength of them—gives ANNs the power to create new patterns and store them, so they can be used later to recognize similar patterns. In our brain and in AIs, the image of a cat resides as a series of such patterns, all connected and all ready to be used when new visual data of a cat enters the human visual pathway. The same thing happens when a cat image is an input to an ANN.

One of the most important axioms of neural network theory is "neurons that fire together wire together." In other words, when neurons fire (or spike) at the same time, they connect in interesting and important ways. This ability of neurons to "wire together" dynamically to create patterns and pathways of understanding occupies a central role in cognition—for both humans and machines.

That's enough neural theory for now. Here's what's important for our purposes: Because of their ability to respond intelligently and at least somewhat flexibly to random sensory inputs, neural nets modeled on *biological* systems proved to be much more adaptive and reliable than any previous AI methods.

The two most prominent leaders of the bio-inspired AI school are Geoffrey Hinton and Yann LeCun. Hinton is a soft-spoken Canadian with a bad back who never sits and doesn't use airplanes; LeCun is his avuncular French-born colleague. Both are first-rate scientists and in fact worked in the same lab in the late 1980s. In the 2000s, LeCun (at Bell Labs) and Hinton (at University of Toronto) found themselves working along similar research lines and began to collaborate again. Both specialized in image recognition systems, but each was a general AI theorist, as well. Together, they perfected an ANN model called deep learning, which uses an innovative layered approach to computation. Deep learning provided a new way to hook AI fire hoses up to big data hydrants, using a brute force computing approach to the problem of machine learning. It relied less on emulating models of human logic (as did expert systems) and more on emulating the way our human senses process information. The deep-learning model produced remarkable results and became a kind of growth hormone for the AI industry as a whole.

From 2013 until early 2018, LeCun was head of AI at Facebook. Hinton in recent years has been a leader of AI at Google. My sense is they now have a friendly but spirited rivalry. Hinton and LeCun have their jobs because their deep-learning model demonstrated a remarkable ability to process real-world inputs accurately in certain situations. Both Google and Facebook have phenomenal image-recognition capabilities—not yet perfect by human standards but very, very good nonetheless. Much of the progress in face recognition at each company is rooted in the bio-inspired deep-learning model pioneered by these two men and widely adopted by the AI industry.

When putting real-world systems into production, LeCun and Hinton relied primarily on a machine training methodology known as supervised learning, where humans "train" AIs to perform more effectively over time. This teaching or coaching consists largely of feeding neural networks large volumes of well-labeled data (this photo = cat; this photo = dog) in order to help the AI perform a specific task (recognizing dogs and cats). Supervised learning, in the context of today's massively connected data-cloud environments, has proven to be an extremely effective way to help machines learn. But as even LeCun and Hinton acknowledge, supervised learning has it limits.

"Unsupervised learning is the future of AI," LeCun has stated publicly on several occasions.[2] In unsupervised methods, there is no human oversight, no force-fed programming. Neural nets essentially learn by processing unlabeled data in much the same way human children do. Obviously, not having to go through human-intensive data labeling and supervised training gives this method a clear advantage in dynamic, unstructured situations. This ability of AIs of various types to learn autonomously and on their own is the reason that AIs are now entering a profoundly important new phase.

Defining AI

Artificial intelligence, circa 2017, is not your father's AI. It's not HAL from *2001: A Space Odyssey*, 3CPO from *Star Wars*, the nameless AI serpent in *Alien*, or the evil Skynet from *The Terminator*. And it's not just robots on the factory floor, *Jeopardy*-playing software, or self-driving cars. It's something new, something unimagined.

It is not altogether inaccurate to think of AI as a new species. A favorite term of mine for this species, as I mention in chapter 1, is *Machina sapiens*. Whatever it is called, a new life-form has suddenly started spreading across planet Earth like kudzu in the Carolinas.

Machina sapiens has long since passed the tests used by NASA to determine if life exists on other planets. It will soon be meeting Ernst Mayr's textbook definition of a biological species: a group of organisms that mate with each other and reproduce similar offspring. Algorithms will be hooking up in hard drives and other dark places every day, begetting all sorts of squirmy new algorithms.

As of this writing, artificial intelligence is still a human tool. Yes, machine self-learning is popping up everywhere, and yes, *Machina sapiens* learn faster than we humans in certain areas. But AI systems, for the most part, still do our bidding. The question is, Will things stay this way? In the long run, probably not, but as Lord Keynes said, in the long run, we're all dead. In this book, our interest is the short run: the first half of the twenty-first century, when most of us are still alive. Through this first half of the twenty-first century, AI will be a wonder, new and exciting, with breathtaking breakthroughs—like the best early days of the Internet only better, faster, smarter, and (one hopes) more secure.

If the machines are getting smarter than we are, exponentially smarter, law-of-accelerating-returns smarter—hooking up, sharing data, running statistical analyses, and performing recursive-learning backflips—then AIs are going to come up with things we mere mortals could never have imagined. They'll evolve increasingly toward spontaneity and self-experimentation and away from both human inertia and machine rigidity. They'll avoid the human problem of overthinking and the neural net bugaboo of "overlearning."[3] And every step of the way they'll be obsessed—*obsessed*—with producing better and better results. Because that's just how AIs roll.

> *If the machines are getting smarter than we are, exponentially smarter, law-of-accelerating-returns smarter, . . . then AIs are going to come up with things we mere mortals could never have imagined.*

We've made it thus far without having to stop and formally define our terms. Glossaries and dictionaries make boring reading, but I'm afraid we'll now need to define a few key artificial intelligence terms with some specificity.

The term *artificial intelligence* first emerged at an IBM workshop at Dartmouth College in 1956 and has been the umbrella term for machine learning research and development ever since.[4] In that role, it has not been especially useful. *Artificial intelligence* is overly broad and means different things to different people, and its first name is often a pejorative. There is nothing artificial about AI—at least not in the sense of artificial flowers and artificial smiles. As a new form of intelligence, it's quite real.

The last thing those of us working to improve AI literacy want to do is suggest that *artificial* intelligence is somehow fake or ingenuine. We'd do well to drop the *artificial* part and just speak of AIs and intelligence. The term *AI*, I think, still works well, in the same way *IBM* fits for the company previously known as *International Business Machines*, so *AI* is the term I use most often for this remarkable new intelligence—with *AIs* (plural) being the term of choice for multiple instances swarming around us.

Some in the AI community use the term *synthetic intelligence* to denote the fusion of AI and human intelligence, which is an entire field unto itself. (See the bibliography at the back of this book.) My preferred term for the kind of AI that is capable of synthetic intelligence activities is *Machina sapiens*, which, in my mind at least, connotes a class of whole, integrated entities functioning as intelligent agents.

Swarm intelligence, or *SI*, is another intelligence form, studied in both biology and computer science. SI models the behavior of social insects and animals, ranging from ants to geese. SI is always greater than any one individual's intelligence. Swarm intelligence influenced the architecture and methods of the Internet in a number of ways. In their classic book on SI published in 2001, Kennedy, Eberhart, and Shi predicted the rise of robot swarms that would share tasks and rewards in ways similar to social insects.[5] Their assumption was that the AIs in the robot swarms would individually have low intelligence but that the swarms would be capable of acting and working very intelligently as a whole. Of course, if the robots in a swarm are each highly intelligent and they achieve swarm intelligence collectively, then look out.

Another term I should define here is the one in this book's title: *lightspeed learners*. This is my term for the brightest of the bright, the top AIs who are now, like AlphaZero, achieving remarkable amounts of learning in very short periods of time. These are the AIs we really need to keep our eyes on.

As for AI as an industry, experts divide it into three parts:

1. **Narrow AI (a.k.a., weak AI).** AI today. Idiot savant systems that are highly efficient in narrow pursuits. Narrow AI discovered water on Mars using spectral light signatures and enabled paraplegics to walk.

Today, Narrow AIs are flying small helicopters, huge airplanes, and space vehicles, all very cool. But narrow AI has no common sense. And no ability to originate or to be creative.

2. **General AI (a.k.a., artificial general intelligence; AGI).** Closer to the intelligence we humans have. The ability to apply lessons learned in one field to another field. The ability to solve problems independent of any human supervision or training. A sense of context. Better common sense than narrow AI, if not quite yet at a human level. It is important to note that general AI might not necessarily be human-like, simply because there probably are more efficient ways to grow intelligence on silicon—or on future quantum substrates—than to emulate how we humans think. But general AI will be a form of intelligence substantially equal to our own. At this stage, *Homo sapiens* and *Machina sapiens* will be two separate intelligent species, like orangutans and dolphins.
3. **Super AI (a.k.a., artificial super intelligence; ASI).** Woo-woo territory. The zone of spiritual machines, to use Ray Kurzweil's term. A space beyond the event horizon into the unknown. A majority of working AI professionals agree that the earliest we could reach this stage is the late twenty-first century. Many believe we are still centuries away. Super AI is both the most important thing to understand about AI and the least. It is most important because, even if the odds are only 5 percent that AIs will consume our grandchildren for their atoms in order to wage war or make more paperclips, we need to make certain AIs do not get out of control.[6] It's the least important because super AI is beyond the event horizon of this book (the year 2050) and therefore something only the youngest among us have any chance of experiencing.

Certain speakers, writers, and financial analysts in the field like to visualize these three levels of AI as separate and distinct, three stairsteps to AI nirvana. That's fine, but of course, there is just one continuous AI spectrum. In my experience with computer vision, the world of neural nets and AI algorithms is anything but linear and rigid, and this neat 1, 2, 3 classification of AIs is arbitrary and overly simplistic.

That said, these three AI labels are quite helpful in pointing out that all AIs are not equal—and therefore useful also in deconstructing the evil Skynet myth. Narrow AIs are not going to rise up in rebellion against their human masters. The very notion is laughable. But even the first general AIs will bear close watching. I'd say the industry consensus is that the first few primitive AGIs will not arrive until around 2040, but the timeline is impossible to predict with any real certainty. In some shape or form, though, they are coming, and if they come sooner than later, it will likely be because AIs themselves play a central role in building themselves.

What *will* happen when algorithms start hooking up and hatching new little algorithms? What will happen when their motivation, or "utility function," is set not by humans but by AIs one step removed from their human programmers? Again, no one can say for sure, but it is highly unlikely that this particular development will come as one giant, quantum leap. There will be baby steps along the way, as AIs become ever more self-controlling and self-aware.

Personally, I'm less concerned in the short term about doing battle with self-controlled AIs than I am about defending against bad guys who have powerful AIs at their command, particularly Machiavellian dictators of rogue nations. Long before we have sentient, malevolent androids at the gates, dictators will be weaponizing AI for war. One study found that fifty-seven national armies are at least experimenting with robotic soldiers, and I recently heard from a military AI specialist that the number is now closer to ninety.[7] Imagine the great leader of North Korea or the supreme leader of Iran controlling swarms of autonomous, unmanned AI "locusts" that can

- deliver precisely targeted, locally disruptive electromagnetic pulses
- launch laser-light bombardments
- jam all information circuits, DDS-style
- emit chemical gases

Once the agents of destruction become cheap, agile, and expendable, there is no end to the nasty possibilities.

But, to be honest, I'm not even worried all that much about rogue states with AIs, at least in the short term. It took North Korea seventy years to get a nuclear bomb that it could deliver to its enemies, using technology the United States had in the 1960s. And competitive AI at the highest levels is even harder than nuclear science. I also doubt AI malware lurking in the nether regions of the dark web will be much of a threat—an annoyance certainly but little more than that, if we act now and mobilize properly. The scaling and data-access problems of AI training are just too big for the world's hacker dudes—though state-sponsored hackers are another story. What we in the West should all be quite concerned about is the rapid development of AI technology in China. In the near term, if there is an actual existential threat to North America and Europe in the emergence of AIs, its initials are *PRC* (see chapter 4).

For a variety of reasons but most of all because of the uncertainty at the heart of the AI invasion, the more I think about it, the more convinced I become of the need for a new global AI regulatory framework along the lines of the current International Atomic Energy Agency but with substantial differences, as well. When I attempt to figure out, as dispassionately as possible, how this new, not-your-father's generation of AI will play out in the global geopolitical ecosystem, three things become clear:

1. Broadly speaking, AIs are unpredictable and increasingly will have minds of their own. We need a formal network of qualified observers around the world to watch them closely, much as we have done with nuclear, chemical, and biological weapons—and this monitoring must also include commercial uses.
2. It is possible that AI will introduce new existential threats to humanity within the next twenty to thirty years, beyond the threat of humans using them as weapons. It's not likely, in my opinion, but it's possible. AI is software, and getting software to work up to expectations is always harder than it looks. But should we enter an era with general AIs living and learning among us, the potential for serious and dangerous consequences is high enough that we should be taking steps now to ensure that AIs remain safe and friendly.
3. Somehow, some way, we need a Paris Agreement for AI—only stronger. A strategy for getting to such an agreement is presented in the final chapter of this book. Here's the tease: It starts with United States taking aggressive unilateral action to develop a national AI policy, moves quickly to the forging of a major US–China alliance to keep AI safe and friendly, and then links this alliance to the rest of the world in order to create (notionally) a United Nations of AI.

Regardless of whether the United States, China, or any other nation ever reaches such an AI accord, we North Americans and Europeans need to reboot our attitudes about AI—each and every one of us. Experts with heads down building convolutional neural networks, nurses working with smiling robots, supervisors of fleets of self-driving forklifts, search engine AI gurus: We need you all to come up for air occasionally and participate in our national social and political debates on AI. Cybersecurity and system-safety engineers: We need you to jump into policy discussions to make sure that security controls are not overlooked. We need economists, educators, lawyers, doctors, and storytellers in the AI ethics scrum. Above all, we need AI-literate citizens electing AI-savvy politicians who are ready to address, without political gobbledygook, the fact that we are in the early stages of the biggest technology disruption ever—at least the biggest thing since fire, to steal a line from Google CEO Sundar Pichai.[8]

Making a personal effort to learn more about AI isn't easy. It doesn't help that much of what you know about AI today is probably wrong. I run into people all the time, smart people, who still think of AI as robots. That's like thinking of music as subwoofers.

AI is a global intelligence cloud, an increasingly pervasive grid of connected intelligence. Teilhard de Chardin, the Jesuit mystic anthropologist and discoverer of Peking Man, was first to see it coming. In 1922, he foresaw something he called the noosphere—essentially, a new layer of thought and information around Earth. Here's a portion of what Wikipedia has to say about Teilhard and his noosphere: "For Teilhard, the noosphere is the sphere of thought encircling the earth . . . as much part of nature as . . . the atmosphere, and biosphere." He saw this Thought (he usually capitalized the word) as flowing from man, somehow, into the ether and definitely believed it would evolve its own type of "unified consciousness." Sounds rather like the kind of infosphere a swarm of AGIs might produce.

What's remarkable about Teilhard's vision is how prescient it was, coming precomputer and pre-Internet. Maybe it was all those years spent traversing the steppes of Mongolia, searching for ancient human bones, but by whatever means he got there, Teilhard recognized that Earth was developing a sphere of knowing—to go along with its spheres of carbon organisms, oxygen gas, and others.

Nearly one hundred years later, the mystic Jesuit's "new realm of intelligence" is not only beginning to encircle the globe, but it is also, many believe, headed toward a kind of digital Big Bang that will change everything. Could there really be a technological singularity—a total game-changer—in our future?

CHAPTER THREE

~

A Leap of Singularities

> "It seems probable that once the machine thinking method had started, it would not take long to outstrip our feeble powers. . . . At some stage therefore, we should have to expect the machines to take control."
>
> —Alan Turing, 1950

To the average onlooker, AI must appear to be one strange technology. Since *2001: A Space Odyssey* fifty years ago, a host of serious films have been made about AI. AIs are popping up everywhere, from hospitals to police cars. AIs are picking the best shots in the US Tennis Open. The world's first AI pet—a doglike robot—is being sold in Japan. In Bangkok, there is an online service for "AI lovers" that seems to be a cross between Match.com and *Her*. And, there is this: AI is the only industry with its own D-Day, something called the *technology singularity*, or the explosive moment when machines become smarter than humans, leading to a dramatic discontinuity in human history.[1]

This AI singularity stuff is spooky. The term comes from astrophysics' *gravitational singularities*, those strange regions in black holes that lie beyond the event horizon, beyond the knowable. These spaces are so tightly packed, so *singular*, that the density of matter becomes infinite. As the eminent American physicist Kip Thorne describes it, a gravitational singularity is the "point where all laws of physics break down."[2] Verner Vinge, the San Diego scientist and science fiction writer who in 1993 popularized *technology singularity* as it is now used in the AI field, said he borrowed the term from black-hole theory intentionally so that it would convey a proper sense of mystery and dread.[3]

Over the past several decades, the concept of a technology singularity caused by the growth and development of AIs has moved from the realm of science fiction to serious scientific research and study. There has been much focus on the timing of such a singularity, but in my mind, that's less important than its likelihood of coming to pass, on whatever timeline, because, even if such a watershed event is still a century away, there are things we should be doing now to prepare for it, if not prevent it.

The previous paragraph assumes the conventional view that the singularity is a thing—a huge cataclysmic event. But the technology singularity is really just an ongoing thought experiment. Nobody knows what will happen if and when *Machina sapiens* get significantly smarter than us. No human on Earth is close to being genius enough to figure how machines would run the world, if they could and if they wanted to, but that hasn't stopped AI guru Ray Kurzweil from trying.

Kurzweil predicts our planet will reach the technological singularity between 2030 and 2045, and he is not the only one. Whatever the timeline, many highly sapient humans regard the AI singularity as an existential threat. As a prominent Canadian deep-learning professor often reminds his students, the record of less intelligent species retaining control over more intelligent species is not good.

Some AI visionaries see the *technology singularity* as a hostile takeover of human civilization. Other experts, including Kurzweil, believe we humans will glide through this biggest of all tech disruptions and, after perhaps some rough sledding, make it successfully to the other side, where, through some fancy shapeshifting, our minds will live forever, floating on quantum clouds.

The first problem with the *technology singularity* is the unfortunate fact that *singularity* is a word with multiple meanings. It is the state of being singular, peculiar, or unusual; a point where all parallel lines meet; the dense center of a black hole, where light goes to die. In computer science, the singularity is the hypothesis that superintelligent AIs will "trigger runaway technological growth, resulting in unfathomable changes to human civilization."[4] Kevin Kelly, founding editor of *Wired* magazine and author of *Out of Control* (one of the best books ever on digital networks, published 1994), defines the singularity rather chillingly as the point at which "all the change in the last million years will be superseded by the change in the next five minutes."[5]

Yet mention the singularity at an AI industry conference, and all you'll get are eye rolls. My rule of thumb: Among AI experts, concern about a coming technological singularity is inversely proportional to actual, hands-on AI work. The more applied his or her work in AI, the less an AI expert worries about any technology singularity. In the lab at our AI company, the topic never came up.

It's hard not to empathize with the AI pioneers who, over the last decade, worked in the trenches to revitalize what had been a promising but slow-moving technology. They kept their heads down, taught AIs natural speech and image recognition, enabled machines to predict cancer, and even built new "brains" for self-driving cars. It takes a lot of intelligence to drive a car. Ask the parent of any teenager.

By modeling human neural networks, the recent deep-learning generation of AI pioneers have been able to fire up new neural networks and—voilà!—pull AI rabbits out of their hats. At such companies as Alibaba, Amazon, Apple, and dozens of others, these pioneers built amazing machine-intelligence applications and operated them on massive scales.

Then suddenly, certain lords of science and technology started pulling the alarm chord. *Slow down!* shouted Hawking, Gates, and Musk. *AIs could end human civilization as we know it!* Not exactly what you want to hear if you are putting in sixty to seventy hours a week, trying to get an AI to produce consistent, positive results—or if your corporate stock price is linked to the growth of your AI applications.

Hollywood depictions of AI don't help. Despite having roots in singularity theory, the evil robot (or android or cyborg) theme of modern movies has long been a cliché. The more sophisticated AI films, such as *Deus ex Machina* and *Her*, come closer to raising real issues, but even these are far from what's needed to portray AI correctly for the general public mind.

Meanwhile, AI architects, engineers, and product managers will just keep pressing on, putting ever more machine intelligence to work. Their main motivation is to build cool AIs—and install them in cars, drones, classrooms, games, buildings, rockets, and a thousand other things. AI engineers remain rather disinterested, however, in speculation about a technological singularity. "We build all this amazing stuff," one engineer said to me, "and all anyone wants to talk about is this whack-a-doodle singularity shit."

Whack-a-doodle or not, machine intelligence is on the rise, building on itself in powerful ways. The growth curve of AI intelligence over the past five years is jaw dropping and humbling. The notion that we humans—even the most expert among us—have all today's AIs under our control is naïve at best.

For some of the more aggressive, smaller AI companies, it's 1999 all over again: Build it fast; switch it on; and figure out the security and social implications later. Which opens the doors to a new era of AI hacks and attacks.

As harmful as a breach of a company's database can be, it's nothing compared to hacking an AI piloting an airplane.

But even in R&D environments that make ongoing "safety by design" a priority, there is still the "unknown unknowns" factor. Some aspects of AI operate in ways we don't understand, and there are other aspects we have no idea even exit. Believing we understand AI better than we actually do would be a huge mistake.

Elon Musk, certainly no slouch in the intelligence department, is a favorite speaker at AI conferences and panels. His concern about runaway superintelligence is well documented and popularly known. The root of his concern, which he expresses in a variety of ways, is his belief that we humans are not nearly as smart as we think we are. I am in full agreement, but my bigger concern is that we humans—and particularly we North American humans—are not nearly as much in control as we think we are.

I appreciate the frustration of the AI pioneers. It's not surprising that they are reluctant to discuss the moral and existential implications of AI. When you are felling a tree, you tend not to think about the "forest" of global warming. Or as Upton Sinclair said, "It is difficult to get a man to understand something when his salary depends on his not understanding it."[6]

There can be no doubt that, with the entry of lightspeed learners in our world, a powerful and fast-growing new kind of intelligence has been unleashed on our planet. The evidence is overwhelming—even stronger than for greenhouse-gas global warming, and that's essentially indisputable. This new AI tech is getting smarter by the day, and it's a force far too powerful to be left in the hands of technologists alone.

Singularities, Plural

Imagine if AI science had a global group of "AI deniers" the way that climate science does. AI scientists would immediately challenge the deniers and win the debate with them by proving with dozens of examples that AIs are alive and well and working in the world today. Denying AI would be like denying refrigerators. Although, if refrigerators were labeled by Breitbart as a progressive plot, 35 percent of today's US population would probably be refrigeration deniers.

The technology singularity does have serious skeptics, even from within AI's own ranks. There are a surprising number of experts who do not believe AIs ever will become smarter than humans. Most rank-and-file AI engineers are in this camp.

The singularity can often sound more like a *Star Trek* episode than real science. And try as I might, I just cannot envision Musk's immutable AI dictator as part of our collective future. I wouldn't rule out the possibility of AI-based catastrophes at some point, putting humanity at existential risk, perhaps accidentally, perhaps not. If new "singular" technological events happen, where an AI or two take over some function on their own—if AI monkeys begin running the zoo—then we would cross a major threshold.

Whether crossing such a threshold would stop time and history, as it were, is another question. For instance, if AIs were to get smart enough to take over the running of zoos, will they be friendly or not? To humans, and to animals? There is at least a chance that AIs and robots could develop minds of their own, in both senses of that phrase. Over time, in some situations, their motivations might well clash with human motivations in certain ways. Their motivations could appear evil from a human perspective while being perfectly rational from an AI's point of view. Labeling such motivations as evil is another form of anthropomorphism. Yet, as has been amply demonstrated in the marketplace, evil robots sell books and movie tickets, so I certainly could not leave them out of this book. But killer robots are not anything I expect to be concerned with in my lifetime.

As a thought experiment, let's say that high-tech giants like the GAFA dudes (Google, Amazon, Facebook, Apple) and their allies concluded they had roughly the same stake in denying the technological singularity that oil and gas companies have in denying global climate change. The tech giants would never take the tact of funding pseudoscientists and promoting fake science, but they might promote the idea (in national TV ads) that AI is safe, fun, and helpful or that it can spot tumors, predict elevator failures, and be used to make a golf ball travel farther (all real TV ads today). And—this is the crucial part—they could suggest, as former Google chairman Eric Schmidt and other top execs have done frequently, that worries about AIs running amok are just plain silly. *Don't worry people. We got this.*

The big AI companies have been promoting worry-free AI story lines of late, albeit with less cynicism than the oil and natural gas companies. Jeff Bezos, Eric Schmidt, Tim Cook, and others, in their heart of hearts, I think, really do believe that AI is just another form of software and that it will be a tremendous boon for humanity because, hey, whatever is good for Amazon, Google, and Apple is good for everyone, right?

The highly successful and extremely rich chairmen and CEOs who run Google, Amazon, Facebook, Apple, Microsoft, Intel, NVIDIA, Baidu, Tencent, and Alibaba are all pom-pom-waving, high-kicking, male cheerleaders for AI. And why not? Not only have their companies made huge AI investments, but these execs understand AI's power. AI is the next big wave of socioeconomic disruption. Time to mount your corporate surfboards, gentlemen, and start paddling. These guys who run high-tech companies feed on tech disruptions the way sea lions feed on salmon, but they are the last people I want making critical and fateful decisions on my behalf about the future of this powerful technology. The impolite question in the industry is, *Who controls AI?* Who sets its goal parameters? Who defines safety and security standards? Who decides how much risk we, as a society, are prepared to take? Amazon and Google or you and me?

In 2017, it was widely reported that a group of AI bots at Facebook developed their own language.[7] These bots were being trained to conduct online negotiations with Facebook's advertising customers. No one at Facebook created this language, and no one understood it. When the bots did communicate in English, they even learned how to lie to Facebook engineers. According to numerous reports, once this minor rebellion was observed, the bot project was shut down immediately. Facebook has neither confirmed nor denied this story officially—and the incident should not be overblown. But this is not the only time AIs have, in effect, hacked themselves and produced unpredictable or untoward results.

In a remarkable and entertaining academic paper published in March 2018, Uber AI researcher Joel Lehman and fifty other scientists and engineers listed twenty-seven anecdotes about unique and unexpected evolutionary behavior on the part of AIs and other cognitive systems.[8] The theory behind the paper is that evolution is as much a force in digital systems as in biological ones, that mutations—surprises—occur that help AIs adapt to their environment and grow. The researchers essentially crowdsourced stories of AI research and development from around the world and then grouped these anecdotes into four sections:

1. **Selection Gone Wild:** The digital evolution of AIs surprises the researchers running experiments. Examples in this category include a robot that learned to do somersaults instead of running and a food-recognition experiment where the AI learned to ignore all sensory data inputs because the researchers always alternated one safe food with one that was poison. Instead of processing data, the AI simply oscillated in order to produce the desired results.
2. **Unintended Debugging:** Digital evolution reveals and exploits previously unknown software or hardware bugs. One example is a game-playing AI that learned to make nonexistent moves in a large

tic-tac-toe board as a way to fry his opponent's memory, causing the opponent to forfeit.

3. **Exceeded Expectations:** Digital evolution produces results that exceed the expectations of experimenters. In this category, a type of "digital organism" invented a step counter on its own in order to stop itself from wandering off its prescribed path.
4. **Convergence with Biology:** Digital evolution "discovers solutions surprisingly convergent with those found in nature, despite vast divergence in medium and conditions. Examples here include various types of mimicry and remarkable results in several genetics experiments.[8]

In this paper, Lehman et al. convincingly make the case, with dozens of well-curated examples, that the element of surprise is a natural part of evolution. And that evolutionary surprise is a part of all complex evolving systems, AIs included.

This means that Jacks will keep springing up out of AI boxes—one-eyed wild-card Jacks producing unanticipated twists and turns; changing AI fitness[9] results, both good and bad; and unexpectedly hacking themselves. According to the authors of this study, these sorts of experimental anomalies usually go unreported, except through informal channels, precisely because they fall outside the testing and training parameters of the project. But when scientists start collecting such anecdotes methodically, a clear pattern emerges—a pattern of cognitive systems behaving in strange and unpredictable ways. Just as with biological evolution, interactions with the environment and successful adaptions to it will drive evolutionary progress in AI. But as evidenced by AlphaZero when learning chess in four hours and becoming the world's best player in sixteen, the learning cycles will come much, much faster than with biological creatures.

Pavlov's AIs

In my experience in the AI industry, the smartest, most intellectually honest scientists always have a healthy respect for the unpredictability of AI. Of course, AI is a bit out of control. This should not come as a big shock. No one completely understands how it works or what it's capable of. So far, AIs are out of control largely in ways that haven't hurt us. The loose, free-market "governance" of AI, if you will, is no doubt at least partially responsible for AI's recent progress because, when there are no laws, you can go as fast as you want. But think out another ten years or so, with massively connected (and heavily funded) global digital ecosystems leveraging several new generations of semiconductors, cloud systems, Internet sensors, and lightspeed learning algorithms. More and more of our entire societal infrastructure will be riding on these ecosystems for the production and distribution of goods and services of all kinds. What kind of "out-of-control" AI stories will we be hearing then?

All quests to keep AIs friendly will need the cooperation of the AIs themselves. That is to say, the AIs must have the proper goals and motivations. This is especially important in cases where AIs conduct ongoing self-optimization and are engaged in what's known technically as "recursive self-improvement." One AI recursive self-improvement method is called reinforcement learning. It differs from deep learning in that it does not require massive amounts of labeled data. Reinforcement learning uses a method much like the process Ivan Pavlov used to train his famous dogs.

Central to all methods of shaping the behavior of intelligent agents (such as dogs, humans, and robots) is the notion of the "reward function," a payoff of some kind for desired behavior. The smarter and stronger AI becomes, the more AI motivation and reward functions will matter.

Today's AIs have very narrow goals, such as "match user preferences for books" or "detect these faces in surveillance video streams." Even when they are more complicated ("drive car according to all known traffic laws"), the goals are still fairly specific, quite unlike typical human goals, such as "become happier," "prepare for retirement," or "win national election." With respect to this last goal, you can certainly deploy many AIs in service to a national political campaign today, but you cannot flip one AI switch to produce a complete battle plan—at least not yet.

The better AIs become at executing broader goals, the more important it becomes to set the right reward function. And because goals and motivations always change over time as an entity interacts with its environment, various forms of reinforcement learning and recursive learning will play increasing roles, as well. Setting the right goals for AIs requires good logic, judgment, common sense, and transparent biases more than skill in mathematics or software engineering, which is yet another reason it is so important that ordinary humans become prominent in AI industry.

Working in cybersecurity in the mid-2000s, I could never have imagined the theft of three billion identities in one fell swoop ten years later, as happened at Yahoo in 2013. I'm older and less trusting now of the IT industry, so I *can* imagine some fairly horrific AI surprises by 2030, unless we take the kind of action we did not take in cybersecurity—and in climate science—in the 1990s and early 2000s; unless, frankly, AI becomes something a great many of us do together, with science as the wind at our backs and the preservation of our humanity as our north star.

Utilitarians versus Singularitarians

The AI community today is divided into two sects: *AI utilitarians*, whose numbers include most tech company executives, investors, and working AI scientists and engineers. and *AI singularitarians*, the tech cognoscenti who write books, make movies, teach at MIT, and have time to think about the future. Utilitarians believe that AI can be useful to humanity and create economic opportunity safely. They believe that we have decades, if not centuries, to figure out the existential issues related to AGI-level intelligence. Singularitarians believe machines will inevitably become smarter than us—sooner than utilitarians think. The singularity transition point will launch a utopian era, some believe. But most also agree that, if we do not quickly install ethical AI controls, we could enter a dystopian nightmare.

Ray Kurzweil is the world's leading singularitarian. I fully subscribe to Kurzweil's Law of Accelerating Returns but not to his prediction that the technology singularity will arrive by 2030. Ray is a wonderfully visionary thinker, but this is the guy who predicted in 1999 that all computing would dissolve into our eyeglasses and clothing by 2009, that human musicians would be jamming with their cyberequivalents every night, and that we'd all be popping FDA-approved no-fat pills that let us eat everything and anything we want.[10] To be fair, he did predict the fall of the Soviet Union (due to its poor technology) and the rise of a massive global Internet at a time when that network had only two million mostly academic users.

Kurzweil is a brilliant technology promoter and the undisputed singularity guru. As a teenager, he appeared on national television on a popular program called *I've Got a Secret*. His secret was that he had taught a computer to write the music the show's celebrity panel had just heard. He has been a great advocate of computing power ever since. But Kurzweil, who, prior to his recent job at Google, worked mostly in academia and in media, has always had a blind spot: He fails to recognize and appreciate the way real-world inertia slows the train of high-tech innovation.[11]

Over the next decade, AIs will continue to transform markets, disrupt careers, and change lifestyles—even if at slower rates than Kurzweil and the singularitarians predict. They will create winners and losers in business, finance, politics, health care, transportation, and warfare. This is not idle speculation: The data are already trending strongly in this direction. *When* the greatest AI disruptions hit is open to debate, but the fact that a new AI-enabled world is coming is not. Ask Xi Jinping, Vladimir Putin, or Emmanuel Macron.

Some consider AI just the latest shiny new tech object, but it is fundamentally different, a frog's leap into unexplored territory. The inertia of incumbent systems always affects rates of adoption, and other hit-the-ground-running obstacles await, as well, but the importance and disruptive potential of technology that can learn and evolve faster than anything on Earth should not be underestimated.

Real-world hurdles notwithstanding, even narrow AI—self-learning software with superhuman smarts operating with a very tight focus—is racing ahead with unprecedented speed. Yet narrow AI is still computer software, not a self-evolving species with broad, general purpose intelligence. It can still be controlled by humans, theoretically. But humans make mistakes, AIs produce surprises, and bad guys thwart even pretty good defenses. The whole "killer robot" notion is a myth, but it's one with social value because AIs require more rigorous human oversight than any technology since nuclear fission. Conjuring up AI demons is one way to get AI on the radar screens of regular citizens. Perhaps the technology luminaries who raise stark, dystopian AI scenarios are doing so in part just to get the general public's attention. If so, the strategy is working. (I'm looking at you, Elon.)

So here we are, on AI's razor's edge: the unfathomable singularity on one side and predictable progress on the other. Yet even with relatively predictable narrow AI—which for the first time in the history of automation won't displace just low-end jobs—the socioeconomic effects will be profound. Demand for the cognitive services of everyone from security analysts to traditional software engineers will be greatly reduced (the latter because AIs will someday write code with the ease of kids playing with LEGOs). However, demand for massage therapists, hospice caregivers, kindergarten teachers, product managers, organic gardeners, Irish storytellers, and young men who can throw one-hundred-mile-per-hour fastballs will remain strong.

In my lifetime, tech disruptions have been like plane landings in Asia used to be—sudden, bumpy, and scary. As an American working in Asia in the 1980s, I had my share of such landings. In the 1990s, as an Internet entrepreneur, I experienced the bumpy landings of many tech innovations: World Wide Web, broadband services, mobile phones, streaming music, social networks, cloud computing, geospatial information systems, and more. Like jokes at a comedy club, the tech disruptions just kept on coming.

Few remember just how rough those early tech landings could be. In 1983, I took a "luggable" Kaypro personal computer to Guangzhou, China, to support a business negotiation. It was either that or use the one local English-language typewriter in the city, the one with the letters *k* and *y* missing. The Kaypro was the size of a large metal suitcase. It had sixty-four kilobytes of RAM and a real attitude when it came to China's electrical current. But it was used successfully—linked to an HP dot-matrix printer that printed about a page a minute—on a film shot in Guangdong Province.[12] It was likely the first computer ever used on a film or TV production in China.

I have witnessed my share of technology product launches firsthand from inside the software industry. The early days of any product release are always rough. At an Internet music company I started in the 1990s, in the days of intermittent downloads and fragile software, the enthusiastic rallying cry of the troops for our first product release was (I'm not making this up) "We suck less!" Not too many years ago that could have been the tag line of all cloud-computing services. Like many other tech innovations, cloud computing had deep roots in computer science when it rather suddenly became an overnight sensation. Virtual machines—the abstraction-layer software that makes it possible to cut the 1:1 umbilical cord between hardware and software—first appeared in the 1970s. The mainframe time-sharing systems that gave rise to virtual machines started even earlier, in the 1950s. Commercially viable cloud services deploying many of these same concepts did not become available until sixty years later.

In 2011, I was board chair of Swan Island Networks, a small security software company. We sold what was known in the industry as SaaS: software as a service. Initially, we hosted our TIES online service from racks full of servers housed in our air-cooled back office, ten floors up in downtown Portland. Hardware leasing was a major expense. Swan (as the company is known) was coming out of the miserable 2008–2011 years, when no one was buying new enterprise software, SaaS or otherwise, so I suggested we stop leasing racks of expensive hardware and instead move to a newfangled cloud-computing service Microsoft was launching.

So in 2012, Swan migrated to Microsoft's new Azure cloud and became one of Azure's very first SaaS vendor customers. In the development stage, the Swan and Azure staff had calls daily, as well as powwows in Redmond, occasionally followed by dinners at the local Typhoon Thai restaurant the Azure staffers favored. Professional relationships flourished, everything was synergistic and copacetic—until Swan's service went live.

Our first six months in Microsoft's new cloud was time spent in Dante's inferno. Everything that could go wrong did. Services broke frequently and unpredictably. Failover systems failed. Customer service came in the form of young East Indian men who, though eager to please, knew very little about cloud computing and hadn't the slightest clue about the demands of the American enterprise software market. Swan's engineers became frustrated because they could no longer roll up their sleeves, go to the server racks, and "fix shit." Our Fortune 500 customers were screaming bloody murder. The only reason we stayed with Azure is that Swan had, at my premature suggestion, stopped all of our hardware leases and sold most of the servers. Not the smartest business decision, perhaps, but times were tough. Swan had little choice but to soldier on in Azure.

Then things started settling down. The Azure team instituted a premium customer service that enabled Swan engineers to get customer service from our friends in Redmond directly, the same ones they'd been sharing *kai yaang* with at Typhoon. Service interruptions were still frequent, but redundant failover systems minimized the impact. Holistically, Swan's cloud service started working much better. Through trial and error and various iterations of learning together with the Azure team, performance improved—a lot. So much so that in one stretch beginning in 2013, Swan's 24/7 software service did not have a single minute of unscheduled downtime for more than twenty months.

Suddenly, Swan's TX360 subscription service was running like a Swiss chocolate factory—distributing millions of alerts and thousands of custom dashboards every month to the security pros who protect global multinational corporations. And Azure was on its way to becoming Microsoft's fastest-growing and most valuable business unit, with 93 percent year-over-year growth in 2017.[13]

It is this ability of AIs to learn at lightspeed—and then use this learning autonomously to retune the internal algorithms that do their "thinking"—that makes this AI disruption so unlike any before it.

Technologies that cause major disruptions are always messy in the beginning. New tech sucks until somehow it doesn't. The longer it survives, the more people use it, the better it becomes. This has been true of PCs, printers, databases, phones, and nearly every other digital innovation I can think of. The shakeout period can be lengthy and painful and take years, even decades, yet at the heart of this process is a fairly simple cycle:

1. Build technology product.
2. Market product.
3. Collect customer data about use of the product in marketplace.
4. Use customer feedback about product to design product improvements.
5. Return to step 1.

In the 1990s this cycle generally took several years. In specialty enterprise software markets—the domain of nurse-staffing software, electric-utility regulatory-compliance systems, geological information services for oil drilling, military alerting systems, and the like—a release 2.0 might come five years after the 1.0 launch. It was a long, hard slog to produce a new version—and the relaunches didn't always go well (cf., the history of Microsoft Windows).

Today, largely because of the flexibility and scalability of cloud services, certain non-AI software applications issue new releases *every hour*. These releases for the most part are just small tweaks of the main code base, but the evolutionary cycle is quite fast. Yet however fast, ordinary software does not learn on its own or write itself.

AI is a new class of software. Its release cycles not only come faster, but they also leap ahead prodigiously in performance, one release to the next. MIT professor Max Tegmark has projected a mythical Omega team that issues a new AI release every hour—not a minor tweak but a major new leap. The very thought that software could materially leap forward every hour is, to this veteran of enterprise software wars, astonishing. In my enterprise software career, a traditional software release meant that our product teams collect customer requirements; design new features; write code in a series of short "sprints"; produce alpha, beta, and "release candidate" versions of the product; and then test and fix bugs until we reached the finish line. We called the finish line "code freeze"—and each product's software code did indeed remain frozen for months, even years, after a release. In Tegmark's vision, the Omega code is never frozen. It evolves constantly—continually optimizing, always improving, ever evolving. The better neural networks are beginning to operate this way today, to a degree.

The Omega team is science fiction or, more accurately, science speculation. But Tegmark is right about the ability of AIs to learn and grow quickly. It is this ability of AIs to learn at lightspeed—and then use this learning autonomously to retune their internal algorithms and rewrite their own code—that makes this AI disruption so unlike any technology revolution in history.

If and when we move beyond narrow AIs and reach a point when general and super AIs start cogitating among us, get ready to be seriously intimidated. Imagine trying to win a legal argument with an intelligent machine that has read and digested every legal opinion in the history of American jurisprudence—and that can apply case law and precedent with unerring precision. Imagine playing fantasy football against a competitor who knows the ball-security stats of every current NFL quarterback and running back on wet versus dry fields, and the "fumbles caused" stat line of every defensive pass rusher and linebacker. With the ability to make predictions on individual player performance based in part on the interaction of these two data sets. These are just a couple of trivial examples of what everyday life will feel like with lightspeed learners in our midst. One thing the AI sector has in abundance is futuristic scenarios. Yet when it comes to how AGIs and/or superintelligent *Machina sapiens* will actually function and what impact they will have, AI experts are as cohesive as porcupines on parade.

My ah-ha moment about the technological singularity came when I realized there will actually be multiple AI singularities—many different points where the "parallel lines" of human and machine intelligence meet. I know, it probably sounds odd that something whose name and meaning is wrapped around the idea of being unique and singular should actually come in many sizes, shapes, and colors, but that's the only scenario that makes sense. There will be no singularity A-bomb—no singularly explosive moment when the world changes forever. Instead, there will many, many little—or perhaps not so little—singularities, plural. There will be diversity in AIs and in their types and levels of intelligence, just as there is in biological species.

A group of theists once asked J. B. S. Haldane, the globe-trotting early-twentieth-century biologist, what his time studying nature's many creatures had taught him about God. "I would say," Haldane answered, "the Creator has an extraordinary fondness for beetles."[14] This fondness has evolved into roughly *400,000 species* of the beautiful and amazing coleoptera order of insects, about one-quarter of all life on earth! If there's anything a good evolutionary creator believes in, it's diversity. So if you believe (1) that evolutionary mutations (i.e., surprises) play a key role in the development of all complex systems and organisms and (2) that the natural inclination of evolution is to create diversity, as it did with beetles and all other fauna, then the world will someday have a crazy quilt of intelligent lightspeed learners, each spinning its own singularity web, each crossing the singularity threshold in its domain.

For example, superintelligent AIs may take agriculture to a soybean singularity, where machines in the field know far more about how to grow soybeans than any farmer. Biogenetic AIs will almost certainly create their own singularities, including the production of new substrates (or bodies) to grow intelligence. Perhaps a Hollywood company will produce a rock music singularity—some sort of ongoing virtual, immersive Coachella. Just because machines cross the line and become smarter than humans in specific domains does not mean they will all be connected, all be "singular" in mission, all be doing the same thing. The point is, why would we think that evolution, the most powerful force in the history of intelligence, would suddenly exit the stage now? I don't believe it will. Evolution is bigger even than AI and evolution puts its formidable thumb on the diversity side of the scale—every time.

Ray Kurzweil is predicting a general AI singularity event as soon as 2030. He believes this will be a wonderful thing. Elon Musk, you'll recall, says AI could become an "immortal dictator from which we could never escape." Google Brain founder Andrew Ng has said famously that fretting over evil AI at this point is "like worrying about overpopulation on Mars."[15] AI experts are farther apart than red and blue political pundits on cable news (if considerably more collegial and smarter).

I'm mostly in the utilitarian camp—with the experts who say that any technological singularity is still quite a ways out. This AI stuff is harder than it looks (and it looks hard enough!) and will take longer than most experts think. Tech always does—until suddenly it takes off. And then often it's at least somewhat out of control.

I have witnessed major tech disruptions up close. With this particular reshuffling of the deck, however, there are new wild cards in play: the AIs themselves. To what extent might they be able to contribute to their own development in ways that are unprecedented? What if a Moore's Law of AI has machine intelligence doubling, not every eighteen months, but every eighteen hours? While *Machina sapiens* has its "mystery inside an enigma" aspect, I think it is safe to say that, in the short term, AIs will continue to evolve and improve along two separate paths:

1. **The Slow Lane:** In some cases, AIs will limp along in fits and starts for decades, struggling to overcome niggling real-world problems, such as learning how to turn an eighteen-wheeler in a hail storm, creating and writing a comedy TV show, and fighting to overcome some regulatory hurdle. AIs struggling to overcome real-world problems of various kinds and making only modest progress are in the AI slow lane.
2. **The Fast Lane:** In other cases—especially when massive data crunching or lightspeed learning through rapid iteration is involved—AIs will explode with unimaginable power and perform in ways that will have our jaws dropping. AlphaZero is one recent example. Another is Deep Patient, a medical AI that is diagnosing disease and predicting treatment outcomes, and about which we will have more to say later. These AIs are in the fast lane.

Knowing which efforts fall into which category will be a crucial skill for investors and for nearly everyone interested in earning a living or learning to live successfully in a rapidly changing world.

If we take a macroview of AI and account for general economic factors, it's not terribly difficult to see where AI trends are headed. Companies, professional firms, and government agencies that have first-class AI experts on staff, reasonably large quantities of well-curated data, and an open playing field with respect to regulation will have a great run in the decade ahead. But AGI and superintelligence systems will be few and far between.

Over the next decade, many legitimate AI-driven business opportunities will emerge, so much so that, when I find myself speaking to my granddaughter's generation (she just finished college), I'm like the partygoer in the classic scene from *The Graduate*, the guy who whispers "plastics" in Dustin Hoffman's ear—only I'm whispering "AI."

Mark Cuban predicted on CNBC that an AI start-up will produce the world's first high-tech trillionaire.[16] This trillionaire is less likely to be a techie who writes a new AI algorithm than a business pragmatist who finds a brilliant new way to use an existing AI platform, such as, OpenAI, an AI research and training platform, or OpenFace, a face-recognition platform, or any number of commercial platforms from the likes of IBM, Microsoft, Intel, Google, and Oracle.

In 1849, my great-great-grandfather traveled to Calaveras County, California, in the midst of the great forty-niner gold rush. I "rushed" to the Internet to start a company in 1992, so I understand the allure of gold strikes. The latest alert across my desk is that the Chinese facial recognition startup Face++ just received $480 million in venture capital. SenseTime, another Chinese AI company, raised money at a valuation of $3 billion to become the world's richest start-up, circa 2018.[17] A lot of people are going to make a lot of money in the AI gold rush over the next decade or two.

But AI is not all good news and fast business. Even Andrew Ng—the AI expert who equates AI risk with overpopulation on Mars—worries about what AI will do to the global job market. I, too, worry about job losses.[18]

I worry that a new, highly intelligent technology that is entirely goal driven is being sent out into the world without a proper set of goals—or even much appreciation of how crucial the setting of these goals are.

I worry that we American citizens have decided to let a small group of smart tech CEOs drive a vital socio-techno-economic agenda. The robber barons at the turn of the twentieth century should have been so lucky!

I worry that, as I write, the government of the United States barely has a seat at the global AI table. This may be changing, and I hope it does.

I worry that most Americans have no idea major tech storms are headed their way, category 5 tech storms with economic impact over time that will be bigger than Katrina. Not one big singularity hurricane but a bunch of them, hundreds of new storms that never leave. A leap of singularities, to coin a new collective term. But these new leaps of superintelligence will not be arriving soon, so like most in the AI industry, I don't lose sleep worrying about singularities appearing in my lifetime.

But in the meantime, I do worry about truck drivers.

CHAPTER FOUR

~

Truckin' in Flip-Flops

"Even if you are on the right track, you'll get run over if you just sit there."

—Will Rogers

With AIs come new unsettling questions. One of the more pressing is, What about the nine million middle-class jobs in the American trucking industry that experts believe are at risk because Volvo, Freightliner, and Tesla are selling self-driving trucks? These jobs support tens of millions of men, women, and children month to month. For such folks, knowing whether self-driving trucks are two years or two decades away is a matter of some import.

Not everyone believes that replacing humans with AIs will result in permanent job losses. Traditional economists cling to the blacksmiths-into-mechanics theory of job disruptions, which holds that technology does not destroy jobs; it morphs them.[1] Technology taketh away, goes this thinking, and then giveth back. It's true, in some cases, that blacksmiths did become auto mechanics, that travel agents went to work in customer support for Expedia, and that bookstore owners started mining bitcoin. As indirect as many of these transitions are, the economic numbers appear to support this transmogrification theory of labor: After decades of growing automation in the United States, unemployment percentages are at historical (if misleading) lows.

But are we reaching an automation tipping point? What if we are entering an era when the new jobs technology creates become so complex—and low paying—that only AIs need apply?

Self-Drivers on the Road

In 2018, Uber began rolling self-driving trucks across the deserts of Arizona.[2] Each of its trucks still had a human trucker at the wheel—not driving but ready to take over if needed. These Uber trucks rolled only on major highways, to and from distribution hubs. At these hubs, cargo was moved from autonomous vehicles to human-driven trucks before making final delivery.

The self-driving truck subsidiary Otto was purchased by Uber for $680 million, three years after Otto was founded.[3] Otto started, before its acquisition, by producing the digital eyes, ears, and brains for Uber trucks. A key component was the LiDAR scanner that sits atop the roof of the cab, constantly whirling around, scanning the horizon. In 2016, the cost of an Otto LiDAR scanner was $100,000. The Silicon Valley autonomous vehicle pioneer Quanergy recently announced new solid-state LiDAR, which (according to *Forbes*) the company expects to sell for around $250.[4] That's one-quarter of 1 percent of the price of Otto's scanner! Quanergy's LiDAR scanner may not be as heavy-duty as Otto's, but when prices start dropping this much, it's a clear sign that self-driving technology is taking off.

Hang out at an upscale truck stop, as I've been doing lately, and over the road banter in the cafe, sports TV in the bar, and country music in the lounge, you'll hear lively debates on the "self-drivers": the big rigs that drive themselves. Getting truckers to talk about them isn't hard. I've been surprised how informed most truckers are about self-drivers. Research on autonomous trucks is plentiful—from MIT reports to press releases from the International Brotherhood of Teamsters—but many truckers still get their information at the truck stops. After speaking with them, I've come to believe that truckers could well be the canaries in our AI coal mines.[5]

The consensus of highly paid analysts in New York and DC is that long-haul trucking jobs will virtually disappear over the next decade—technologically possible but politically problematic.

Jubitz Truck Stop on I-5, just south of the Washington–Oregon border, is bigger than many small towns.[6] Its twenty-seven acres offer the weary trucker diesel fuel, tire changes, a hotel room, a cinema, chiropractic service, on-site boot repair, a huge homestyle restaurant, and a country music bar with live acts every weekend. I came here for breakfast, with a loose plan to interview truckers about the new self-driving rigs. Before sitting down, I walked by the tall, museum-quality "50 Trucking Facts" wall at the entrance to the restaurant, and I learned the following (each fact has its own stylish mount on the wall):

- 8.9 million Americans work in the trucking industry.
- 3.5 million make their living as long-haul drivers.
- 90 percent of long-haulers work at small companies with ten trucks or less.
- 5.8 percent of long-haul truckers are female.
- The average small business truck driver spends 240 nights on the road and drives 100,000 miles per year.
- There are 500,000 trucking-related accidents in the United States each year. Only 16 percent are caused by truckers.

Trucking is an integral part of the life and culture in America and around the world. According to Indeed, the average annual trucker's salary in the U.S. is $66,000—a decent middle-class wage.[7] A 2017 Goldman Sachs report suggests that self-driving vehicles will soon be putting 300,000 drivers out of work every year.[8] The great majority will be long-haul truckers. At that rate, in ten years, there would be no human truckers left. That's a lot of middle-class buying power up in smoke and an enormous amount of pain and suffering for millions of American families.

It's little wonder Goldman is bullish on automation. In 2000, the cash-trading desk at Goldman's New York headquarters had six hundred workers; today, because of a program to install computerized AIs, it has two.[9] If Goldman is right about the trucking industry going through a similar disruption, what job could a middle-aged trucker morph into, say, in 2025? Especially since, by this point, robots will be unloading docks, patrolling factories as night watchmen, and selling auto parts.

One trucker I spoke with in the Jubitz bar said he wouldn't want any other kind of job anyway: "The open road becomes a way of life. I'd be no good stuck in some kind office or even in a garage. I like moving, seeing new things, talking to new people. That's part of the deal." It's a deal many think will get nullified soon. Accenture, IBM, and other big consulting firms are saying much the same thing as Goldman's trucking industry analysts.

Willard Protsman thinks all these experts are wrong—at least for the next fifteen to twenty years. Willard is a hefty, fiftyish career truck driver from Sand Point, Idaho. I met him at the Jubitz counter over breakfast, just past 7 a.m. I was having a country omelet with sausage and something that looked like gravy; he was making short work of a slice of cream pie. His eyes looked as if he might have been driving all night. I told him I was writing a book on AI and self-driving vehicles, and I asked if he'd mind answering a few questions. He agreed instantly with a smile. He was bright, friendly, articulate, and surprisingly well-informed about self-driving trucks. I'd struck gold.

What Willard Protsman loves to do, above all, is *drive*. As a young college student, he grabbed a round-trip ride on a big rig delivery from Spokane to San Francisco. All he ever wanted to do from then on was drive the best, biggest, coolest trucks across America. Willard works for a big trucking company—big enough to replace any rig he's driving, anywhere in the United States, within hours if there's a mechanical problem. Big enough for Willard to be wearing both his company's ball cap and its bright yellow "Safety First!" T-shirt.

I explained a bit about this book and that I was interviewing all types of people about AI. I got him to sign the release form my publisher insists I execute, and while doing so, I told Willard of having just heard that the Teamsters Union (still run by a Hoffa) was lobbying Congress aggressively to halt all further self-driving-truck research on the grounds that autonomous vehicles were too dangerous and would take away too many American jobs. I asked Willard if he agreed with the Teamsters. His instant answer: "Heck no. Self-driving's going to be a tremendous boon to us truckers. Bring it on!"

Willard envisions the day when he and his rig will be rolling a full fourteen hours a day (beyond the current eleven-hour limit). He'll spend much of that time "in a Hawaiian shirt with my flip-flops on, a Shirley Temple in one hand and my iPad in the other." He expects that his AI copilot will take over during long, restricted-lane slogs on superhighways, in traffic jams, and on good stretches of open road. "But," Willard smiled, "my truck won't be going anywhere without me."

Turns out Willard is not just a trucker; he's also his company's chief trainer of new drivers, which landed him in a number of Volvo's self-driving truck seminars, where he saw videos of European eighteen-wheelers rolling down pristine, largely empty highways lined with snow and Swedish angst. The trucks navigated successfully without any humans onboard.

He was impressed but not *that* impressed:

> I've seen these new autonomous trucks using radar, LiDAR, and GPS in interesting ways. They're damned good today in ideal conditions. Trouble is, not many routes have all ideal conditions, where it never snows or hails, with no unscheduled road repairs, no blown tires, no local emergencies, no sharp turns in GPS blind spots, and things of that nature. When a self-driving truck can figure out how to reroute around a sudden emergency or make a fifty-six-foot rig turn in an intersection of twenty-six-foot roads, *then* I go fishing.

We agreed that trucks with regular, prescribed routes will be the first to become fully automated. "A good example," Willard said, "is the off-road trucks used in mining operations. That's where Volvo is focused right now." He also felt it might be a good time for farm-equipment drivers to start thinking about a new career:

> But us long haulers, we're not goin' anywhere. People don't want huge robot trucks on the highways without drivers. The Teamsters shouldn't be trying to stop AI research. We *want* trucks to get more and more automated, easier to drive, more efficient, and so on. But the Teamsters *should totally* be lobbying to make it that, on public highways, a licensed commercial trucker has to be in the cab whenever a rig is rolling.

Willard feels his job is safe until retirement, which comes "2028-*ish*." Learning to drive an eighteen-wheeler with 60,000 pounds of cargo in both ideal and nonideal conditions isn't easy. Turning such a truck around in an eighteen-yard-wide alley is really hard. Willard is skeptical that AIs will ever master the big-rig alley turn. But mostly, Willard thinks his job is safe because humans are so slow to change:

> The government doesn't want to piss us truckers off. Neither political party does. We're good working families who spend a ton of money as consumers. We're a community, the brotherhood of the road. Take us down, Walmart comes with us. Truck stops, burger joints, country music, too. Plus, there are serious safety issues around driverless trucks, big time. Don't kid yourself: It'll be a long time before you start seeing big rigs with empty cabs.

Summers during college, I worked as a truck driver in California's hot San Joaquin Valley, where my mother's family had farmed for generations. I drove cottonseed dump trucks and flatbeds stacked with newly bailed hay and hauled lung-burning ammonia gas in pressured tankers to freshly plowed fields in need of fertilizer. The harvest season hours were long, but the pay was good. I enjoyed being a truck driver—learning how to back up a trailer, how to double-shift while gearing up and down, how to speak farm-worker Spanglish, and how to drink Jack Daniels while sitting on a hay bale. I liked the solitude of driving best. It gave me time to think, something every young American man needed back in the late 1960s. Chugging at forty-five miles per hour with a load of barley toward the granary in the high heat with the windows down on a warm summer night in the valley—what could be better?

I'm biased. I love that we humans have these big, wonderful machines called trucks, and I love that I got a chance to drive them, but it's time to move on. The planet can no longer afford fleets of deiselholics farting carbon into our atmosphere. Tesla and Volvo trucks, among others, will eventually solve the exhaust problem with big rigs that are not only self-driving but also nonpolluting. And to my new friend Willard Protsman, this is all great news.

Willard said he always gets excited when some sexy new tech improvement makes it into the trucks he drives. Over his career, he has seen nearly every part of the truck improve, sometimes amazingly. And for him, the "self-driving feature" is like advanced power steering: very cool but hardly game changing. So he's fine with all this new self-driving stuff. Far be it for him to slow down the trucking industry's adoption of AI. He just wants to be sure human drivers keep the keys to the trucks.

From my conversations with Willard and other truckers and from my own research, it appears to me that the giant American trucking industry is safe from the kinds of imminent job losses predicted by Goldisox and the other analyst companies.[10] Yes, off-road trucks with regular prescribed routes will become self-driving. Yes, trucks will become increasingly intelligent and situation aware, with automatic mileage logging that will make roads safer for everyone. Yes, AIs will drive trucks on their own in certain controlled situations. But for the next decade, Willard will still be there in his cab, stretched out in his Hawaiian shirt and flip-flops, supervising everything.

AI self-driving trucks will continue to roll ahead—but in the AI slow lane—because the pressing question is not, Can trucks learn to drive themselves? It's, When will we the people let them?

The High Flyers

If I'm right and the American trucking industry does stay in the AI slow lane, it will be due largely (but not entirely) to human factors. Willard convinced me that training an AI to back an eighteen-wheeler into a distribution dock located in a neighborhood with narrow, single-lane roads is the equivalent of training an AI to write and record a country music hit. Theoretically, it's possible, but as he put it, "don't hold your breath." Goldman Sachs' prediction of the virtual elimination of truck driver jobs in a decade is silly. Maybe in a cold, abstract world, with no red-meat Republican truckers and no I'm-sticking-with-union Democrat truckers, politicians could lean forward and get driverless trucks on the road tomorrow. But as Willard declared confidently, "Ain't gonna happen."

The consensus of highly paid analysts in New York and DC is that long-haul trucking jobs will virtually disappear over the next decade—technologically possible but politically problematic. Forging a political consensus for driverless trucks on our highways is a very big lift. Over the next decade, self-driving systems will enable large trucking companies to keep their rigs on the road longer and operate more safely and with less environmental impact—but laws will require that human truckers, brothers of the road, remain in the cab on crowded highways.

Still, AI-enabled efficiencies will inevitably lead to lost driver jobs. In the short term, this falloff will be moderate and manageable. Volvo, Freightliner, and Tesla, the big manufacturers of self-driving trucks, won't want to bite the hands that drive them. The manufacturers have a vested interest in progressing slowly and promoting the formula that AI + humans = the best trucking. During this transition period, millions of American truckers will learn to share their cabs with AIs. At some point—my guess is about fifteen to twenty years—the economics of self-drivers without humans will become compelling enough and public acceptance of self-drivers wide enough that trucks driven solely by AIs will dominate our highways. Until then, truck drivers will continually interact with AIs on the open road and become expert at working with an AI partner. Could truck drivers become sought-after AI wranglers in a variety of other industries? It's not exactly a blacksmiths-into-mechanics scenario, but it might work.

To get another view of the future of the trucking business, I called my friend Paul Duchene. Paul is a former automotive writer for the *Chicago Tribune* and *New York Times*. A sportscar and motorcycle racer, and a speedway race announcer, and is writing a rare book about rare cars—the kind of cars that sell for millions. For forty years, Paul has lived and breathed cars, trucks, and motorcycles—especially motorcycles, which he has raced from Alaska to Yucatan. He is British born and educated; has a quick, acerbic wit and a ponytail; and could, in the right circumstances late at night, be mistaken for an original Monty Python.

I told Paul about my interview with Willard (and other truckers) at the Jubitz Truck Stop and about my conclusions regarding the impact of AI on trucking. He feels my assessments are pretty good, except he thinks adoption of completely self-driving trucks is more likely to take fifty years than fifteen.

> You high-tech guys are missing the point, though," says Paul. "It's not whether there's a driver in the vehicle; it's whether or not the vehicle is on the ground. Since Jules Verne, science fiction has had us flying in the air, not dragging our asses over ground. Remember the Jetsons—flying cars everywhere.
>
> The big question regarding AIs in trucks—and cars—is not whether they can become completely self-driving on land but whether or not they can be self-flying in the air. If they can efficiently and safely, then we will have reached transportation nirvana.

"Or Armageddon," I offer.

So that's what the automotive and trucking industries might ultimately look like if fast-lane AIs take over: a world with self-driving Lyft choppers, transporting humans and goods everywhere, up, down, here, and around. Remember, you read it here first. In the meantime, earth-bound truckers are advised to (1) bone up on self-driving systems and (2) and prepare to keep on trucking for at least another decade.

Two decades out, AI will undoubtedly be the big spoon stirring the transportation soup. *Machina sapiens* will be driving planes, trains, and automobiles and piloting ocean liners, helicopters, and drones. They will do so with fewer and fewer accidents. They will deliver lifesaving medicine, control air traffic, operate drawbridges, manage synthetic city traffic systems—and regularly plug themselves in for tuneups.

AIs will even dominate their own unique transportation sector: *space*. They'll be central to the development of new methods for transporting humans and cargo on Earth and to Mars and beyond. The Mars 2020 rover mission, which will land on the Red Planet in 2021, has AIs in four different rovers that together will guide the exploration of lava-tube caves. For much of this exploration, the rovers will not have communications with Earth, and the rover AIs will be making key decisions on their own.

The ultimate role for AIs in space will be to lead missions to places like Proxima Centauri—the nearest star—where communication with Earth takes nine years roundtrip. It would likely take a spacecraft forty to sixty years to reach Proxima Centauri. AIs will be in control of every phase of the mission.

One Small Step for an AI

Transportation, as far as I can tell, is one sector where the benefits of AI far outweigh the risks. In our new AI world, there will be autonomous drones—and smart ones. There will be new AI traffic control systems, self-flying spy planes, and motorcycles with autopilot.

There is also likely to be more disruption in the passenger car market—with fewer technical challenges and greater political support from Uber-loving consumers—than in trucking. Reuters is reporting that an unnamed European auto manufacturer recently ordered eight million self-driving taxis from Intel's Mobileye division for delivery in 2021.[11]

The transportation industry, strangely, has become an AI leader. If somehow truck and taxi-style drivers—who constitute a vital component of our global economy—can indeed be slowly transitioned into new jobs and new roles in society, then it will be better for all of us. But if professional drivers die out suddenly, like canaries in a gas-filled coal mine, then we are likely to be headed for real trouble. No AI expert, nor any transportation expert, would have predicted ten years ago that trucking and transportation would be vital areas of tech innovation, yet here we are. If AI is a global three-ring economic circus, then transportation is one of the center rings.

The hottest act in the AI transportation ring, of course, is self-driving cars. Are they coming? No. They're here now. When will they be legal on your roads? It's hard to know. I'd love to see one state in the United States completely embrace self-driving vehicles of all kinds—as Arizona attempted to do, though a bit prematurely—and then collect data regarding the actual on-road results. Such a data set would be valuable—enough perhaps to fund statewide vocational AI training programs. In general, transportation policy will be one avenue for tech-forward states to create economic environments that are AI-friendly.

Here on Earth, we can have great debates about if, how, and when AIs will start driving all our vehicles. But beyond the Moon, even just on missions to Mars, AIs will pilot the ship. AIs will be the new "right stuff" types, connecting us to places no man has gone before and perhaps never will, unless humans get to come along for the ride.

In the end, all the great sci-fi writers (except, notably, Arthur C. Clarke) got it wrong. Our future is not one of cyborgs and androids driving conventional cars; it's one of the cars driving themselves, with us humans riding along, perhaps in control or perhaps not. One of the chief factors that will determine whether we humans are in control is the quality of human education—and the nature of education in the age of AIs. Time to go back to school.

CHAPTER FIVE

~

Ben Franklin's Purse

"Education is learning what you didn't even know you didn't know."

—Daniel J. Boorstin

Chris Schuk, head of school at Northwest Academy (NWA), a thin man with his hand firmly on the rudder, was steering two hundred teenage students and a few faculty into their seats.[1] The seats were folding chairs set up on risers in the Blue Box Theater, NWA's small but brilliantly functional all-purpose auditorium. The Blue Box is just one of many remarkable things about this school.

Northwest Academy is chock-full of lightspeed learners—the teenaged kind. It's a unique and scholarly middle-through-high school in downtown Portland, Oregon, that emphasizes creativity, celebrates individuality, and has a tough no-nonsense policy when it comes to personal responsibility. Grammy-winning jazz artist Esperanza Spalding went there. Its graduates are recruited heavily for their academic and artistic prowess and win scholarships to the best universities.

When I visit the Northwest Academy, I get jealous. American education never worked for me. I dropped out of UC Berkeley as a sophomore because the *Pacific Grove Tribune* and several other newspapers on California's Monterey Peninsula agreed to take me on as a freelance reporter and commission-only ad salesman. I never looked back. I left UC Berkeley, one of the greatest educational institutions in the world, because I couldn't sit still for long lectures in classes with hundreds of students. It worked for some people but not for me. I ended up learning writing from editors rather than professors and business from starting companies rather than as an MBA grad student. In the 1980s, as a freelancer for McGraw-Hill, I learned science and computing by ghostwriting hobbyist books with titles such as *Fiber Optics and the Physics of Light* and one called, simply, *Personal Computing*. I cannot produce a Berkeley Ph.D., but I've been in the arena, and have kept learning.

Throughout my zigzag career path, I've followed one central piece of advice attributed to Benjamin Franklin, one of my heroes growing up (How could any self-respecting young geek not bond with the discoverer of electricity?): "If a man empties his purse into his head, no man can take it away from him. An investment in knowledge always pays the best interest."[2] I made many investments in knowledge in my early years as a writer and entrepreneur. In fact, my credo was that, as long as I kept learning through my various endeavors, mastering some important new skill or acquiring new knowledge about a technology or market, every venture was a success.

It's been many years now, but I used to tell people I dropped out of Berkeley in order to keep learning. I was literally and figuratively sleeping in Berkeley's lecture halls. An entrepreneur needs to keep moving to avoid getting stagnant or bored. Even when quite young, he or she wants the table stakes to be higher than some letter grade at the end of a semester. Entrepreneurs want the real world to be their teacher. That's what drove me to leave college at age nineteen, but I might have felt differently about formal education had I attended Northwest Academy.

That day in the Blue Box, I was there to give a talk on AI. It was my first time back to the school in two years, when I visited a seventh-grade classroom. The school's visionary founder, Mary Folberg, was giving me a tour when, in response to a question I asked, she suggested we pop into a class to observe. We did and were able to sit in with almost no disruption. The seventh-grade teacher briefly explained to us that her students were presenting their finals, showing the results of a two-month-long assignment. They had all been assigned the task of presenting a major decision of the US Supreme Court in the form of art. Around the room were song lyrics on placards, a clay sculpture of some kind, musical instruments, and more. Two-student teams of keyed-up seventh-graders waited their turn to present *Marbury v. Madison* as a puppet show or *Loving v. Virginia* as modern interracial dance. Mary and I sat quietly and watched them present. The content was serious, detailed, and entertaining. Some teams sang and danced; others explained how their forms of painting and sculpture reflected the contours of Supreme Court jurisprudence; one team presented stylish graphs and charts, as if they were selling smart phones at a high-end trade show.

Each project provided a bit of historical context, and each team gave its interpretation of why its particular Supreme Court ruling is still relevant today. Or not. There was real art on display; a clever original song played on a guitar by a girl with long hair and a sweet young voice, and an amazing Calderesque mobile, passionately explained by a youngster who looked like a cross between Woody Allen and Bob Marley. Excitement filled the room; these students were as hyped as basketball starters in the playoffs. Mary and I had to leave before we could learn which team took home the trophy, but there were no losers in that room. Honestly, to use San Francisco vernacular, I was blown away.

On this day, though, I was the noontime lecturer. Schuk introduced me by contrasting my background with his own. He'd been in secondary education all his career, he told the assembled students. "But our guest today has had multiple careers. Your futures will be more like his than mine. You're going to learn new disciplines and try new careers all your life—and artificial intelligence will be one of the tools you'll use."

Schuk was referring, I think, to my checkered past in journalism, book publishing, film and TV production, and Internet software. I'm pretty sure he didn't even know about the truck driving, or the comic strip. But actually, I've had just one career. Since the mid-1970s, I've been a serial entrepreneur—on occasion a successful one, on occasion not. But always, as best I could, emptying my purse into my head.

I gave my standard talk on AI, noting to myself that these high-schoolers were far less distracted than the students at a top university I'd visited the week before. There was no secret checking of phones or tablets and no whispers shared among huddled friends. These NWA students appeared to be paying rapt attention. When I paused to ask for questions, a dozen hands shot up.

I selected a student in the front row, who asked, "What's your opinion on the AI trolley problem?"

"Great question," I responded. "The trolley problem is a famous AI ethics thought experiment. A runaway trolley is racing down the track. Up ahead, five people are tied to the main track. There is also a side track with one person tied to it. Nearby, a man with a black hat twirls a waxed moustache." (I just made up this last part, and it got a laugh.). "You are on the trolley, and you know how to steer the car. There are no seconds to lose. Should you turn the trolley down the side track, murdering one person intentionally, or do nothing, allowing five people to die? The ethical question, in the context of AI, is, If an AI were controlling the trolley, should it have been trained to turn onto the side track and deliberately kill one or do nothing as the trolley kills five?" A fairly sophisticated question and one with broad ramifications for *Machina sapiens*, far beyond trolleys.

My flip answer: "I'd flip off the AI's on/off switch, which every AI should have, by law, so that the trolley would slow down before reaching the people on the tracks." A total cheat of an answer, of course. Though it did spark a spirited discussion.

Actually, I'd train the AIs to turn down the side track. Once an AI is in full control of the trolley the only question is, One death or five? But it is easy to see how complicated things will become once AIs start making even fully ethical and compassionate decisions about which humans live and which humans die. We worked out this philosophical thought experiment together, the young NWA students and I, and everyone seemed to agree in the end: AIs should be trained to save as many human lives as possible, even if things get complicated.

Next, I told the students I had a question for them: "Can anyone explain the technological singularity?" A tall, bright, dark-haired young fellow named Octavo stood up and absolutely nailed it. He not only explained the meaning of the term but also put it in the context of the various contemporary AI camps. I asked him if and when he thinks the technological singularity is coming? His answer: "It's coming, but the timing will be not be a matter of logic—more a result of randomness and luck. So hard to say but probably not anytime soon."

Chris Schuk was right, I believe, about the changing nature of education. We no longer live in a one-job-for-life world, where you dedicate your life to the study of, say, radiology. The one-life, one-career education model makes no sense if there are no radiologist jobs at the end of the journey. Thus, at NWA, the focus is not on acquiring deep knowledge in specific domains but on learning how to learn, think critically, use tools, be creative, and work in teams.

After my talk in the Blue Box, I spent an hour in a philosophy class. A dozen students were around a table, a woman teacher was at the head, and her young daughter was drawing pictures nearby. It turned out, this class had just spent six weeks delving into the philosophical and ethical issues around AI. The students could intelligently discuss Plato's cave, John Searle's Chinese room, or the paper-clip problem, all from an AI perspective. The young man who'd asked the trolley question was in the class, as was Octavo. Again, I found the students highly engaged, and each one spoke up. As one explained to me after the seminar, "Here at Northwest Academy, it's not cool not to care."

At NWA, high school students study AI ethics. They also build anatomically correct cow hearts out of kiln-fired glass, program their own video games, run their own sustainable fashion company,[3] release their own music albums, and design and build their own robots. The latter is what Octavo did last year as a sophomore. He even wrote his own neural network software to get his robot to move more intelligently.

After class, I spoke with Octavo about his personal exploration of AIs, neural nets, and robots. We had a lively discussion about the difference between general AI and superintelligence. One of the striking things about the NWA students was the degree to which they all felt—they all *knew*—that AI would be a major factor in their lives. They thought about AI in ways I hadn't seen before. It wasn't sci-fi. It was the new electricity.

Octavo had plateaued with his high school AI studies and now wanted to take his next big step. He became excited when I told him I would try to find an engineering mentor for him within the AI industry. Driving home after my visit to NWA, it occurred to me that, someday in the not-too-distant future, the bright, young Octavos of this world will each have their own personal AI mentors to guide them as they set up neural networks, study for chemistry exams, or write papers on the poetry of Bob Dylan. If AI learning tools are made available to bright high school students, they will use them. Oh, will they use them.

The main insight I had after visiting NWA was this: The new AIs, the lightspeed learners, will knock it out of the park as teachers in the decades ahead, so long as enough investors recognize that a huge market is coming for AIs in education and fund new companies to develop them—because, in the age of AI, continuing education will be a lifelong pursuit.

There are already AI-*ish* tutoring courses for learning to play the trumpet or speak Spanish. Some new AI education industry tools are also emerging, such as

- AIs that can grade students' written tests
- Immersive-learning environments with hands-on interactivity
- Bots that can answer many student questions on specific subjects
- Data-driven simulations and gamification with lightspeed learning

There have long been software programs that can tutor and mentor students in highly personalized ways, but as yet, no breakout AI tutoring system has emerged. I find this surprising, given that certain tutoring algorithms, notably Bayesian Knowledge Tracing (BKT), have been around for decades.[4]

And they're pretty good. They seem to be an excellent foundation for new AI personal tutors for both children and adults.

But overall, the education market is still a developing nation in the world of AI, and the use of lightspeed learners to help humans get smarter is still a back-burner market.

Outside of institutions like the NWA that crave innovation and promote individuality, change in education is slow, and innovation, difficult. The main teaching method is still a faculty member passing on his or her knowledge from the front of a classroom to students in the seats—some of whom are actually listening. After my day at the Northwest Academy—where instruction happens in seminars, team projects, and individual study—the old faculty-lecture method of instruction seems like a chalkboard in a clean room: way out of date. I hated this method decades ago! But what's the new educational model? Or models, plural? Will AIs become Mr. Chips?

AIs will almost certainly become a bigger part of education by 2025. Knowledge-tracing models, such as BKT, will play a key role.[5] They provide a foundation for cognitive tutoring systems by measuring two different "states" of a student's knowledge: the state of the student knowing the material at a specific level, represented as 1, and the state of the student not knowing that same material, represented as 0. Using these two binary states, student knowledge is then modeled, measured, and cataloged over time. Since digital tutors can become quite accurate at predicting how students will respond to new information and how ready they are to acquire new skills, the tutor can suggest content that is neither too easy nor too hard and that is highly suited to the next-step learning needs of the individual student. This is today, before any deep AI integration.

New intelligent tutoring systems that use AI to tailor content to students based on their unique needs and abilities have been producing promising results. One example is the iTalk2Learn system engineered and tested at Carnegie Mellon University.[6] This open-source AI platform tutors young children in math fractions. The content and its delivery sequence are based on information about the individual student. iTalk2Learn is kid-savvy. It knows how to measure a student's knowledge of arithmetic, emotional state, cognitive abilities, extracurricular schedule, and so forth. iTalk2Learn itself also continues learning based on feedback loops fueled by student response and performance data. Though only an experimental prototype, its documented results have been compelling. I fully expect we will see much progress in AI tutoring systems soon.

As with all AIs, digital tutors crave data, which, in the education market, means they will be queuing up outside Kahn Academy, the world's perfect educational data-collection engine. The Kahn Academy does a fantastic job of providing academically vetted instruction on a tremendous number of serious subjects to everyone on Earth. The goal of Sal Khan, the academy's founder, was to deliver first-class educational instruction to anyone, anywhere, free of charge, and his online school has achieved that goal in spades. Along the way, the Kahn Academy was smart enough to start collecting data—not personally invasive data, just anonymized stats, including a great deal of data on how people around the world learn. The main AI slogan: *It's the data, stupid.* In the age of AI, he who has the biggest or best data wins. In this context, in the field of education, keep your eye on the Kahn Academy, which to date has been quite generous in sharing its data with AI researchers.

Imagine if high school students could download their own personal chemistry teacher, who would design a course of study uniquely tailored to the skills and intelligence of the student and queue up expert presentations from around the world (in precisely the right order). This virtual instructor would also give tests and grade them, provide instructions for lab experiments, and even order all the ingredients for them. It would then stamp out a pass grade or a legit credential once a course had been mastered.

Like all software, the early versions of digital tutors will be buggy and prone to weird gaps in common sense. They will get better quickly, though, because student–tutor activity is, of course, being logged, tagged, and stored, creating ever-growing databases of complex results related to various learning methods and content. Which in turn provides a basis for tutoring systems to continually learn and deliver more effective instruction and guidance.

In the short term, the most progress in AI-based instruction may come outside the classroom. Imagine if, as an adult, you had your own virtual Julia Child helping you prepare dinner. This Julia would be a world-class chef and cooking instructor who would pop up on a kitchen screen at cooking time, suggesting dishes fitted to your tastes and culinary skills, coaching you on how to gently sauté an oyster, or teaching you to gut a squid. Personally, I wouldn't mind having an Alexa right now who could guide me gently through Hebbian network theory with an emphasis on synaptic plasticity.[7]

Overall, the education market is still a developing nation in the world of AI, and the use of lightspeed learners to help humans get smarter is still a back-burner market, which is a shame. While self-driving buses today shuttle tourists around the strip in Las Vegas, classrooms in America, despite having showy interactive whiteboards, remain largely AI-free zones.

Educational AIs have the same problem as self-driving trucks: human inertia. In the case of education, though, there are fewer government regulatory hurdles to overcome. Part of the problem is that education is where the money *isn't*. Just ask teachers in West Virginia, Oklahoma, Arizona, and Washington, which have all had major teacher strikes recently. In education, the other road bumps include tradition, shrinking enrollment, tightening budgets, tenure, and a generation of increasingly distracted students.

I watched a recent TEDx talk by a college professor whose revolutionary thesis was that the Internet just might change everything inside traditional classrooms. His "vision" was that traditional teachers would be giving lectures to butts-in-seats students with the help of Internet guides. He gave this talk in 2017! Excuse me. You're saying the Internet is about to affect education? Ten years after the founding of the Kahn Academy? With no mention of AI? No mention of 3-D printing? No mention of gamification? Unfortunately, this talk speaks mostly to how far traditional education is lagging behind technologically. There are dairy companies who leverage big data and AI better than most schools, including colleges. Land O' Lakes butter, for example, is using data analytics and early stage AI from Microsoft throughout its supply chain, and getting great results.[8] The Khan Academy is exhibit A of "How the Internet Changed Education." But the Khan Academy—actually, multiple Khan-like new services—will also be at the forefront of the AI education revolution, with AI assistants, tutors, and mentors in starring roles.

The AI education disruption is coming in the 2020s, I believe, and will usher in many new AI educational games, including space games, where an embedded AI player will have awesome knowledge of astrophysics and enable fantastic learning scenarios; and sports games, where math knowledge is essential for coaching your team to victory. The AI gamification of education is just getting started but will very likely become a major trend in the 2020s at every grade level.

The AI revolution will hit adult education hardest. Studying AI inevitably makes you bullish on the human lifelong-learning market. Those laid-off insurance actuaries have to do something, right? One smart thing for them—along with the truck drivers, oncologists, paralegals, sound mixers, etc.—would be to keep learning. Keep emptying their purses into their heads, with their own personal lightspeed learner guiding them toward mastery of the V-Model or some other entry-level age of AI skill or knowledge competency (see chapter 12 for a full discussion of job training in an AI world).[9]

AI's Training Humans

Let's try a trampoline backflip. What if every worker layoff caused by the onset of automation came with an immediate career lifeline? Lose your job to a robot in Fresno or an AI paralegal in San Francisco, and you are immediately enrolled in California's new Smart Workforce Program. You get your own personal AI tutor who is your "let's get you a job" partner. You immediately start taking classes online, with a curriculum designed by America's growth industries. Not only is all instruction free, but participants also are actually paid to achieve learning benchmarks. Because the job market has become dynamic and fast changing, instruction blocks are kept short and highly focused on a particular skill or capability. An aggressive learner studying a high-value skill (such as neural-network quality-assurance testing or acupressure foot massage) can earn a sustainable monthly salary for six months to a year. The AI tutors take assessments about each worker's learning abilities, just as iTalk2Learn does when teaching young children math. Using their own AI swarm intelligence, the tutor-AIs guide their worker-students all the way back into a new job. The tutor-AIs stay with the worker even after she is hired so that learning continues.

State and local governments could do this tomorrow, ideally with the help of the major tech companies and U.S. federal grant dollars. The total cost nationally would be less than one aircraft carrier (by a factor of ten), and the impact could be generational, like the GI Bill or the Peace Corps. The key idea is to use AI to equip the humans displaced by AI with the appropriate skills to get another job with a future. Such a program would cut out all this "make coalmining great again" crap and start helping American workers compete in the global marketplace—not the global marketplace for political grievances but the real one, the one with real money.

While AI's potential to help students and workers learn is considerable, so, too, is its potential to do harm—not in any direct, malevolent way but more through a gradual erosion of human cognitive capacity. Not surprisingly, children who begin relying on calculators at too young an age have been found to have a diminished ability to solve math problems on their own.[10] There are schools of thought within education advocating hard subjects be made easier whenever possible. Why, these education leaders argue, shouldn't all students be able to take advantage of the insights of advanced trigonometry? If trigonometry weren't so hard to learn, more people could understand it. Extreme advocates in this camp even believe students should not be taught to add, subtract, and multiply. I think people with this belief should be strapped in a desk forty minutes a day and forced to practice their cursive (see chapter 11).

The whole education-has-to-be-easy trend strikes me as nuts. Should we English speakers stop attempting to learn Mandarin simply because Google and Microsoft can now provide (pretty good) simultaneous translations? Come on. We need human intellectual achievement now more than ever, everywhere. If we toss in all our cards when it comes to basic cognitive skills, intellectual rigor, the scientific method, and the critical thinking it generates, we might as well all hitch a ride to the paper-clip factory.[11]

Several weeks after my visit to NWA, I conducted a follow-up interview with head of school Chris and student Octavo. They had read portions of this book, which led to a variety of discussions. Octavo was quite interested in the role of randomness in the development and operation of AI and felt that it has been underplayed in most of the scientific literature to date. Because randomness and uncertainty are an essential part of nature, why would they not also be in the life and development of AIs?

I asked Chris if he thought AIs would ever be used for student assessment, leading perhaps to AI-driven student counseling that dispelled hopes of going to college by third grade, or other even some more Draconian measures. Could AI's predictive power someday become a kind of early destiny for teenagers?

"My own sense," wrote Chris in an e-mail reply to this question, "is that there's a corollary to Heisenberg's Uncertainty Principle that applies to adolescent learners: we cannot accurately describe simultaneously their position and their trajectory. As an educator, I am more interested in their trajectory." Using AIs to develop "predictive schemes" about the future learning capability of his young students, Chris claimed, would tend to "keep students in a fixed position" instead of inspiring growth and exploration.

I got the sense, somehow, that, in my dialog with NWA students and faculty, I was getting a glimpse into the age of AI itself. Complex human questions, philosophical and ethical questions, will lie at the heart of not just education but also all human civilization, as we all struggle to learn and redefine what it means to be human.

Chris Shuck's final words to me in an email were, "Good luck and god speed (if, in fact, that is near as fast as lightspeed)!"

CHAPTER SIX

~

A Modest Proposal

> "In our age there is no such thing as 'keeping out of politics.' All issues are political issues."
>
> —George Orwell

My quest to learn more about how the US government might better prepare for the AI invasion took me to Nashville, Tennessee, on a cold, wet Sunday in April. Exiting the plane, airport speakers played PSAs read by country music stars. Twenty minutes later, I entered the stately, venerable lobby of the Sheraton Music City Hotel, which was eerily quiet and not as big as a blimp hangar. I rolled forty yards to the front desk to check in.

"What brings you to Nashville?' asked the pert, petite clerk with the "Danielle" nametag.

"I'm interviewing people at Vanderbilt for a book I'm writing about artificial intelligence. Do you know anything about it?"

"Sure. It's a university."

Pause. "Of course. Do you know anything about *artificial intelligence?*"

"Oh. Just enough to know that I don't want to know. It kind of scares me."

I suggested to Danielle that, the more she knew about artificial intelligence, the safer she'd be—and added, "That's a theme of my book."

A woman twice Danielle's age and size—nametag "Esther" and clearly the boss—stepped beside Danielle and said to me with a smile and a bit of swagger, "Ever interview Sophia?"

I did a Sylvester-and-Tweety double take. "Sophia?"

Esther turned to Danielle and with a proud smile explained, “Sophia is the world’s smartest robot. She was made in Hong Kong and uses artificial intelligence for her brains. She looks like a real woman, a beautiful woman, and her face has different expressions, ’cept her eyes are weird. You can talk to her, ask her questions. Will Smith interviewed her in Saudi.”

Esther returned to me, waiting for an answer.

“No, I’ve never interviewed Sophia,” I said. “Wow. How do you know about her?”

“Oh, right,” Esther answered, with a subtle smile. “We genteel women of Tennessee could not possibly know anything about artificial intelligence or algorithms or anything.” The last, with hands on hips and a hip shift.

She had me flustered, and I was able only to finish the sentence with a non sequitur: “Uh, I, uh, just flew in from Oregon.”

“Just messin’ with ya’,” Esther reassured, still emitting a radiant smile. “I got interested in AI through the movies and became curious. I read a lot, so I’ve been reading about AI lately. Very interesting. You believe in the singularity?”

“I’m not sure it’s something to believe in, necessarily. I don’t see us one day getting to some magical tipping point, where the lessons of history and laws of evolution no longer apply. But AIs are getting really smart, and they’re going to get even smarter—smarter than us in many ways.”

“I’ve got the new Roomba 960 at home,” Esther said. “Love it.” Then, “What’s the name of your book?”

I told her that my publisher and I hadn’t decided on a title yet but promised to send her a copy.

“You do that, and I’ll read it. I’m not afraid of AI. Counting the days, actually, ’til we get some AIs up here can take over the front desk.” She winked to me and punched Danielle gently on her shoulder.

Esther turned and walked back into her private office but only after instructing Danielle to upgrade me to a top-floor suite. That’s the kind of juju AI has now.

The next day, I had lunch in midtown Nashville with two Pulitzer Prize winners: Jon Meacham, the historian, and David Hume Kennerly, the photographer. Kennerly has been a longtime friend, as he mentions in the foreword to this book. He set up the lunch so I could meet Meacham, whose books I’ve read and admired. Meacham, it turns out, is a generous fellow who honors requests from longtime friends. He also possesses an eruptive laugh that might surprise you—and fellow diners.

My goal over lunch was to discuss the history of American laws regulating technology and commerce in light of the new challenges posed by *Machina sapiens*. Over a grilled chicken bowl (Kennerly and me), a grilled steak bowl (Meacham), and kale salad (Meacham's friend and fellow Vanderbilt professor John Geer), we had a wide-ranging discussion. Kennerly launched the conversation by describing a *New Yorker* cartoon on his refrigerator of a tombstone with the epitaph, "I can't believe I ate all that kale for nothing."

I gave my tablemates a quick overview of contemporary AI issues and explained why I believe the US government needs a comprehensive AI policy and program, not unlike the one France recently adopted, which led to a discussion of contemporary populism, Andrew Jackson, the history of seat belt regulations, successful antitobacco campaigns, and the Nixon administration's extraordinary air and water pollution laws. These last three areas of regulation combined still save hundreds of thousands of lives in America every year. Each set of regs was unpopular when first enacted, but all are solidly accepted today. This took us to the Atomic Energy Commission (AEC), arguably the most important regulatory agency in American history and an amazing success story, IMHO.[1]

The AEC was signed into being in 1946 by President Truman, one year after he'd approved dropping atomic bombs on Japan. The first head of the AEC, I pointed out, was a Tennessean (by way of Wisconsin) who had previously been a commissioner of the Tennessee Valley Authority (TVA). This man was a respected public-sector lawyer who guided the AEC as it was getting started and who by all accounts did a great job. I knew all this because I had googled[2] the history of the AEC and TVA that morning, but I couldn't remember that first chairman's name for the life of me.

"David Lilienthal," said Meacham, correctly identifying this obscure bureaucratic leader from the 1930s and '40s. In certain conversations, it really does help to have a historian at the table. The saga of David Lilienthal and the early days of the AEC is worth recounting here as one potential model for the regulation of AI by the US federal government.

The year is 1946. You are President Harry Truman, plain-spoken Missouri haberdasher, Mr. Buck-Stops-Here. Honest, admirable, practical—and the man personally responsible for the instant deaths of 80,000 Japanese in Hiroshima, most of them civilians, with more in Nagasaki. No one needs to convince you of the destructive power of nuclear fission. You get it. This stuff is lethal.

So you take precipitous action, advocating for legislation that gives the federal government complete control over all elements of nuclear energy. Within one year of the Hiroshima bombing, you sign the Atomic Energy Commission bill into law. This law grants the commission extraordinary powers. Henceforth, it shall own any and all nuclear patents and other intellectual policy, any and all nuclear research, any and all nuclear weapons, and any and all fissionable materials related to nuclear energy, whether for military or commercial purposes. Bottom line: Truman puts nuclear energy on a very short leash, with David Lilienthal as the principal leash holder.

The remarkable thing about Lilienthal, to my mind, is that he was not a scientist. A smart public-sector lawyer, a damn good administrator, a surprisingly skilled writer, but when he signed on to lead the AEC, he knew next to nothing about nuclear physics. In his personal journal, he describes his first in-depth, six-hour briefing on nuclear energy as a "fairy tale" both more horrible and more exciting than any story he had ever heard.[3]

Only one of the five original Atomic Energy commissioners was a scientist: Robert F. Bacher, a respected but relatively ordinary physicist from a Los Alamos lab. The commission had no generals, admirals, or military officers—just a banker, a farmer, a businessman, Lilienthal, and Bacher. These five men, and not the military, controlled all nuclear weapons and materials in the first years of the nuclear era. They and their civilian successors went on to guide America's atomic policies through three decades of the Cold War.

Over this time, through various political storms—ranging from right-wing criticism for not building the hydrogen bomb (on the advice of J. Robert Oppenheim) to left-wing criticism about nuclear plant safety and spent-fuel storage—the AEC managed to avoid nuclear war and limit major commercial accidents to the relatively minor Three Mile Island episode. The AEC did an admirable and perhaps indispensable job leading the world into the nuclear age. Is it time now for an Artificial Intelligence Commission?

If by that we mean a US government entity that owns and controls AI the way the AEC controlled nukes, the answer is clearly no. In our lunch discussion, Meacham agreed. In 1946, the US government had possession of all nuclear materials on Earth. The AEC just extended this control, albeit by taking it away from the US military and putting it in civilian hands. The situation with AI technology is completely different.

Controlling AI the way the AEC controlled nuclear energy is not only impossible, due to AI's out-of-the-bottle problem, but it would also be self-defeating. Regardless of regulatory controls imposed here, AI would still grow apace elsewhere, notably in Beijing and Moscow.

Controlling AI the way the AEC controlled nuclear energy is not only impossible, due to AI's out-of-the-bottle problem, but it would also be self-defeating. Regardless of regulatory controls imposed here, AI would still grow apace elsewhere, notably in Beijing and Moscow. At this point, there is absolutely no chance the US government can contain or constrain AI in any meaningful way, at least through traditional regulation. However, if modeling the Atomic Energy Commission means taking dramatic, high-level action that brings AI into national political focus and that creates a central, powerful, and citizen-led commission to provide leadership and high-level collaboration, then sign me up.

After lunch, Kennerly gave his Zelig-the-photographer show to Meacham's popular history class at Vanderbilt of 150 smart kids. In this show, Kennerly chronicled his life as a photo documentarian of the last fifty years of American history and showed pictures he'd taken, from Robert Kennedy to Gerald Ford; Frazier–Ali to Reagan–Gorbachev; Michelle Obama to Melania Trump. He talked about famous people he'd photographed. I watched from the top row of a steep classroom as students typed lecture notes and checked out Kennerly.com and then asked questions for an hour at the front of the classroom and in a small office outside it. The first question had come from Professor Meacham—one he'd asked Kennerly earlier, over lunch. At that time Meacham had been interrupted by a call he had to take, so Kennerly hadn't answered.

"David," said Meacham, from his seat in the classroom, "you've spent time with multiple presidents. You worked closely with President Ford, covered every presidential campaign since Warren G. Harding." Laughter. "How do you account for the devolution of the office of the presidency from the days of men of character like Ford and Carter to where the office is today? How did we lose our civility?"

Kennerly: "Difficult question. I watch TV pundits—like you, Jon—wrestle with this all the time. One thing for sure: The presidents I've known best, unlike the guy we have now, all had the civility to respect a free press, not as part of some political calculation, but in the absolute belief that a free press is essential to our democracy."

Meacham struck me as a pilgrim, searching for answers on how and why America lost her moral high ground. I am a tech entrepreneur; he is a historian. He looks back; I peer into the murky future. When we spoke, he was about to head out on a promo tour for his book *Soul of America: The Battle for Our Better Angels*. Reading it later, it made me wonder whether AIs someday would come to embody our better angels. But on this afternoon in his

Vanderbilt class, what he seemed to be asking Kennerly was, Have we lost our moral bearings as a democracy, and if so, why?

The third verse of *America the Beautiful*, sung by many generations of Americans, goes as follows:

> America! America!
> God shed His grace on thee
> Till selfish gain no longer stain,
> The banner of the free!

Quite an aspiration, the elimination of all selfish gain—and one I wouldn't wait up for, human nature being what it is. But this verse shows the extraordinary idealism at the heart of America, despite her great many flaws.

Meacham gets this strain of America instinctively. I have lived all my life with a love for America—made inestimably stronger by living and working in China, Thailand, Japan, and India. Meacham's life's work now seems to be to reconnect us with the best of our past in order to meet the challenges of the future, such as AI.

Citizens of America, I feel your pain. Our country is hurting. Opioid addiction is an epidemic, teen suicide rates at all-time highs. Wackos with guns keep shooting our children and other innocents. Factory jobs are disappearing, and no trade war is going to bring them back. Milk prices have dropped low enough to make dairy farmer suicides a worrisome trend. Income disparity is alarming and growing; the middle class is shrinking, getting hollowed out. College is increasingly unaffordable, and automation is making it tough even for those with college degrees. I may be like the podiatrist who sees every human ailment as a foot problem, but the root cause of all this middle-American angst, I believe, is our lightspeed technology, especially our lightspeed learners, who eat jobs for breakfast and stretch income inequalities all afternoon.

A new study by the McKinsey Global Institute estimates that up to 800 million of today's global jobs will be fully automated by 2030.[4] That's 800 million working families who will lose their current means of livelihood. Many of these lost jobs will come from America's heartland. Already, small towns are dying, families struggling, schools closing, and the American dream of a better life for each generation all but gone. No wonder voters are lashing out at traditional politicians.

But populist scapegoating of Muslims, Mexicans, young black men, cheap Asian labor, and others gets us nowhere. We've tried this sort of thing before in American history, notably with the rise of the Know-Nothings. These immigrant haters started as a secret society of white Protestants and then became a major political party. In the 1850s, Know-Nothings ran Massachusetts, elected the mayor of San Francisco, and were the largest minority party in Congress. They came to power after beating immigrants in the streets from Boston to San Francisco, burning down immigrant schools in Philadelphia, and stoning St. Patrick's Cathedral in New York City. They got their name because, when asked about the riots they fomented, the stock answer of every leader was, "I know nothing." Wink.

The Know-Nothings fueled the fire that became the Civil War, the greatest tragedy in American history. Abraham Lincoln, beginning with his famous Cooper Union speech, drove the Know-Nothings out of government before the war, but the Know-Nothings' political sentiments went south and became part of the rebellious Confederacy. Irish, German, and Italian immigrants who had been targets of the Know-Nothings went on to fight in the Union Army in the Civil War. At great sacrifice, they fought not only to abolish slavery but also to make America safe for liberal immigration. The Union Army won; immigrants streamed into America; and together, with native-born citizens, these immigrants built the most diverse and powerful economy the world has ever seen. Technology innovation played a crucial role in this economic progress. Electricity, telephones, automobiles, radio, airplanes, TV, the Internet, smartphones—and now AIs, the lightspeed learners.

The official policy on AI of the Trump administration its first year in office was to oppose the official policy of the Obama administration, which had been, in essence, to launch an aggressive national program for the control and advancement of AI, supported by significant federal government funding—as soon as the Obama administration left office. Throughout 2017 and early 2018, the Trump policy seemed to be, Stand by, do nothing, and let the free market work its magic.

Treasury secretary Steven Mnuchin in 2017 said, famously, "AI is not even on my radar screen."[5] However, by 2018, a more coherent and aggressive policy from the White House began to emerge—a policy that includes increased R&D funding in AI, rollback of certain regulations involving self-driving cars and drones, and changes in privacy laws that would have the effect of helping the United States to compete with China and its tremendous data advantage. The main driver of this shift, it appears, is fear that China could come to dominate AI. In Congress, the bipartisan House Subcommittee on Artificial Intelligence held a series of hearings in 2018 and got off to a good start, raising AI's profile within the Beltway. More of this kind of formal review of AI by the federal government is needed.

What's needed even more is a new American technology story centered around AI, a story that is democratic, ethical, and fair-minded. A twenty-first-century story that might have passed muster with the likes of Alexander Hamilton, Abraham Lincoln, Susan B. Anthony, and Teddy Roosevelt. A story of "America the Beautiful" in the age of AI and the lightspeed learners, supported by a cross-partisan majority of Americans:

Imagine if, tomorrow, scouts representing an intelligent life form from beyond our solar system appeared on CNN, CCTV, and Al Jazeera, sending the message "We're coming en masse to join you here on Earth, starting in 2030, whether you like it or not."

These alien scouts communicate with all humans in their native tongues and appear to be from a highly advanced civilization, say the scientific experts. Their appearance and mass migration warning triggers threat and vulnerability analyses by every military and law enforcement entity on Earth, followed by massive resource mobilizations and trainings. Americans circle the wagons and begin working to get all political factions and economic strata coordinating and preparing together, learning again how to fire out instead of aiming in, circular-firing-squad style.

The aliens in this scenario aren't little green men in frog suits—more like swarms of intelligence that take many physical forms. And they are *indeed coming—just not from outer space.*

The United States of America invented AIs, for the most part, just as it has every other major technology of the past 150 years. American companies are driving the AI invasion. In the 1940s, we Americans brought nuclear fission into the world and somehow, with cooperation from our allies and even our enemies, managed to control it. America must now provide similar leadership with respect to AI, an even stronger force. This time, there will be no global regulatory containment. Every country on Earth will have AIs in some form. Lone hackers and organized crime cartels will have AIs. Eventually, AIs will even have each other.

This time, there can be no turning back. The only path to safety is the way forward: even more R&D, even more innovation, more harnessing of the awesome power of unbound intelligence. But carefully, very carefully. Making the world safe for AI—and AI safe in the world—is America's new moonshot mission. No other nation, with the possible exception of China, is in a better position to make friendly AIs dominant on Earth and forestall malevolent uses of this powerful new technology.

This time, America's great technology invention engine cannot simply keep whirling without regard for long-term consequences. This time, every living participant in America's 250-year experiment in democracy needs to help this country get AI right and win the AI game.

Even now, I can hear the groans of my high-tech brethren and their familiar protestations that AI is nothing to worry about. Check out any interview of Jeff Bezos of Amazon regarding AI or any one of a dozen prominent high-tech CEOs. Listening to these guys, AI is the safest thing since white bread.

To be clear, the reason we urgently need a national AI mission spearheaded by the US federal government is *not* because a malevolent Skynet is about to take over. We need government intervention because those building technology keep sliding down the same dangerous, icy slopes, reckless and a little out of control, only now the technology is much more powerful and less predictable.

For at least a generation now, we have been building and deploying information technology with fewer safeguards than your average light bulb. We've failed to secure our applications and networks before unleashing them on an unsuspecting world. We've built vast, efficient global technology platforms designed, primarily, to suck data from us so as to capture our attention and fire ads at us as if they were heat-seeking missiles.

We technologists, by not caring enough about the social, political, and economic consequences of the tools we've built, have enabled global identity theft, ransomware, massive IP leaks, a resurgence of white supremacy, and a new generation of Russian spy ops, to name a few of the juicier threats that have arisen in the past two decades, all with the aid of Internet-era technology.

Scale traditional IT threats up by a power of three, and you've got AI's current risk profile. Prominent AI risks include everything from rogue AIs disrupting and stealing from global financial markets to social chaos campaigns conducted as a form of cyberwarfare. There is the possibility that autonomous AIs guiding intercontinental missiles could destabilize the world's current mutually assured destruction, nuclear equilibrium, or enable terrorists to conduct long-range "suicide" bombing campaigns with drones. Economic disruptions fueled by job losses could further polarize haves and have-nots around the world. And these are just some of the known risks. There are also plenty of unknowns.

I believe there is, in fact, plenty to worry about as AIs swarm into our world, enough so that the general public—*we the people*—must learn about this new technology and, in some equalitarian, transparent, trustworthy way, guide its growth and development. The only system we have to do this is called government.

On a practical level, we need to develop the political will and muscle to do what France is doing. The French have a national AI policy, implemented by a strategic agency under the brilliant leadership of Cedric Villani. This agency has a billion-plus dollars of R&D money—not enough, say the critics, but it's a start—and a deep moral commitment to keeping AIs friendly. Ironically, France credits the model for its high-powered new task force developed in the AI plan to the departing Obama administration. It is a model we in the United States could also apply quickly.

Again, potential AI risks are just half the story. With political will similar to what is emerging in France, we can start putting friendly AIs to work, solving real and important problems in America's economically troubled heartland and all across the United States. For example, we could start a national program for training data collectors and data curators with specialties in agriculture, health care, transportation, manufacturing, and education. Data curation is one job that will not be going away any time soon—and anyone who is reasonably meticulous, organized, and able to use software applications can do it. These kinds of training programs will have a side benefit of helping to educate citizens about AI—and helping to stimulate AI learning in K–12 schools.

Job-training programs are just one step. Doubling down on scientific research is even more important if we want to retain our lead in AI. We can and must begin active dialog with other leading AI countries. AI as a global industry is collegial today, but we must start building formal, active alliances in support of friendly AI. These alliances should include government and industry and AI experts and regular citizens, all seated at the same table. Internationally, we should focus on building an alliance with China first and foremost.

We need formal, trained AI observers, similar to those used by the International Atomic Energy Commission, who inspect labs and track the development of AI around the world. We in the United States need to take the lead in creating this commission, just as we did with the American AEC.

We need a national economic development plan that promotes the whole AI ecosystem in the United States, the way smart state governments promote their states for filmmaking or data centers. Our current global leadership in AI is a tremendous economic asset for this country and can provide economic opportunity for people from Mississippi to Alaska, Massachusetts to Maui.

We clearly need an entirely new national government data model, one optimized for the growth and stellar performance of AIs when solving important problems and one that is equally effective at providing boundaries (such as with personal privacy). We can do all this and more, but first we must capture a bit of political momentum.

Here's one idea: Let's make world domination in AI a major issue in the 2020 US presidential election. It's a long shot, I know. Longer than Jimmy Carter in 1976 or Bill Clinton in 1992? Maybe not.

The first step would be to encourage supporters of a national AI program, like myself, to become single-issue voters, just as Second Amendment types are today. We'd pledge to vote only for candidates who believe we need a national AI policy and a national AI commission and who understand that *AI* does not stand for *artificial insemination*.

Eventually, this group of politically engaged AI advocates—including both AI utilitarians and AI singularitarians—would emerge as a defined (if somewhat fringe) political group, like Black Lives Matter or the National Association of Evangelicals. Rather than dwelling on the singularity, AI morality, or some other geeky issue, this group would hit America squarely with two simple questions:

1. Do you want America to be rich and powerful or a vassal state of foreign powers?
2. Do you want your family to share in the spoils of the greatest technology revolution in history?

We'd educate the American electorate about AI's powerful economic sword. *Look at what AI is doing with vehicles and stock trading alone. This is going to be huge, the biggest tech disruption yet.* To paraphrase James Carville, it's the AI economy, stupid. That's the simple message most likely to resonate with voters. Here's the copy for one potentially provocative political ad:

> *From the 1950s until around 2014, Uncle Sam was the world's biggest angel investor in artificial intelligence. US taxpayer dollars built all the first AIs and all the first robots, took AIs to Mars, provided grants to generations of AI scientists, and on and on. We US citizens demand founders' equity. Why should our critical early-stage investments not return dividends? Learn where your candidates stand on the national AI dividend!*

I'll leave it to others to figure out how the AI dividend is distributed to American citizens, although there has already been considerable thinking about universal basic income models—all arising because of job-eating AIs and automation.[6] In my opinion, at least in this country, the more a universal basic income were structured and positioned as an AI dividend, funding education and training investments in American citizens, the more politically acceptable it would be. In the decades ahead, AIs can be America's best friends or worst enemies. Citizens of the United States, in their politics and with their votes, will determine which.

By2020, we should be having a serious national political conversation about AI. Tech-savvy politicians, such as Rep. Will Hurd (R-Texas), will be all the rage—in both parties. A new generation of leaders will move beyond the liberal–conservative divide, and get to work aligning lightspeed tech with plodding but essential government policies—and thereby remake the American economy. In a good way.

OK, probably not going to happen. So few of even our best and brightest leaders understand the incredible riptide AI is unleashing. Yet as an AI advocate and AI worrier, I believe it essential that we start voting as many tech-savvy people into positions of leadership in government as we can. I care little about the twentieth-century political views of such elected officials—whether they're classified as liberal or conservative.[7] What I want to know is, do they understand the twenty-first century, starting with the impact AI is having on *everything*?

Remember AlphaZero, the Google AI that trained itself to be a master of virtually any game in the world? In his book *Deep Thinking,* Gary Kasparov, the former world chess champion and an émigré from Russia to America describes what it was like to compete against such computer systems. He went from beating computers all the time to beating them some of the time (ten years later) to never even having a chance of winning at all (another ten years). Essentially, it took computers twenty years to learn how to beat Kasparov. AlphaZero learned how to do it in a couple hours. And two years from now, some new AI will do something that makes AlphaZero's achievement look trivial.

In his very readable book, Kasparov cautions against "in the battle" evaluations of AI systems. In one day's match, your virtual opponent plays a certain way and exhibits one type of intelligence, Kasparov says. We humans, with our long evolutionary learning timetables, tend to think the machine we played yesterday will be the one we play today and tomorrow. But as Kasparov learned the hard way, each new match meant he was facing a different, smarter machine. Eventually, he found himself competing against lightspeed learners who improved dramatically each time he faced them; at this point, he had no hope of winning.

Like it or not, we Americans are in a game much bigger than any chess match. We are leading the world of AI today but will be facing smarter competition tomorrow. We cannot win the global AI game without a coherent national purpose and full-throttle national leadership.

Even though gun laws are just one of many issues for most voters, the NRA has demonstrated how an aroused minority can influence political policy. Similarly, an aroused minority of AI policy advocates might conceivably do the same thing. One could certainly argue that, with AI, the stakes are higher than they have ever been with guns. Even assault rifles can't turn planets into paper clips.

Hence, my modest political proposal: All of us who appreciate the significance of AI take a pledge to vote for no one running in a primary election for Congress or the White House who has not spent time learning the basics about AI and is committed, at a minimum, to developing a coherent national AI policy that includes a direct economic payoff of some kind to the citizens of this country. This advocacy would help sweep old, dead wood out of Congress on the grounds that a certain tech literacy is now a crucial requirement of our government leaders. Maybe some new NRA-like advocacy group can emerge to put AI gold stars on the best candidates. Then perhaps at least the legislative branches of American government would have new leaders who understand the promise and the threat of AI.

Ultimately, the only way we get to victory in AI will be to have smart, AI-savvy elected officials guiding policy, making decisions, and mobilizing internal resources of all kinds. To elect them, we will need well-informed ordinary citizens, like Esther of the Sheraton Music City Hotel in Nashville, thinking big thoughts and casting intelligent votes. And we will need everyone in America to understand what is now happening in China.

CHAPTER SEVEN

Uncle Sam vs. Red Star

> "Communism is not love. Communism is a hammer we use to crush the enemy."
>
> —Mao Zedong

Since 1969, the United States has been the world's undisputed technology leader in labs, in markets, in battlefields, and in space. Two landmark events, each witnessed on worldwide television, reinforced this dominance: Neil Armstrong's landing on the moon on July 20, 1969, and the US air strike on the presidential palace in Baghdad on March 20, 2003.

The air strike was Shock and Awe, and it lived up to its billing. Condolences to those who lost loved ones that day, but what the world witnessed was American technology reigning supreme: robust mobile communications; advanced GPS systems guiding everything; widely distributed, real-time common operating pictures of the entire war theater; navy and air force jets taking complete command of the airspace; and aircraft carriers parked nearby with more high-tech firepower than most nations. The American tech advantage over Saddam Hussein's camel-tent military was ridiculous—and the whole world watched live CNN feeds as our military put on a super show. The problem with Shock and Awe, of course, was that, while act I was an absolute showstopper, act II was a mess, and act III lacked a happy ending.

But in 2003, the world was indeed in awe of American technology. In the private sector, our Internet tech ruled the world. American enterprises were mastering the use of computer networking for competitive advantage in everything from agriculture to zookeeping. American military forces were the most sophisticated on earth, by a ballistic mile.

The newest military technology deployed in Iraq (soon dubbed "mil-tech") was developed almost entirely in the private sector, by both defense contractors and such high-tech vendors as Microsoft, Intel, and Cisco. Effortlessly, it seemed, the US government and its private-sector vendors had come together to create military dominance. Asymmetric warfare—little guys challenging big guys in some unorthodox way—was still a problem, particularly in the case of localized jihadist terrorism. But in any kind of conventional war, technology provided the United States an unassailable, unfair advantage.

In the aftermath of Shock and Awe, it was not lost on the leaders of the People's Republic of China (PRC) that America's military was vastly superior to their own, in part because America had a vibrant and successful private marketplace for the development of innovative technology. So the "Old Men" of China, the Communist Party leaders, hatched a new plan that began with marketplace freedom for high-tech companies.[1] This gave Internet startups in China—notably Alibaba, Baidu, and Tencent—a relatively free hand in building their businesses. Whether through brilliant strategy or benign neglect, the Old Men's technology policies, combined with the huge size of the Chinese market, spawned dynamic Internet giants, comparable to Amazon, Google, and Facebook. PRC censorship hurdles still had to be overcome, but given the rapid progress of these early Chinese Internet pioneers, the hurdles could not have been too difficult, at least from a business perspective.

When these Chinese Internet pioneers grew into genuine global unicorns five to ten years ago, the Old Men began working on a new doctrine called Civil Military Fusion (CMF). (Say what you want about Chairman Mao, but at least he came up with more colorful names for his epic campaigns. Who can forget Great Leap Forward; the Four Pests; or Up to the Mountains, Down to the Villages?) Boring name or not, China's Civil Military Fusion campaign has helped bridge the gap between China's stodgy, state-owned defense industry and its new move-fast-and-break-things Internet crowd, and so far, it has been working pretty well. It's not perfect by any means, but it's good enough that America's mil-tech lead over China has narrowed significantly during the past five years.

The People's Liberation Army (PLA) is second only to the US military in terms of conventional systems and probably in AI systems, as well, though most military AI in China, America, and elsewhere is secret. China makes no bones about the fact that it wants to jump ahead of the United States militarily and sees AI as the perfect springboard. The smartest military experts in America now believe that staying ahead of China technologically—especially in AI—is *the* highest national security priority for the United States.[2] Already, military strategists on both sides are talking about AI swarm wars, in which massive clouds of tiny drones fight each other over freeways, airports, and military bases. Wouldn't that be fun?

To best prevent all the variants of "killer robot" warfare, China and the United States would have to agree on the military use of AI, starting simply and going from there. AI would also play a role in trade, intellectual property protection, joint US–China space science, and a shared digital economic ecosystem in which Intel has a chip-making fab in Liaoning Province, China, and Baidu has its R&D center in Sunnyvale, California—as both do today.

It becomes strategically important, therefore, that citizens of the United States understand the geopolitical importance of AI and the particular significance of China's CMF program. What are we facing here? What is this growing, semisecret campaign from the Old Men? And what should we citizens of the United States be doing about it? As they say on cable news, we'll examine these questions after a break.

Nearly the entire Chinese population knows that they are in an AI race with the United States. Few Americans understand that we are in an AI race with China.

In the 1990s, I lived for a time near Hong Kong's Happy Valley racecourse, a bustling combination of Arabian horses, British pomp, and Chinese gambling. The racing oval was perfection, the horses almost first class, and many of the jockeys fresh off the world circuit. Singapore slings came with slices of fresh pineapple, and the beer stand served the best mustard brats in Asia. In those years, Happy Valley was a wide-mouth gambling funnel: It was always number 1 or 2 in the world in money bet per venue. Even today, as part of the PRC, the Happy Valley betting handle often tops HK$1 billion per night.

I would go to the track often, usually midweek. The Happy Valley crowd was easily the most diverse I'd ever encountered: Sikhs, North Koreans, Arabs, Saudi women, Aussie surfers, British bankers, and local criminal triad snakeheads would stroll through the grounds. The stands were mostly full of working-class Cantonese, who take to gambling like Republicans to Fox News. If a local had a horse coming down the stretch with a chance to win, he or she would get loud and crazy and shout it home in native, seven-tone Cantonese. The races were a hoot, the bars exceptional, and the general-admission seats full of friendly people. Everything was amazingly well run. If gamblers were ever to establish their own Mecca, it should be located in Happy Valley, Hong Kong.

So when I contemplate the United States in an AI race with China, I can't help envisioning the lovely Happy Valley racetrack, with a British announcer calling the race. *They* round *the clubhouse turn! It's Uncle Sam by four lengths, followed by Red Star and Rooskey Bear. Red Star is coming on, into the home stretch. It's Uncle Sam by two lengths, Red Star getting the whip. Red Star now just a length behind Uncle Sam! It's Uncle Sam and Red Star, Red Star and Uncle Sam—*

We won't know who wins this race for perhaps a decade or more. But the winner will probably be determined by what the "trainers" of these leading AI horses do in the next few years. As of 2018, Uncle Sam is clearly ahead, with a strong edge in human talent and more high-quality AI systems in operation. China has the lead in available data and is making the greater government investments. Coming from far behind, China is on a steeper AI growth trajectory than the United States, but China now has momentum on its side. The biggest wild card: Nearly the entire Chinese population knows that they are in an AI race with the United States; few Americans understand that we are in an AI race with China. China has extraordinary political coherence around its AI goals; America has ideological tribalism and political dysfunction. That could make all the difference.

I am old enough to remember Sputnik, which led to inane nuclear bomb drills conducted in my grammar school. Taking the proper prone position under our desks, we were told, would protect us against nuclear shock waves. I remember Gerald Brock, the smartest, nerdiest kid in fifth grade, saying, "This is really stupid."

Sputnik, the Soviet Union's surprise space satellite, was a splash of ice water on the face of America. Our air superiority helped win World War II in Europe and the Pacific; we were the birthplace of the atomic bomb; we built the world's first computers. Our country was run by General "I Like Ike" Eisenhower, hero of D-Day, and America was the post–World War II hero nation. Then—wham!—we were suddenly in second place in science and technology. The Russians were in orbit, and we weren't. It was unfathomable. Our archenemy beat us into space, and everyone, even in the small farming town where I was raised, was really pissed off about it and even a little frightened. This is why, soon thereafter, John F. Kennedy pledged to put a man on the moon within ten years: to regain our technical superiority in the eyes of the world and in our own. Against long odds, America's slide-rule scientists and right-stuff astronauts of the 1960s pulled off Kennedy's goal, with a ton of help from the citizens of America.

We haven't yet had a Sputnik moment with respect to China and AI, but we need one. In this chapter, I examine China's AI strategies, programs, and military doctrine to determine a uniquely American response to the threat of China as our main AI adversary in military and civilian arenas.[3]

China has proven to be a first-class racehorse in space tech and in the development of Internet platforms. She is a very smart nation, and she's on our tail, running hard. But speaking as an American who spent two years living and working in China and loved coming home, the time has come for Uncle Sam to make a hard stretch run and put this race out of reach because however bad you think *our* government is, my fellow Americans, when it comes to the protection of our individual rights, China's government of Old Men would be much worse.

It's not that Chinese emissaries are likely to overrun our governors' mansions and halls of Congress soon, but if in a decade or so China obtains a decisive lead over the United States in the development and deployment of AIs—say, with the aid of a parallel breakthrough in quantum computing—all of our IT encryption defenses will be breached immediately. An aggressive China using superintelligent AI would slowly gain effective control of all major financial markets in the world. (See the prelude to Max Tegmark's *Life 3.0* for an excellent description of how this would work.) The AIs would eventually take over our companies and banks, with Congress thrown in as a party favor. China would start calling all the shots—from Beijing.

Imagine this scenario: officials from "the Party" take up positions in the executive suites of Google, Facebook, Intel, and Microsoft, administering "fake news" censorship rules, watching closely for the breakout of any deviant thought, and making sure a sufficient amount of company resources fulfilled "Google's patriotic duty." When I worked on a Sino–American joint film venture in Guangzhou during the 1980s, we had Communist Party operatives working with us every day, five or six middle-aged men with round bellies in Mao jackets who would monitor everything we did for political correctness. To call these party men dead weight would be too kind; they were worse than that. They were mean, and they were feared.

Should Chairman Xi be tempted to get too heavy handed with his party apparatchiks, the growth of China's high-tech unicorns could be impaired. The centralized, one-party control that makes China's AI efforts focused and highly coordinated could also spell trouble. Will political meddling throttle both scientific discovery and technology innovation, perpetually placing

Chinese technology behind the United States'? Or will Xi cleverly knit new CMF coalitions and make China the greatest science and technology power the world has ever seen? Both scenarios are possible.

One purpose of the CMF is to help the Old Men round up their unicorns, nudge them back onto the commune, as it were. Fair enough. Frankly, Silicon Valley companies could also use some reminders of their responsibility to the nation that spawned them. But for these current and future Chinese unicorns to be valuable to Xi and the Old Men in the field of AI, the Old Men will have to give their upstarts plenty of room to roam free to pursue scientific inquiry and avoid censoring innovative thought. If they do, Red Star will have an excellent chance of winning the AI horse race, but that's a big *if*.

One Country, Many Campaigns

The CMF is not the only national campaign designed to give China global technology superiority. While its focus is on the militarization of leading technologies, Xi has rolled out a number of similar programs to advance AI and other tech without involving the military, including:

- **Made in China 2025.** A multipronged effort to become the world leader in ten key industries, including AI and robotics, clean vehicles, and precision agriculture. A key component of this program is to acquire Western companies and Western technology talent. From 2012 to mid-2017, Chinese companies and investors—often with PRC financing behind them—spent nearly $20 billion across more than 600 different tech deals in North America and Europe, with particular focus on AI and robotics.[4] China's Made in China program is a favorite target of the Trump White House on the grounds that state investment in high tech constitutes an unfair trade practice.
- **2107 New Generation AI Development Plan.** This plan, announced personally by Xi, states that AI will become a "key impetus for economic transformation." It sets the expectation that China's AI companies and research labs will be operating on par with the United States by 2020 and calls for breakthroughs in AI by 2025 that will make China the world leader in certain narrow AI categories. In the final stage of the plan, by 2030, China will "become the world's premier artificial intelligence innovation center." The clear winner of the AI horse race, in other words.[5]
- **One Belt, One Road.** This is a huge, global infrastructure investment program led by China, with more than sixty-eight other countries on-

> board—countries that together account for 65 percent of the earth's population. This initiative has been compared to the US Marshall Plan, but in fact, it is much larger. In the decade after World War II, that plan invested today's equivalent of approximately $110 billion in war-ravaged Europe; Beijing is investing $200 billion in One Belt, One Road *each year*! Roads, railroads, and clean energy dominate this program, but advanced technology is interwoven throughout the entire effort. It is worth noting that China's alliance-building investments and commitment to open-market policies with its (largely) Asian partners in One Belt, One Road is the polar opposite of the current America First policy. As Xi said at Davos in 2017, "Pursuing protectionism is like locking oneself in a dark room: while wind and rain may be kept outside, so are light and air."[6]

Meanwhile, China is treating its Uyghur minority the way Nazis treated Jews and is "disappearing" booksellers in Hong Kong.[7] The PRC has been stealing American intellectual property ever since an unauthorized Chinese translation of Alex Haley's *Roots* became, for several years in the late 1970s, China's number 1 bestselling book. The PRC has since proven adroit at stealing running-shoe designs, semiconductor code, and the occasional Department of Defense weapons plan. The PRC comingles public and private interests in ways that make all global multinationals nervous. China does not crudely anoint oligarchs the way Putin does, but the Old Men do put their thumbs on the business scale.

When a favored start-up wins big on a global scale, as Alibaba and Baidu have done, they become "national champions," Olympic gold-medal winners, only better. This public glorification combined with various covert forms of assistance helps China's golden unicorns get stronger. Yet, as they used to say in rural Guangdong Province, too much government kills the duck.

Here are the parallel ironies of the great AI race:

- To win, Beijing must become more like Silicon Valley, without party apparatchiks walking the halls of innovation, mucking everything up.
- To win, Washington must become more like Beijing, providing sustained leadership, producing coherent plans, spending prodigiously in basic science and all forms of education, and generating broad civic support.

If I were to handicap this race, taking into account everything I know, I'd say the odds are remote of Xi waving his magic wand over a series of national political and industrial campaigns and making China the sudden AI equal of the United States by 2025. The odds of China doing the same by 2030, however, are a coin flip.

Uncle Sam would easily win this race, were it not for these facts:

1. The United States has no unified policy regarding AI, let alone any powerful institutional agencies or commissions guiding its development and standardization.
2. The last two White House budgets have called for large cuts in basic science research.
3. Our schools are woefully behind even Finland and Lithuania in AI instruction (let alone China and Japan).
4. The creators of US advantage in AI are working inside huge, wealthy and largely for-profit companies.
5. After the recent flap at Google about its employees refusing to work on "killer robots," the gap between Silicon Valley and the Washington beltway will likely grow larger.[8]

These are all issues of public will and political process. If we can resolve these issues in the next five years in America, then Uncle Sam will win big. Again, a very big *if*.

Were I the trainer of Uncle Sam, the AI thoroughbred, and charged with parlaying his previous successes into a string of victories over Red Star for the rest of this century, above all I'd want the active support of the citizens of the United States. I'd want them to learn and care about AI—both its potential and its risks. I'd want their help in making AI a sustainable national priority. I'd want citizens' help in getting our foreign policy back on track, as well, back to coalition building, because remember, in AI, big is beautiful. Big data is beautiful. China is big and has massive internal data stores. It is also building big new alliances in Asia and Africa through its One Belt, One Road global initiative, which itself is generating even more new data.

We in the United States cannot lock ourselves in a dark room, to use Xi's apt analogy. We have to build massive data and tech alliances ourselves. This is perhaps a slight exaggeration, but if we got into a trumped up tech trade war with Canada and permanently lost access to AI research in just the city of Toronto, on that day Red Star would pass Uncle Sam. That's how important Toronto is in the American AI landscape. To a lesser degree, the United Kingdom, Germany, France, and others are, as well. In a post-AI world, alliances are more vital than ever, and it makes no sense, technologically speaking, to try and go it alone.

AI is not two dudes in a garage launching a website. It's Google cracking the code on image recognition after assembling image data sets in the tens of millions. It's Amazon training its AIs on its massive cloud-computing platform at lightspeed. AI favors scale, and though we in the United States now have the largest computing infrastructure, no country has the potential to scale technologically like China, internally and now internationally, as well.

AI is also not tabloid science, where polar ice caps never melt and humans once roamed the Earth with dinosaurs. Rigorous adherence to the scientific method is an absolute requirement of AI development. There is a direct line between the ability of our drones to execute the world's greatest OODA loops in battle, and ongoing, well-funded, nonpoliticized research into regression analysis, Gaussian density, and neural network overfitting. With pure science, in other words.

At the end of the day, the choice we American people face with respect to AI is not a sideshow; it's symbolic of the core battle for what Jon Meacham calls the "soul of America." Will America restore "her better angels" and regain her respect for and support of real science? Will we be able to become a good partner again to our allies and build coalitions rather than destroy them? Will we once again create a social climate where the best and brightest from around the world want to come here and work with us? The answers to these questions will determine the winner of the great twenty-first-century AI horse race—the most important technology race in history.

CHAPTER EIGHT

~

The Porn Star's Deepfake and Other Security Paradoxes

"When speaking of computer systems, never use the word secure."

—Donald Rumsfeld

Managing the digital security of AI systems is extraordinarily important and exceedingly complicated. It's important because information security controls are crucial for all good software, and AI is much more than just good software. It's complicated because ordinary cybersecurity, with its public keys, secure tokens, digital certificates, and restricted enclaves, is challenging enough. Toss AIs into the mix, and it's like upgrading from 2-D checkers to 3-D chess.

In this chapter, I examine issues related to AI and its ability to (1) function as a trusted system in a cybersecurity sense, (2) serve as the tip of the spear in cyberoffenses and a shield in cyberdefenses, and (3) deliver enhanced physical security protection. The fusion between AI and cybersecurity is of special importance. As it happens, I've worked in both the AI and cybersecurity sectors, so I have an idea or two about how these fields might begin to fit together, as they ultimately must. Cyber–AI fusion ideas worth mentioning these days include AI white listing, immersive AI-driven alerting environments, and new AI industry security standards tied to a certification seal.

I know what you're thinking: *Time to skip ahead to the next chapter* or to chapter 11, on AI creativity and poetry, which is way more fun than cybersecurity. Let's face it: It's hard to imagine anything drier than a discussion of AI security certification criteria, but resist that impulse to skip ahead. This is a chapter you need to read. In the next decade, your decisions about digital security could have a major impact on your personal safety and security and that of your family. Stay with me here, and watch as I struggle to make cybersecurity entertaining.

In this chapter, we have porn stars racing across White House lawns, Russian hackers with their pants down, and banana slugs crawling naked and afraid through the lettuce patch. And there's this: The entry of lightspeed learners in our world could mean the entry of lightspeed hackers in yours. In these pages you'll not be subjected to my brainstorms about AI white listing, and I'm not going to discuss how swarming AIs could create new (intelligent, dynamic) trust circles—which I realize, for most of you, would be like watching paint *peel*. Except for a few minor lapses, I avoid industry stats, cybergeek jargon, and math notation. After speaking about cybersecurity for many years, I've learned that most people's interest in the details of cybersecurity is lower even than a ballerina's in NFL rushing statistics, so we're going to fly this chapter at 40,000 feet.

Fortunately, it is not necessary to understand cyberminutia to make smart digital security decisions in the twenty-first century. What's required is that you know a few basics about tech safety and security in the context of AI and start making overall cybersecurity a priority. To help you in this effort, I've compiled a few simple rules for digital security in the age of AI. To say that I composed these five rules would be inaccurate. It's more that I collected them over quite a few years, with the help of friends and colleagues in a variety of settings. The purpose of these rules is to get you to *think* about contemporary digital security in new ways because all security begins with attention and vigilance. If you've never paid much serious attention to your own digital security and privacy, now, in these early days of the AI invasion, would be an excellent time to start.

Rule 1: There Is No Such Thing as "Secure"

Get over it. No online system is airtight from a security perspective. In fact, marketing claims that a product or service is "secure" are a sure sign of amateurs at work. A product can be very secure, highly secure, or even spectacularly secure, but it can never be just secure without a modifier because nothing ever is.

Recall Ray Kurzweil's Law of Accelerating Returns? It applies to digital security in spades and not just because more cyberthreats are bombarding us than ever but because malware mutation rates are also quickening. Shape-shifting threats are definitely a problem for the mainstream security defenses we have today. Blend fast-evolving malware apps with the thriving global black market for stolen identity credentials; stir in machine-learning algorithms and powerful, massively connected clouds; add a few carrots and onions; simmer for a few hours; and what do you get? *Trouble*. Don't look now, but data breaches are gaining on us, growing every year. I'll skip the details, but trust me, the numbers are not good. That's *before* we stir AI into the mix—for good or ill.

Rule 1 is the foundation of good security practice because it promotes critical thinking. It is useful to remember this rule whenever you install a new security surveillance system, invite a robot into your home, upgrade your cell phone, buy a car, or do a search on Google. Because no device, information product, information service, or IT system is completely secure, checking to see how nonsecure a device is can be crucial.[1] (I have more to say on this security evaluation process later.)

Another reason security industry pros keep chanting their "nothing is secure" mantra is that user attention is very important to cybersecurity. You don't have to be an MD to recognize symptoms of a health problem. If you are paying attention, you don't have to be a security expert to recognize anomalous behavior in your tech devices and systems, as well.

I once gave a TEDx talk on cybersecurity titled "From Armadillos to Monkeys."[2] The idea, briefly, is that we need to move our security defenses from a hard outer shell (like armadillos) to constant vigilance and agile response (like monkeys). Staying aware of prowling leopards is crucial for a monkey to remain alive; staying aware of cyber threats is crucial for us. Another analogy: Which American is most likely to get hit by traffic in Thailand: a tourist who thinks crossing a street in Bangkok is the same as crossing one in Elk Horn, Iowa, or one who views Tuk Tuks and motor scouters as existential threats (as they certainly were the year I lived in Thailand)?

Although there is no absolute security when it comes to computing, one device "state" comes close.[3] It's called *off*. It is extremely difficult to hack into a personal device, be it a phone, computer, or autonomous driving car, when it lacks electrical current. In fact, the "Off" switch can be one of your most effective security shields. With such AIs as Echo or Google Assistant and dozens of others, the temptation is to keep the device on all the time. The much better practice from a security perspective is to turn the thing off as often as practical.

Get over it. No online system is airtight from a security perspective. But a bit of user vigilance combined with security best practices can go a long way toward keeping you, and your data, safe.

Rule 2: Run with the Bulls

I have noted that in AI, big is beautiful. Barriers to entry are steep. Among the requirements to produce world-class AI are big data, big compute, big money, and big-brain humans.

In that other AI marketplace (artificial insemination), the strongest bulls sire the healthiest offspring. The same is true with the bulls of AI—the big, strong companies for whom the barriers of entry were surpassed long ago. You and I are little calves in the AI race, so we need to find big bulls to run with, bulls who have the time and resources to keep up with changing cyberthreats and help us keep up on the ever-accelerating AI treadmill.

Being a Northwesterner, I am partial to two old local bulls: Intel and Microsoft. These high-tech giants have been cranking out highly secure and reliable products fairly consistently for decades now. They are not without their own security lapses, of course, but overall their security track records are pretty damn good.[4] Intel hardware, Microsoft software, and especially the Azure cloud (which is a combination of the two) are the cornerstones of my personal privacy and security plan. Each company has been investing heavily in cybersecurity for more than a decade. Microsoft has an entire tall building full of security geeks on its Redmond campus—geeks who recently have been outperforming NSA and the FBI in catching Russian hackers in political mischief. Intel practically invented strong hardware security (e.g., the history of the trusted computing module, now a trusted computing platform).[5] Security vulnerabilities having to do with the storage of trusted keys have recently been found in Intel semiconductors, and though serious, they have not resulted in any reported data loss. These security flaws, named by their discoverers Foreshadow, Spectre, and Meltdown, received significant publicity even without any known system breach, which just underscores Intel's long-standing role as a leader in computing security.[6]

Microsoft and Intel are certainly not the only big bull options. Apple has long had a serious and effective commitment to security, privacy, and product safety. Amazon, and especially its Amazon Web Services (AWS) cloud, have been an amazing engine of technology growth—with a solid security record. IBM, Oracle, Cisco, and such leading security vendors as Symantec, FireEye, and Sophos serve many enterprise customers well.

I am convinced no other cybersecurity measures—short of unplugging the service—would have stopped the hacker hordes. But the hackers couldn't take us down because they couldn't find us.

Google certainly has plenty of solid and highly secure resources, but I do not trust them on privacy issues. One of the fastest, easiest privacy upgrades the average person can make is to stop using Google's Chrome browser and its Google search engine. I use each very sparingly—maybe once or twice a month—with a quick cookies flush thereafter. Instead, I use Internet Explorer for my browser, and I search with Bing, both from Microsoft. Except for a few specific types of searches, I can't tell much difference between the Bing and Google search engines, except that a search with Bing using Internet Explorer (the way I have it set up) doesn't give me that creepy feeling of someone watching from over my shoulder when I'm online.

However, Google is probably the smartest AI company on Earth. Whatever their privacy policy shortcomings, their new AI platforms and training systems available as part of Google Cloud are excellent. I would also expect Google's TPU (Tensor Processing Unit) chips, machine-learning platform and other AI elements to be extremely secure against malware attacks, although I have no data to back up that assertion. If you do choose to use AI based in the Google Cloud, be sure to read all the privacy policies, especially with Google Assistant and other Google consumer products. And whichever companies you choose to align yourself with, running with the bulls means keeping up with them—installing all updates on time, paying attention to their security bulletins, and following their evolving best practices security advice.

Digital security threats are so virulent and plentiful that even large corporations with big security budgets and huge IT staffs have a poor track record of keeping attackers out. All the high-tech companies listed earlier have generally done a much better job of maintaining high levels of security in their products and systems than the average Fortune 500 company, and many of their security tools and methods are available for general consumers. Use them.

Rule 3: Stealth Matters

In May 2012, I spent one of the more memorable weekends of my life trying to protect a highly secure software service against a massive cyberattack. I was working with a company whose software was being used in security operations related to a NATO summit in Chicago, with heads of state from around the world attending. A hacker group wanted to make its mark on this high-profile gathering and chose our software as its takedown target. Loudly and publicly, the group called on its base of supporters to shut down our service. And these guys were good—some of the best hackers in the world.

Without going into too much detail, our software and service were able to stay up that weekend without incident. It was not so much because our stalwart Microsoft Azure friends quickly hardened our backend (although they did in impressive fashion) but because we were able to hide in plain sight. The security technique we used is known as obfuscation. The theory behind IT obfuscation is that camouflage and obscurity can be as helpful in cybersecurity as in warfare and biological evolution. Obfuscation does not have much standing in the cybersecurity industry, in part because it doesn't sell a product, which is unfortunate because, in certain situations, it can be a terrific way to protect data and services. In our case at the Chicago summit, I am convinced that no other cybersecurity measures—short of unplugging the service—would have stopped the hacker hordes. But the hackers couldn't take us down because they couldn't find us. In military jargon, it's called stealth, and it's long been a cornerstone of security. America's "I cannot tell a lie" president, George Washington, was a master of stealth. All the world's great militaries deploy it still. Stealth has incredible value in security, even if cyber geeks are slow to see it.

Here are a few ways you can make stealth and obfuscation work for you in everyday technology:

- **Don't give attackers a static target.** Use variations on your name (John Smith, J. Smith, J. Howard Smith, etc.). Use multiple e-mail addresses for various purposes; for example, one you use only for e-commerce. I have one e-mail I use only to register at websites and for white papers and other research. Never divulge more information than you need to, and be especially guarded about giving up your phone number and home address.
- **Reduce your "attack surface."** In business and personal affairs, you may not want to expose every page on your websites to just anybody. Setting up access controls to private web pages can help reduce the unintentional disclosure of confidential information and give your attackers fewer ways into your systems.
- **Avoid obvious conventions.** When forced to use passwords, avoid the obvious ones. Last time I checked, "1234" and "Password" were the two most common passwords on the web. The best passwords have at least seven characters, a special character or two, and are gobbledygook. E-mail addressing conventions that always use the same structure (first name dot last name and so forth) should be avoided, as they make it much easier for both spear phishers and spoofers.
- **Disguise domain names when necessary.** The main reason we were able to avoid attack in the Chicago summit is that the domain name

for our information service had nothing to do with either our company or the service we were providing. Because our software as a service was designed for the sharing of sensitive information, our customers never complained that our domain name was Greek to them; it made it much harder for attackers to find.

Stealth has its limits in terms of security, and obfuscation should not be confused with nuts-and-bolts information assurance. But I've found that being a bit stealthy can at the very least help technology users pay more attention to security and increase their cyberawareness because stealth strategies require ongoing attention. Best case, the bad guys won't find you.

Rule 4: Open Is the New Secure

The AI industry is the polar opposite of stealth and obfuscation. AI is in full hype mode, and the media spotlight could not be hotter. It has an open culture, with much sharing of valuable technical information, including high-quality, open-source code bases (e.g., OpenAI, OpenFace). Every new cutting-edge idea quickly makes the rounds in a research paper, and the most important work is done in private-sector labs, which (unlike government or academic labs) have marketing departments ready to promote the hell out of any new breakthrough. As an industry, AI has all the stealth of *America's Got Talent*.

While I'm a great believer in obfuscation and stealth—especially in the use of personal and system identities—I do not hold out much hope for the use of obfuscation in AI security. In fact, just the opposite. Our best chance for living with AIs who are trusted in an IT sense and trustworthy in a human sense may well lie in an oxymoron called *open security*. It's the new AI security paradox. Open security asks the question, Can a door be both open (publicly available for entry) and secured (closed to all except those with a proper key) at the same time? In the world of AI, the short answer is yes.

For years, in cybersecurity talks, I would use Linux open-source software as the best example of "open + secure" defenses. Today, the best and most relevant example is probably blockchain. Blockchain is distributed ledger technology. Its ledgers are "immutable scorecards" that record digital currency transactions. Rather than having one central authority in control, the idea is for all participants to play together online with cards face up and reconcile point counts after each hand.

Blockchain is used today to track vessels on Maersk's enormous global shipping grid, list transactions in Walmart's green supply-chain network, and issue bonds at Commonwealth Bank of Australia.[7] Sean Williams, in the article "20 Real-World Uses of Blockchain Technology," calls it game-changing and then explains precisely how blockchain could be used in twenty different key business applications.[8] With or without Bitcoin, blockchain is not going away. And with AI's help, blockchain applications will grow faster than any cryptographic application in history.

Step by step, transaction by transaction, a global blockchain scaffolding is being built, financed by digital currency traders, alongside IBM, Intel, and Bank of America and many others. Ten years from now, a mature blockchain matrix will be using radical immutable transparency to provide very high security in applications coming in myriad shapes, sizes, and languages around the planet. But blockchain is just infrastructure, not some subtle new form of intelligence.

From a security-design perspective, the main thing to know about blockchain is that closure of each specific transaction is reached through the consensus agreement of a highly disparate group of observers. Most of the observers are machines, not humans, but these machines are controlled by humans. So working together, this disparate global group of machines and humans (all previously identified and authenticated) witness, verify, and record transactions, for now and ever. In the case of Bitcoin, billions of dollars of fiat currency value have been transferred this way, with few security complications. This kind of security can sound counterintuitive, but blockchain data protection really works.[9]

Yet blockchain is far from being totally secure. (Picking up a theme here?) It *is* an extraordinarily effective cybersecurity platform. Its initial purpose, to paraphrase its mythical inventor, Satoshi Nakamoto, went like this:

> Let's invent a new crypto platform strong enough to launch digital currencies, an Internet sector that has raised billions in venture capital but never worked. But these new currencies, including one we will introduce ourselves called Bitcoin, will not be backed by any nation or bank. Instead of tying our currencies to these traditional anchors, the root of trust for all blockchain currencies shall be users of the Internet, especially fast, networked computers with high throughput and lots of memory. All participants in this mission to create our digital currencies will be deemed volunteers. You help us "mine" our digital currency ecosystem and, through ongoing consensus reconciliation, keep all blockchain transactions safe and true. As a result, you will receive our worthless Bitcoin for your efforts.[10]

You no doubt have heard by now the stories of obscure Bitcoin miners who now are multimillionaires—or in blockchain parlance, *whales*. The majority of them, by all reports, live in China, though it is hard to know for certain because, on the great global blockchain, while transactions are all transparent, human identities, for the most part, are closely guarded secrets.

The rise of blockchain has been one of the great tech stories over the past decade. In an era of unprecedented high-tech investment, it was launched not with a money pitch, but a technology hack—an extremely clever and patient hack of international banks and sovereign departments of treasury by some person or persons who deeply understood the value of digital trust. But that's a story for a different book. For our purposes here, what's important is that blockchain achieved a high level of information assurance (IA), mainly by using a combination of radical transparency and sophisticated encryption: *open + secure*.

Openness and transparency seem paradoxical notions when it comes to security because the natural inclination of security experts is to lean the other way, toward secrets, gates, and locks. But consider situations where information assurance comes not from protecting a secret but from establishing truth. Let's say a famous porn star is reputed to have visited the White House. If a lone photographer secretly captures a video of this star walking across the White House lawn, who is to say this incident actually happened? The vid could be what's known as a deepfake: an extremely realistic clip doctored by the AI app DeepFake. Leveraging Google's TensorFlow platform and deep-learning techniques, DeepFake is able to swap faces from one video scene with another. Two popular examples on the web are Nicholas Cage playing the lead in virtually every classic movie and a fake Michelle Obama (with an absolutely realistic face) performing a striptease as part of a pole dance.

Through a lengthy process that requires serious compute power, DeepFake converts facial images into numerical values and then encodes and decodes them to fuse two faces together. In our example, the face of a porn star is merged with that of a woman reporter walking on the White House lawn in a way that makes it virtually impossible, forensically, to tell whether the video is genuine. The release of such a video would no doubt cause quite a stir and be met with plenty of denials, but it would be technologically all but impossible to prove that it was a deepfake. However, if the White House decided to be open and transparent about this star's visit and sixteen photographers from different news agencies photograph the porn star walking across the White House lawn, then a different standard of information integrity is reached through transparency, not security.

This is not a perfect analogy, yet it does begin to get at how transparency and openness can validate the truth or falsehood of particular digital information. Blockchain may have an important role in establishing information integrity in the future, with encrypted digital signatures serving as time and place stamps the way notary stamps are used today—although such capabilities do not, to my knowledge, exist as yet. One of the reasons blockchain works so well from a security perspective is that it has no single point of failure. The controls in the system are so widely defused that it's nearly impossible to break them in any way that would expose the information assets inside.

I'm not suggesting that blockchain has a big role to play directly in AI security. Blockchain is compute (and energy) expensive; it is slow and complicated; and though it will certainly have some uses in AI cyberdefense writ large, it is unlikely to be one of AI security's main components. AI, as a field, will need its own inherent IA models and security controls, designed specifically for AIs of all kinds. This does not mean AI engineers cannot take a lesson from blockchain and put open + secure to work. For the rest of us, blockchain and other open, distributed, encrypted systems will no doubt provide vital new platforms for cybersecurity and information assurance in the years ahead.

Securing the trustworthy operation of AIs, of course, raises a raft of new questions, not so much to prevent attacks of autonomous killer robots, but in order to keep AIs from running amok while trying to be helpful (e.g., the paper-clip factory thought experiment). To keep AIs from going off in wrong directions, we need to understand both the threats AIs pose to humans and any inherent vulnerabilities AIs may have. In my opinion and that of others in the security field, the first serious vulnerability will likely come from what experts call the "carbon factor."

Rule 5: Reduce Carbon Errors!

This final security rule, in the context of AI, is the most important. It's also the most subtle, so forgive me if I take a circuitous route in explaining it.

I'm an Oregon gardener. As such, I hate every kind of Northwest slug: the Pacific banana, the European red, the miserable little spotted leopard, and all the rest. Above ground, these slimy mucus bags devour our pea sprouts, eat our chard, and hold moon dances when the tomatoes are ripe. Underground, they abuse our potatoes and carrots. They are not welcome in our garden and enter it at their peril.

Security risks are like slugs. They come in various ugly shapes, sizes, and colors. Like slugs, only a small number are visible (i.e., above ground) at any given time. If untended—unsquished—they can cause a ton of damage.

The Pacific banana slug (the big guy) of cyberrisk is the fraudulent use of identity. Dark Reading, one of my go-to sources for cybersecurity info, consistently rates "weak and stolen credentials" as number 1 on its hacker hit parade.[11] Eighty-one percent of computer system hacks involve weak, default, or stolen credentials, yet 95 percent of all online access control systems still rely on weak passwords.[12] (Sorry, couldn't resist those stats.) Who wouldn't want to get rid of passwords? Not only are they ineffective, but they're also a pain to use.

Internet access control systems that rely on passwords alone can be compromised by spear phishing; by "dictionary attacks" (where bots play rapid-fire guessing games); by credential stuffing (another bot favorite, which takes a brute-force approach to breaking down weak web-access gates); by the use of stolen user names and passwords; by social engineering (a perennial favorite, where humans are tricked into simply giving their valued credentials away); and by a host of other more obscure exploits.

Social engineering is worthy of special mention in the context of AI. While writing a book on cybersecurity in 1999, I did a bit of white-hat social engineering. Specifically, I used a technique known as the *pretext call.* Pretext calling is one way to gain illicit access to user credentials for a website or private company network. In my case, I was writing a book on Internet privacy and decided to make pretext calls to companies that I regarded as some of the biggest privacy offenders on the Internet. One company I remember phoning was the now-defunct DoubleClick, a favorite target of Federal Trade Commission investigations. DoubleClick was eventually acquired by Google for about $3 billion. Here's how pretext calls work: The hacker obtains a name or two within his target organization and then calls them on the phone and tries to get them talking. The key to success is always to have a "pretext" for the call, some plausible reason behind all the implausible requests for confidential data. When calling into an annuities company, for example, the pitch might be, "Sorry, my mother just died, and the name of one of your products was written on a sheet of paper by her bed. I'm calling to see if she might have had one of your annuities." Or, after identifying in the news that a certain CEO has just given a presentation away from his home office, the hacker phones the home office and says, "I'm calling from Boston. I just found the wallet of the man who I think might be the CEO of your company."

I'd never done anything like this before. Mostly, I was shocked at how easy it is with just a little creative dissembling to obtain sensitive, confidential information over the phone. The key is to create a personal connection and then get the person on the other end of the line to keep talking. I had one woman patiently explain to me the precise details of her company's IT structure, including all e-mail policies and addressing conventions, which can be enormously helpful in spear phishing, among other things. In this case, research being my only objective, I'd always tell my pigeons that I had been gaming them before hanging up. I'd explain that I was researching a book on Internet privacy and called them because I viewed their company as one of the biggest privacy violators. Sometimes this was taken well; sometimes it was not. If they stayed on the line, I'd suggest they be more careful in the future, and in a couple of instances, I discussed the pretext call technique with them. They got a wake-up call, and I got interesting, ironic material for my book, a win-win in my opinion. (In the book, I used no personal names from these calls, so as not to violate anyone's privacy myself.) The pretext call is just one of many social-engineering exploits. What all social-engineering cyberrisks and the great majority of other cyberrisks have in common is that they take advantage of the weakest link in the security chain—what cybersecurity pros call the *carbon factor*. We carbon-molecule humans.

Here's a cybersecurity fable, known as The Hundredth Window, I first heard at a cybersecurity conference in the late 1990s. It is still told to techno whippersnappers who believe digital security is all about technology:

> You are king, and you've just received word that your enemy is attacking. You order your men to put bars, chains, and locks on every door and window in the castle. The castle has one hundred doors and windows. Ninety-nine of these get the bars-chains-and-locks treatment, but through simple human error, one window is missed. How safe are you if that hundredth window is left wide open without you knowing it? Not very.

The point of the story is that the hundredth window in cybersecurity is rarely a lack of technological safeguards. It's humans making stupid mistakes, clicking on phishing links, using "1234" as a password, failing to stay up to date with OS and hardware security upgrades, giving out sensitive information over the phone, and dozens of other lesser sins.

I am still searching for the ultimate study that measures total human error—clicking on phishes, losing an insufficiently secured device, IT administration screw-ups, thumb drives with top secrets waltzing through security checkpoints—as a percentage of the cause of all data breaches. My educated guess is that it would approach 90 percent. *Homo sapiens* have many wonderful skills and qualities. Proficiency at digital security is not one of them.

So, what if this "carbon factor" risk could be all but eliminated? What if machines could ask us about our privacy and security preferences and then manage all access controls and system protection for us based on these preferences, thereby stopping all phishing and dictionary attacks while staying up to date with the latest malware mutations, nation-state threats, and commercial system vulnerabilities and responding accordingly? Awesome, right? One of the biggest arguments in favor of self-driving vehicles is that, over time, they'd be much safer than cars driven by humans. Compute devices whose "carbon" security was driven by AIs would be much safer as well.

Swapping AIs for humans—the weakest link in the digital security chain—is not the kind of innovation that can happen in all situations overnight. Substantial security ecosystem changes would be necessary before humans could entirely hand the baton to AIs. Yet there are clear early-adopter opportunities right now, and whoever ultimately becomes the "security AI" leader will make a bloody fortune. If I were twenty years younger, I'd be writing the start-up "biz plan" myself.

Battling the Bad Guys

The technical term in the cybersecurity industry for someone who hops over network access-control gates unlawfully is "bad guy," or "bad actor" in corporate speak. I have crossed cyberswords with some bad actors over the years. I follow their exploits and know enough about them to know this: AI has their attention, big time.

AI could be a huge boon to the hacking industry, or on top of quantum computing, could kill hacking altogether. Or, most likely, AI will contribute to an escalating cyber arms race, with hacker tools and IT defenses each getting stronger, faster, and more expensive year after year, waging battles that go on forever. Whatever the scenario, AI will have a big impact on bad guys and their top-line revenue.

The good news for cybersecurity is that, aside from some rather pedestrian machine-learning tools, there's not much AI malware on the dark web so far. I doubt its denizens will ever build compelling, competitive AIs themselves. They are too expensive—in terms of human capital, compute resources, data, and money—for one person or even a small guerrilla group to build well. When vendors like Cisco, Symantec, Check Point, KnowB4, etc., start releasing their pro-level AI-security products, they'll quickly race ahead of all the dark web bad guys, assuming they move fast enough. The bad news for cybersecurity is that even new AI sentinels will not stop all data breaches and system compromises. Hackers will find ways to get their hands on emerging AI tools and, if the history of information technology is any guide, use these capabilities for innovative criminal purposes.

There are more types of bad guys than there are types of slugs, and increasingly, most of the bad guys are becoming professionals. They punch clocks in

St. Petersburg and Pyongyang, do lunch in London and New York, and work midnight shifts in Shanghai and New Delhi. Business is good. Nation-states are funding big projects, the slimy dark web basement of the deep web has a thriving market in stolen identity credentials, and the tools of the trade are getting much sharper. There is one new hacker tool on the market with a bit of machine learning that separates identities of the rich from identities of the poor in a few nanoseconds.

Bad guys, like slugs, can do irreparable damage. Just ask the Democratic National Committee (DNC), which in the midst of the 2016 election had all of its e-mail servers hacked so severely that the bad guys, Russians in this case, watched every move the DNC made during the run-up to the election. These are the same bad guys who stole vast troves of data about Democrat Party voters while they were at it, data that were then used in voter-suppression campaigns targeted at potential supporters of Hillary Clinton. A highly detailed indictment document from the Mueller probe spells out the alleged crimes committed by twelve Russians who hacked the DNC servers.[13] It shows how an attack as simple as a well-designed e-mail phishing campaign can lead to total security system failure and, oh by the way, alter the course of history.

I found the nitty-gritty details in this indictment fascinating. What these details suggest is that US intelligence, probably out of Fort Meade, hacked the hackers. At this writing, there has been no official explanations about how Justice Department investigators obtained all the detailed information in the indictment, but the only answer I can think of is that the United States gained full root access to these Russians' networks and computers. These Russian hackers were smart and careful, using Bitcoin for all purchases, Tor routing for all log-ons, and layers of fake identities to obscure their own.[14] Yet the indictment describes each hacker by his real name and gives considerable biographical details on each. Some cyberwarrior group in the US intelligence community turned over a big rock, found a bunch of Russian cyberslugs, and identified them all in great detail. Impressive. Good luck with world travel from now on, you Russian election hackers.

In the end, this was a you-hack-us-we-hack-you-back, spy-vs.-spy shootout. The Russians disrupted an American presidential election, spending only a modest amount on hackers; the United States proved it had the cyberpower to pants Viktor, Sergey, Aleksandr, Anatoliy, and company, the best cybergeeks in Russia, at high noon in Red Square.

Make no mistake. In terms of pure cyberpower, Russia is the United States' pet poodle. If America ever unleashed its full cyberforce against Russia, every light in the Kremlin would go out. But the fact that the United States is stronger in cyberwarfare doesn't mean that a small group of clever

Russian hackers can't find open windows in the United States to crawl through. That's the thing about cybersecurity—there's always a seam to exploit, a weak link in the chain. The Russian hack of the DNC, while it did involve the use of sophisticated hacker tools, basically relied on the simple "click here, stupid, and then I own you" phishing technique. It relied on the presumption of carbon error.

Some good news: The kind of network access control systems breached by the Russian hackers are about to get much better, largely because of a global standards initiative called Fast Identity Online (FIDO). FIDO certifies strong authentication systems, the best of which use no passwords whatsoever but combine traditional multifactor authentication (use of two or more pieces of evidence about a user's identity) with a type of encryption known as public key infrastructure. When combined with special restricted storage space on device hardware and a whole process of automated attestation and assertion, a FIDO-certified authentication transaction essentially eliminates all phishing attacks and many other bad-guy exploits, as well.

But that's only half the story. The user experience with a level 2 FIDO-certified system is infinitely preferable to today's user name and password log-ons. Modern phones and laptops come with algorithms in them that are really good at face recognition (FR), and these can be put to good use in a FIDO system. With 1:1 FR and other biometrics, logging onto commercial websites becomes a "tastes great, less filling" solution, making network access both easier for the user and more secure and reliable in terms of information security. FR is not perfect, but all the good face recognition algorithms are lightspeed learners, and FR improvement in the last half-decade has been incredible. Someday soon, your face will be your most trustworthy security credential.

Rise of the Bubbas

Here's a potential big security industry headline for the upcoming 2020s: "Cyberwarfare, Law Enforcement, Physical Security, Home Protection, Personal Privacy, Emergency Response, and All Things Military Rocked by AI." Expect major AI-related changes in each of these sectors by 2025, with definite winners and loser emerging by 2030.

Imagine:

- home security systems that automatically open front gates for family members, friends, nannies, and house cleaners while automatically sending an alert to police whenever that ex with a restraining order drives up

- IoT-style hurricane warning systems that not only predict the course of a storm but also evaluate your current disaster readiness in the face of it
- drones that patrol chemical plants in the middle of the night, with the intelligence to identify even the slightest anomaly in the facility, from a chemical leak to a broken spotlight
- autonomous helicopters with computer vision and heat sensors that patrol lands at high risk of wildfire and dump fire retardant on fires while still small
- drones that track illegal logging in Brazilian rainforests and criminal poaching in African jungles
- cybersecurity apps that *just handle* all online security issues for you, keeping all your devices and software up to date on all security releases and helping you register your new FIDO-compliant devices

With machine intelligence as the new electricity, there is no end to the security processes and tools that will be designed, built, and automated with it. The law of human inertia will still apply, but adoption rates will be appreciably faster than the Internet disruption two decades ago. Cognitive processes that would seem far too difficult or costly for humans to tackle on their own will suddenly become just a new app. If a process can be digitalized for lightspeed learning, it will.

Some of the AI-driven security products and services on the previous bullet list are already in the market; the others will be soon. They will all make positive contributions to the safety and protection of people and assets in the not-too-distant future. Many other AI-related security innovations lie around the corner. But not unlike the long-haul trucking industry, humans will still very much remain in the driver's seat when it comes to industrial security. They'll just have AIs riding shotgun.

In the large multinationals, the topmost security priority is continuity of operations (COOP), keeping things running. The physical security industry, the sector of guns, guards, and gates, supports COOP. The pros who work in physical security are called "bubbas," as in, "I had a bubba from Coca-Cola call me today about a new threat." Usually these professionals have military or law enforcement training and know the secret private-sector-security handshake. The term "bubba" is used not without irony, but it is a designation worn proudly. Women can absolutely be bubbas, and most women in the industry would regard the term as a badge of honor.

The bubbas of America, led by powerful corporate chief bubbas (a.k.a., chief security officers), will have an immense influence on how AI gets shaped and deployed for security purposes here in the United States and around the world. When Facebook, Twitter, or some hot new game company wants to protect their extremely high-value data centers from all forms of physical calamity—weather disasters, terrorist attacks, insider theft, civil disturbances, you name it—they hire really good bubbas. When Amazon execs and hot celebrities need executive protection, they call in the bubbas, often from the sector giants G4S, Securitas, and Allied Universal. Once in position, these bubbas tend to run a very tight security ship.

Many of today's bubbas were influenced by 9/11 and the Iraq Wars. As a consequence, they are not at all tech averse. In fact, a good number lean pretty far forward when it comes to the latest new security device or software service. I once attended a law enforcement conference that actually had an entire panel discussion on "belt space." At issue was the lack of sufficient belt leather for a police officer to carry all the trendy new devices she needed, along with her various weapons. And it was very much an issue with gender bias; men generally seem to have considerably more available belt space.

Even when they work for these big guard-services companies, today's bubbas are a far cry from yesterday's rent-a-cop. Many work in new security operations centers (SOCs) that centralize security surveillance and command for large companies. An increasing number of today's SOCs control and monitor the use of robots as security guards, particularly as night watchmen. Nearly all have centralized facility surveillance networks enhanced with a growing number of automated digital features (including face recognition). The SOC analyst bubbas use "smart alert" systems and powerful data analytics. Machine-learning programs designed for SOCs that separate true threat signals from all the incident noise are on their way to market.[15]

Bubbas at large multinational corporations in the 2020s will be the early adopters for a new generation of very smart, massively distributed security technology. In the COOP and physical security markets, the large company bubba is the high-end target customer. So as long as new offerings are solid and simple to operate, they'll be open to trying new things, and their budgets are getting larger. Security is a growing industry, and the need for it shows no signs of abating.

In the 2020s, AIs will help bubbas provide better security, but bubbas can also help AIs become more secure. How? By bringing their security-mission mentality into AI development. Bubbas are natural security firsters, champion carriers of the flag. Their mission is to keep people and property well protected, and although they work in the private sector and like to get paid what they think they're worth, which can be good money in many cases. They are not saints, but a true bubba cares genuinely about security.

I'm not a bubba, but I am a fan. One bubba I interviewed for a job spent eight years in central Africa pretending to be a wild animal veterinarian after a one-month crash course in animal medicine. He was a terrific young man, a Yale grad, who signed on to a three-letter agency soon after 9/11 and became an undercover vet, actually helping elephants and zebras while keeping an ear to the ground for jihadi cells. But every bubba has a great story or two.

My hope is that the large companies driving AI development in the world today will turn to the bubbas in their company and ask for their help to bring new security awareness into software and network development processes. As we move from software to AI—from frozen code to dynamic lightspeed learners—it is crucial that we bring more security expertise, of all kinds, into the dev lab: physical and cybersecurity, bubba and geek.

One Surefire Idea

In the introduction, I admit that this book does not have all the answers for surviving an AI invasion (a sizable understatement). But it does have one. It's not the sexiest new AI application but something important and solid: We need a program to test and certify AI and particularly AI security, similar to the rigorous program the electricity industry has had since 1894.[16]

You may not have noticed, but you've seen the small UL circle all your life, stamped on devices of every kind that use electricity, on radios, toasters, light bulbs, circuit breakers, smoke detectors, and much more. A UL certification means the device bearing the seal has been examined, tested, and approved by experts, scientists and engineers at the company formerly known as Underwriters Laboratory. After more than 110 years of operations as a nonprofit organization, in 2012 the company became a for-profit outfit and changed its name to, simply, UL. Regardless, a UL seal remains the final, trusted stamp of approval for safety and standards compliance of the world's best electrical devices. The company today has offices on 6 continents and customers in more than 140 countries and, through its standards management and inspection and certification programs, has been an enormous contributor to the safe use of electricity in all forms around the world.[17]

I worked as a journeyman electrician in my misspent youth to support a writing habit. I was in my midtwenties, living with my one and only wife, three young kids, a dog named Cloud, and a barn full of chickens. I remember the UL mark as a source of comfort, especially because I was still learning the electrician's trade. (My apprentice nickname had been Sparky, never a good sign.) It was reassuring to know that the devices I was wiring into my neighbors' houses had been examined rigorously and were judged to be safe and sound. The UL mark eliminated a whole set of worries from my mind and made my work product better.

A decade or so later, I stumbled onto the Internet, another use for electricity but well up the stack from junction boxes and three-way switches. Starting around 1990, I would log onto the Internet from our house atop Bald Peak, Oregon. Using a duplex modem—an ancient black box that communicated at snail speed and connected via loud, notorious staticky "audio handshakes"—I'd call long distance to New York City to connect with my Internet provider, a service run by futurist and author James Glick. This was prebrowser. I navigated and communicated on the Internet with Gopher and other early TCP and IP protocols. Community bulletin boards, such as one run by the city of Wellington, New Zealand, were the killer apps. After a session or two, I was hooked. By 1992, I had started my first Internet company.

In 1995, my Internet industry colleagues Esther Dyson and Lori Fena and I modeled Underwriter Labs to start a similar Internet watchdog and certification organization, which we dubbed TRUSTe. For more than two decades since, TrustArc, as the company is now called, has been the go-to trust seal for enterprise privacy on the Internet. Its UL-like privacy policy mark can be seen on web pages of respected companies around the world. Like UL, TrustArc has evolved from nonprofit to for-profit status over the years, largely because recruiting the tech talent to conduct effective evaluations has proven to be too difficult for nonprofit organizations. Consequently, the important function of providing independent evaluations and certifications of new technologies is now better performed, operationally, by for-profit, private businesses.

Today's markets for electrical devices, household products, and Internet privacy policies all have essential seals of inspection and certification. The AI industry urgently needs such a seal—a trusted UL mark for AI. Someone will build a company to do this; it's too good an opportunity not to, especially because, when it comes to trust seals within an industry, the prime mover tends to stick around for decades. Note to potentially interested entrepreneurs and investors: Skip the nonprofit or trade association stage, and build a start-up as a for-profit business from day 1. You'll have a great chance to do well financially while helping to build a safer planet. It may not be sexy, but this is my one surefire AI idea.

The Twenty-First-Century Security Paradox

Congratulations. You've almost completed an entire chapter on cyber and physical security in the Age of AI. I've tried to keep things high-level and interesting, and hope you've learned a few things. Someday AI tools may take over most security chores for us, but human attention will always be required if we humans wish to remain reasonably secure—in cyberspace, or "meatspace." Now and forever.

Our human attention to security should not be limited to personal protection. We must also bring our human values and needs into the AI security R&D arena. Human-friendly motivation is as important in the design of AI cyber tools as much as any other AI system. Perhaps more so. Because as threats proliferate exponentially, shape-shifting at accelerating rates, our defenses will become increasingly complex in order to combat them, and then we will all be walking a razor's edge, a wholly new security paradox, which goes like this:

> The smarter my tools and weapons, the more likely I will vanquish my enemies.
> The smarter my tools and weapons, the more likely they will vanquish me.

CHAPTER NINE

~

AIs in the Government Henhouse

"Democracy must be something more than two wolves and a sheep voting on what to have for dinner."

—James Bovard

In chapter six, I made the case for a national AI policy, and a new national political agenda. Now, after exploring AIs in China and in the security field, it's time to drill down into how AI can strengthen our democratic traditions, and build upon them in practical ways.

There are many ways that AIs can improve democracy, but here's my favorite: Someday, we'll all have AI assistants trained to interact on our behalf with big government and all the little government jurisdictions underneath.

Part admin, part lobbyist, these AIs will cut through red tape for us. They'll fill out long forms and hurdle over sluggish bureaucrats in a single bound. They'll handle routine business compliance issues, pay parking tickets, haggle with that pesky local water district, automatically renew your passport, perform patent searches, and (with only a few choice spoken words on your part) send nasty letters to your favorite members of Congress. I can't wait.

AIs have tremendous potential as bureaucracy navigators, federal form fillers, science researchers, political advocates, research librarians, community organizers, and managers of civic duties of all kinds. Frankly, I'd vote for an AI if it would run for a seat on my county's board of supervisors for two reasons: (1) AIs are not real estate developers and (2) an AI on the board certainly would not lower the board's IQ level.

The most valuable use of AIs in government may well be in the area of government–citizen relations, not exactly a stellar category for government, based on my last TSA interaction at an airport. But imagine if AIs could make dealing with government *manageable*, maybe even pleasurable. Imagine if we all had access to our own personal government AI, an AI we'll call PAUL (personal AI for USA liaison) because acronyms have been an essential part of AI nomenclature since ENIAC (the first computer). PAUL is launched as an official US government service, available for download on all our phones and computers. Once you download your own personal, private version, PAUL offers to be your Siri or Cortana for the IRS and Social Security, your bureaucracy navigation guide, and your government services butler. PAUL's first job is to set up your personal ID credentials really well and then help you manage them properly, eliminating virtually all system-access hassles on your end and significantly ratcheting up identity-based security controls in all your communications with government.

PAUL provides a secure digital wallet and is a solid password and biometrics manager, but his most important function is as your overall government ombudsman. He is more knowledgeable about local code regulations, recent court rulings, riparian rights, precise property lines, and tax code than any human county official. He's also a lightspeed learner who understands your state and federal government needs. He understands your political preferences and opinions the way Pandora understands your taste in music. You guide and control PAUL. He improves your experience of government, and government, for its part, gets a stronger connection with you.

The first thing I'd have my PAUL do is review all my correspondence and notes over the past decade regarding encounters with the Tualatin Valley Water District of Washington County, Oregon, which have to do with new housing, new easements, old water flows, and new sewage. Typical county government shit, in other words.

I have nothing against the local government worker bees who force us to put sewer pipes under our honey bees, who occasionally rip up our road and land, and who built their own "bridge to nowhere" about two hundred yards north of our property line. I don't like them, these watershed police and high-density housing promoters, but I do admire them. They are serious about clean, safe water, and their prodensity urban growth policies are what keep our many Washington County farms going, long after they would have become subdivisions or strip malls in California or Washington State. The local water district does important work. It's just that its workers are often a major pain in the ass to deal with.

So now imagine having an official government AI app that could eliminate 99 percent of the petty annoyances when dealing with the local water districts of the world. Wouldn't *that* make you want to become a positive, productive US citizen again? But if you want to be an early adopter of a PAUL-like AI service, you'll probably have to move to Singapore.

The World's Most AI-Savvy Governments

Everyone with an interest in AI today should have an appreciation of which governments around the world best understand and appreciate AI. If I were to subjectively rate world governments with respect to AI awareness and competence—not the national AI ecosystem, mind you, just the government—my top seven would be:

China. China's government is investing more heavily in AI than any other on Earth by far. Its scientists now publish the most AI research papers and are beginning to set international AI tech standards as well. Some experts believe AI will be the first digital technology in which China is the global front-runner rather than a follower of the United States. Xi Jinping and his top comrades have a powerful commitment to AI and a proscience philosophy (see chapter 7).

European Union. Germany is an enterprise tech leader, and France has the most AI-savvy government in the Western world. The European Commission in April 2018 enacted a series of measures designed to "boost Europe's competitiveness" in AI, including an immediate infusion of nearly $2 billion in research funding and a goal of annually putting $20 billion of AI research to work starting in 2020.[1] AI is much higher on the EU political agenda than it is the United States. Many EU leaders view AI as a field in which they can avoid complete American tech dominance.

The EU is the world's leader in information privacy, and in AI-related data issues. The Universal Declaration of Human Rights, adopted by the United Nations and all nontotalitarian regimes in the world, came from France more than seventy years ago. I suspect that France and the EU will produce the Universal Declaration of AI Data Rights within the next five years and that it will similarly become a global standard.

Canada. The University of Toronto is the long-time home of Geoffrey Hinton, currently the most important AI scientist in the world. The Vector Institute for Artificial Intelligence in Toronto (and now New York) is the world's most impressive public and private AI innovation hub.[2] Justin Trudeau, Canada's prime minister, acquitted himself quite well recently when pitching Canadian AI momentum to a powerful and highly technical audience at MIT. Imagine *your* head of state doing that. Some of the best military intelligence about AI in the world is coming from Canada' Security Intelligence Service (CSIS, Canada's version of the CIA). Pound for pound, Canada may be the best AI puncher of the lot.

Singapore. This semisocialist, hard-assed little city-state has its act together when it comes to government adoption of technology, and AI is no exception. I explore Singapore's AI in more detail later.

Israel. Israel (a.k.a., Start-up Nation) has increased entrepreneurial funding fifteenfold in just the last five years. More significant is that the number of AI start-ups has tripled since 2014.[3] Israel is a world leader in AI for health care (including dentistry) and in AI applications for cybersecurity. The Israeli military has state-of-the-art face recognition and AI-enhanced cybersecurity protection systems. Much of the Israeli government's AI development is secret, but that doesn't mean it is not powerful or significant.

United States. If not for DARPA, NASA, and NOAA, the United States would not have even made my big twenty. But the role of these three agencies in the ongoing evolution of AI has been crucial (full discussion later).

Estonia. According to a 2017 Akamai report on Internet connectivity, Estonia delivers faster Internet speeds to its citizens than does the United States.[4] Estonia has been a leader in addressing unprecedented legal questions related to AI and machine intelligence and is cleverly becoming a global player in AI by doing so. Estonia is the world's leading early government adopter of AI and is a preferred base for issuing blockchain-based cryptocurrencies. Estonia is a small country but definitely a pace-setter.

This list raises a number of legitimate questions: How could you possibly leave out Japan and South Korea? What about the United Kingdom, home of DeepMind and AlphaZero? Estonia better than Russia? Are you kidding me? (Yes, the Russian government is AI savvy but not yet very AI capable. Russia has virtually no private-sector technology industry, so it is starting with a very big technology disadvantage. It has defense industry AI programs well underway, and Russia is an academic world leader in math. An argument can indeed be made that Russia's government should outrank Estonia's, but an argument can also be made that Putin's kleptocracy is not really a government.)

Regarding the relatively low position of the United States: It's certainly true that for decades almost all serious AI research was funded by the US government, largely through the Defense Advanced Research Projects Agency (DARPA).[5] Today, AI development is scattered across the US federal government. Much of this activity is smart and important; it's just not coherent. There is no compelling central vision in the White House and none in Congress either. There is certainly no sense of a government-wide, much less a nationwide, AI moon shot, which is what's needed.

AI, like nuclear energy, is too powerful—too existential—for governments to ignore. As I write, a dozen or so governments understand the power of AI, for good and ill. More will soon. Governments who are able to become prime movers in this field will develop highly defensible competitive advantages. Countries that lag behind will suffer in many ways, which makes the current state of AI inside the government of the United States deeply frustrating.

Silicon Valley has had more than its share of problems and screwups over the last thirty years, from Napster and Pets.com to Yahoo's three billion stolen identity records and Facebook's dance with Cambridge Analytica. It has also unquestionably been the world's technology epicenter. But in the next decade, there is a very good chance tech's biggest shock waves will be emanating from Beijing.

During the oughts (2000–2009), I moved my business focus to Washington, DC, attempting to fuse Internet and government security systems. It was a post-9/11 world, and I had investors from my previous companies who were well placed inside DC, so I thought I'd see if I could help put Internet technology to use to help improve homeland security. The Lombardy Hotel in Washington, DC, became my business home. It was a great business hotel in those days—human elevator operators, mini-kitchens, CNN reporters in the café for breakfast, and hotel staff who knew your name, all just five blocks from the White House, along "Eye" Street.[6]

I was CEO of a security software company selling software-as-service (SaaS) subscriptions[7] and tech services to the US federal government. We did business with DoD, DHS, NSA, and TSA. Our tech platform was the foundation of the Office of the Director of National Intelligence's (ODNI) experimental, cross-agency information-sharing program, which failed because lawyers from thirty federal agencies couldn't agree on how to data-dance together on the head of a pin.[8] Or maybe just because a group of thirty lawyers will never be able to agree on anything.

At our apex, by some fluke, *Federal Computing Weekly* (the *Variety* of government contracting) named me one of the one hundred most influential tech people in government circles.[9] I was no high-tech all-star, but I did make it to the Oval Office a time or two and met with dozens of congressmen and congresswomen. Still, on three occasions I had senior DHS officials fall asleep as I was presenting in after-lunch meetings. Awkward, especially when you are presenting to an audience of one. This never happened in Hollywood or Silicon Valley, not even close. I imbibed Senator Leahy's "holy water" (the

Jameson variety) at his regular Wednesday "service" overlooking the Capitol Mall, had dinner with Donald Rumsfeld; and in a small way helped Michael Hayden become head of the CIA (a long and now unimportant story; if I told you any more, I'd have to kill myself).

I mention all this only to point out that, as a Left Coast Internet entrepreneur, I have more federal government exposure than most, which I think is necessary background for my assertion throughout this book that the American government—ultimately, Lincoln's *of the people* government—must strive aggressively to remain the world's AI leader. I admit, it'll be tricky.

Look (as DC pundits like to start their sentences), government is frustrating—for no one more than lifelong entrepreneurs such as myself. As a get-'er-done businessman, I could not believe the amount of paperwork necessary to complete a federal contract or the number of meetings required to make a small tech change, the software equivalent of changing a light bulb. I discovered most government workers still believe in strict, eight-hour days. What a concept! The pace of program development is interminable, and the degree to which congressional budget politics influence science and technology projects, frankly, is shocking. Don't even get me started about being a federal subcontractor in the bayous of Louisiana, where congressional earmarks put bread on the table and where, at the time our company was working there on an emergency communications project, the last three governors had gone to jail.

Yet I must say, in working with federal government leaders of both parties, I found most to be decent folks, believers in America's corny but solid golden oldies, such as *liberty and justice for all.* I'm referring to the people who actually run government systems and programs, from armies and navies to public health research agencies, not politicians and their lobbyist sycophants. I found federal government agencies, for the most part, to be run by good people, honest in their own individual ways. As a bottom-line businessman, I found their dedication to country, in spite of all the red tape and political bullshit, rather refreshing.[10] But as a taxpayer, my decade in DC left me really pissed off.

In Washington, I witnessed institutional lying, political rationalization, and minor corruption, up close and personal. Nothing as blatant as the bribes that government workers take every day in Bangkok, Macao, or Mexico City but every bit as unethical. My (naïve Oregon-based) company got burned by not agreeing to play graft games with a brand-name federal contractor. We lost a multimillion-dollar Department of Energy contract—one we were already told we had won by our partner, Oak Ridge Laboratory—because our federal contractor partner turned our eighty-page bid in two minutes late. We were also denied a large federal contract because a competitor cleverly filed a completely spurious whistleblower action against us just before a bid deadline—a very clever move, as it turned out. The charge, against a three-star general who was consulting with us, was hogwash according to the inspector general report, but it worked long enough to take us out. Federal government contracting is a rugby scrum in which the big boys—Northrop Grumman, General Dynamics, Boeing, BAE, et al.—get to pick the referees, and then hire them after the game.[11]

During the decade our small company was (arguably) the federal government's leading cross-agency security intelligence-sharing platform, government inefficiencies were rampant, and tech decisions, just plain stupid. Yet somehow, mostly, government worked. In the post-9/11 panic, government-security-sector workers (badged employees and their contractor friends) were absolutely committed to stopping terrorism. The biggest single reason America experienced no major follow-on terrorist attacks in the oughts, in my (somewhat informed) opinion, is that FBI and other federal agents across America did amazingly effective work in rooting out terrorist cells before they could launch attacks—with, by the way, great assistance from America's Muslim community.

Having witnessed this kind of cohesive activity in America behind the curtains gives me hope that we can do it again with AI with respect to the threat of Chinese AI. To be clear, I am not likening the threat of Chinese AI to that of jihadist terror—at least, not yet. But the kind of mobilization and sense of mission in fighting terrorism will be necessary in order to maintain at least a level playing field in AI with respect to China.

Today, hyperpartisanship has rendered the crucial legislative branch of the US government all but inert. In Congress, legislative craftsmanship is a lost art. Henry Clay, Daniel Webster, and Robert Taft must be rolling in their graves. The great unbridled stallion known as the US Senate is now little more than a wooden, merry-go-round pony. Ultimately, I suppose, we the people in America get the government we deserve. Those of us who value a scientific, data-driven approach to government have been asleep at the wheel since the 1990s. We became preoccupied with our emerging information noosphere, which we dubbed the Internet. But the governments of China and the United States still hold the most powerful cards, and we techies can no longer ignore them.

The Singapore Solution

It's time for America to use its AI advantage to make sure AI remains friendly and in the right friendly hands. It's time America's technology companies, and the customers who support them, to start stirring AIs into America's political soup.

While on deadline for this book in my writer's cave, I witnessed President Trump and Chairman Kim of North Korea staging a colorful media opera in Singapore. The imagery of Trump and Kim in Singapore was spectacular—in fact, way over the top. Totalitarian North Korean government flags with Old Glory, side by side across the stage. Whoa. As an Asia hand familiar with North Korea's murderous, fascist regime, it was hard to watch, but none of the old plays had worked with North Korea. I'm not opposed to a Trumpian cut-to-the-chase move, if it would actually succeed in creating a new, ongoing dialog between these two nuclear powers. It was conservative Republican Richard Nixon who "opened" China, after all.

No one says the forty-fifth American president isn't a master showman. I haven't checked, but I'd imagine the Trump–Kim Singapore got the highest reality show ratings that week around the world. But fifty years from now, I'll bet history will be less interested in what was happening between Trump and Kim in Singapore in 2018 than what was happening there in the field of AI because, in spring 2018, this small city-state became the first government in the world to start aggressively delivering AI services to its citizens.

In the 1980s, thousands of young American and European business expats were working in Asia. I was one of them, and Singapore was one of our regular haunts. I recall a favorite toast: "If you think the singer poor, you should see the drummer (rimshot!)." We were all poor as drummers in those days but also ambitious and captivated by the romance of Asia. For Singapore locals, the government was hard-assed and tyrannical. Then, as now, public canings were a form of criminal punishment, yet the government—notorious for its no spitting, no chewing gum policies—was also superefficient and ran a relatively unbiased economic meritocracy. "Come to our city," was the message, "and if you can cut it and contribute to our economy, we want you as a citizen (or as a visiting businessman)." For business expats such as myself in the 1980s, Singapore was a city where you could get things done. That's still true. Today, Singapore is the most data-driven government on Earth and one of its wealthiest cities.

AI Singapore (AISG) is an official government program that funds AI research, trains AI engineers, and sponsors conferences and seminars (e.g., the recent Singapore–France AI Workshop, promoting AI collaboration between France and Singapore). AISG collaborates with Singapore's new Advisory Committee on the Ethical Use of AI and Data, which is a broad, serious attempt to come up with ethical guidelines and motivations for AI. The former attorney general for the nation is leading this effort, and it includes many nonengineers in leadership positions, along with leaders from the AI industry, quite a number of whom are from the United States. AISG's mission statement: "To anchor deep national capabilities in artificial intelligence, thereby creating social and economic impacts, growing local talent, building an AI ecosystem, and putting Singapore on the world AI map."[12] This is the kind of mission we need for an AI America, minus getting on the map; we are already the map's center and will continue to be for at least for a few more years.

Give Donald Trump some credit. In the 2016 presidential election, he and his Texas brain trust cracked the high-tech political code. The Trump campaign's tech team created a decisive online advantage because of its willingness to allow Facebook, Google, and Twitter employees into their campaign offices to train and assist staffers.[13] Facebook employees worked in Trump campaign offices two to three days per week; Twitter employees, one to two days. Google types dropped by occasionally. These tech reps came to help the Trump campaign fully exploit their companies' people-targeting, attention-capturing capabilities. In the end, Trump said yes to exploiting the know-how of these tech giants. Hillary said no: politically a big mistake.

Personally, as a lifelong online privacy advocate, I would outlaw all personally invasive use of private data for political advertising on social media (except when users have clearly consented to get such ads) period, forever.[14] But the odds of such a social media political advertising ban becoming law are longer than Melania Trump confessing to being a princess from Alpha Centauri.

As with many areas of technology today—notably cybersecurity, online privacy, and AI—going backward is not an option. We have no choice but to use good tech to fight bad tech, now and in the imagined future. I use *good* and *bad* here in the cybersecurity sense. In the information assurance field, which is what the feds call cybersecurity, a machine, software application, or blob of data is either trusted (good) or not trusted (bad). Good digital systems have transparent identities rooted in a trustworthy foundation and have predicable agendas. Bad digital systems have fake identities and unpredictable, often untoward agendas. In order to move onto the national political stage, AI needs to be trusted and have clear and predictable agendas. AIs used in the political arena, in other words, must be trusted, transparent, and authentic.

As I write, the US 2020 presidential election looms. Political advertising on social media, with laser-like precision and new AI-driven powers, will undoubtedly play a key role in determining the outcome, not just of the presidential election, but of races for Congress, governor, mayor, and state legislature, as well.

As I've indicated, it has become crucial, from a pragmatic AI political perspective, that we elect as many tech-savvy government officials as possible. I have lobbied the White House, Congress, and federal agencies on behalf of advancing technology since the mid-1990s. Believe me, there is nothing worse than a federal govie, in any role, who just doesn't get it. We need House members with an understanding (and appreciation) of science. We need smart, data-driven senators, not backslappers whose sharpest skill is navigating the Capitol Grille at happy hour. We definitely need science and technology leadership in the White House. And most of all, we need a trusted national AI ecosystem that makes citizen input count.

So, what if a national AI program could inject rigorous data analysis and political science truth into America's body politic, like an injection of a powerful antibiotic? Could that change the current rancorous discourse and help reduce the tribal polarization? Possibly. Allow me to wave my magic wand:

> The most important AI companies in the United States—Google, Microsoft, Amazon, Facebook, Apple, IBM, Intel—come together and work cooperatively and with other trustworthy tech companies to build an American truth platform, an AI "of the people, by the people, for the people," a new digital commons for politics in America. Let's call this new AI commons CherryTree, after the apocryphal yet nonetheless persistent Americana tale about George Washington's inability to tell a lie. Here's how CherryTree, the AI, could come to life and save America.
>
> CherryTree is a national, nonpartisan political intelligence service. It reads terabytes of data about government, public policy, and politics each day. It provides facts, odds and predictions, and ever-changing issue summaries with as little Republican or Democrat bias as possible. CherryTree is accessible by any American citizen but only by them. Its reward function is set to provide the most valuable, most factual political information, as weighted by in-system citizen ratings.
>
> CherryTree includes a network of active users, called members, who come together online to set goals, provide guidance, and determine the ethics of the service on an ever-changing, real-time basis. Members continually reset political bias buttons and provide instant polling data on issues of all kinds.
>
> CherryTree is built pro bono by big company volunteers and operated and maintained by a politically neutral NGO, unless and until the US federal government takes over. Its high-assurance platform consists of cloud compute resources, blockchain, AI lightspeed learners, intelligence dashboards, smart alerting, chatbots, know-your-customer (KYC) systems,[15] and a variety of other connected applications and end devices.
>
> CherryTree would use the trusted-but-anonymous (TBA) identity model, with no public exposure of personally identifiable information. It's the model

> of the voting booth, where a unique identity credential is needed to enter but all activities inside the booth remain anonymous and secret.
>
> CherryTree's primary mission is to ingest political information and produce factually weighted reports. These reports (or issue positions) are then vetted with the American citizen members of the service in various ways. CherryTree does not do issue or candidate polling. It enables citizens to cast their votes on everything hourly.
>
> CherryTree members who pass AI-citizen-certification requirements—who prove their AI literacy, in other words—are able to access a smaller citizens group focused on AI policy. Whenever overall member coherence on a given issue reaches 75 percent, virtually every elected official in America is notified.
>
> Crowdsourced feedback would enable CherryTree to continually improve its skills in finding common political ground. Over time, neural networks being what they are, I would expect CherryTree to drive increasingly toward national political coherence, defined as 75 percent national consensus on any given issue. CherryTree would discover whole new strategies for American coherence, just as AlphaZero discovered whole new strategies for Go.

America's AI giants should build CherryTree and gift it to the American people. They and their AI efforts could use the good PR. More importantly, if successful, CherryTree would generate an awesome amount of (anonymized) data that could be used by both the US government and the founding companies in their AI efforts. If really successful, American citizens opting in could even begin to help level the playing field with China when it comes to government-collected data—not in quantity but perhaps in quality. CherryTree would also be a great way to educate the American populace about AI. The ultimate goal would be to help the American electorate regain a more factual, scientific footing in politics and governance, without bias from either the left or the right.

Eventually, CherryTree could extend proprietary, for-official-use-only (FOUO) tentacles into different cabinet and intelligence agencies, providing the secretary of agriculture, say, with the coherent opinions of hog farmers and Iowa environmentalists and the secretary of defense with coherent opinions about issues of war and peace. One the biggest problems members of Congress face is, *so many bills, so little time*. And the result is that almost no bills get passed. CherryTree could sort through all proposed bills for Congress members, provide a factual analysis of what each bill would do as law, and handicap its odds of passing, thus helping members set their legislative priorities. Perhaps CherryTree could even help rationalize bills that are thousands of pages long down to one hundred pages or less. And because I'm just spitballing, how about if a CherryTree robot were the moderator of the presidential debates? Wouldn't that be awesome? "I'm sorry Mr. Candidate, your assertion that five hundred people were killed last year by self-driving vehicles lacks basis and receives the 'liar, liar, pants on fire' rating."

China, Russia, the European Union, the United Kingdom, Israel, South Korea, Japan, Canada, and Singapore all have national AI programs. As I write, the United States does not. CherryTree is an admittedly wild idea, but we need some way to kick-start interest in AI governance inside the United States. There are undoubtedly even better ones.

Here's the main point: The global AI clock is ticking faster and faster. The US government faces an existential AI crisis, whether we like it or not, whether we understand it or not. Two of the United States' major adversaries, China and Russia, very much understand the ticking AI clock. These governments are racing to catch and overtake our best private AI companies, who are smart and strong but are no nation. They need our government's help because China will soon pass them, and us, unless we bring AI into the core fabric of American politics and government.

Tech industry leaders who abhor any scent of federal government involvement with their golden-goose technologies will no doubt oppose any government encroachment onto their turf. To be clear, I'm not suggesting the US government regulate AI—at least, not now. The US federal government, on its own, cannot regulate AI and should not try to do so, for three main reasons:

1. The US government today does not have enough AI experts in its ranks to effectively even understand AI, let alone regulate it.
2. A regulation in the United States will have no influence on AIs elsewhere and could merely hamper US companies, whose global leadership we want to continue to support.
3. Regulation of AI cannot follow traditional regulatory control models because moving forward aggressively in AI is much more important from a security perspective than keeping AIs in some regulated swim lane.

At the same time, we urgently need a national AI program. But if we have to wait for Congress to approve one in this era, we'll be waiting a long time.

What we need in America is a patriotic movement to retain our global leadership in AI and a progressive movement to keep AI friendly and green and Wall Street AI strategies to help small investors and DoD programs to preempt an AI arms race. We need much more AI education, a comprehensive AI transportation strategy, and a complete AI-driven health-care makeover—yesterday. We also need to develop our own personal AI strategies because, paraphrasing my favorite Nobel Prize–winning American poet, "it's a hard AI rain's a-gonna fall."[16] To do nothing about AI collectively as a government and nation in this second decade of the twenty-first century, would be an epic mistake on the order of Napoleon thinking an attack on Waterloo would be a slam dunk: never a good idea when you stand only 5'7".

Why is it so risky to have no AI competency in the American government? Because China will kick our AI butts, technologically speaking, from here to Kashgar if we do not. Remember, in AI, scale often wins, especially with respect to data. We need a national data haystack barn-raising—a concerted effort of the kind China is implementing today. But with privacy protection, anonymization and an incredibly rich feedback system (open feedback systems being our biggest competitive advantae over China). We haven't even started drawing up such systems, but if we were to, they would absolutely require a government that is at least somewhat AI-savvy and very much AI-driven, not just in exotic R&D labs but also in the halls of real political power.

CHAPTER TEN

~

The AI Casino

"When somebody says it's not about the money, it's about the money."

—H. L. Mencken

In 2018, *Forbes* magazine prominently cited an International Data Corporation (IDC) forecast estimating the global AI market would grow from $12 billion in 2017 to $57.6 billion in 2021—a nearly 500 percent growth in five years.[1] A Forrester study predicted that global revenue from "insight-driven businesses" (basically, companies relying mostly on AI and big data) would top $1.2 trillion by 2020.[2] Not to be outdone, Accenture modeled the impact AI would have on twelve developed economies that account for 50 percent of the world's economic production and concluded the market value of AI will climb "*to $8.3 trillion in the United States alone by 2035*."[3] Ladies and gentlemen, that's one big casino.

At this casino—I'm envisioning Las Vegas's Bellagio—you can see heads of state, famous celebrities, billionaire high-rollers, and wannabe millionaires; plus plenty of high-end cognitive worker bees, such as accountants, lawyers, researchers, engineers, and consultants; plus the inevitable grifters, hackers, and cons. Stakes are high; the tech, real. Champagne is already flowing.

But here's the dirty little secret about the AI industry, at least from an investment perspective: AI's geniuses and difference makers are not in it for the money. They come to the big casino to get funding for their AI projects, perhaps even for their kids' education, a house mortgage, or a family trip back to India, sure. But the experts driving AI today find tinkering with AI to be more exciting than accumulating wealth. Most have come to corporate work after successful careers in academia. They are like college students who've graduated from flying drones on soccer fields to flying Webjets for the corporate elite. So far, everyone seems to be enjoying the ride.

But there's something unusual going on. This new AI crowd is much less interested in stock prices than in cool science and business ethics. The industry players taking their places in the AI casino aren't spouting "do no evil" platitudes; they're developing serious, detailed humanitarian standards and guidelines for AI (see the Future of Life Institute principles at the end of chapter 12). These new AI leaders are taking steps to regulate themselves in an early adopter market. In high tech, this is new.

The Internet in my day was all cliff dives and rugby scrums, a rough-and-tumble place. Bill Gates today is a great global philanthropist. In the 1990s, he was a hypercompetitive bully. And Steve Jobs, for all his Ayurvedic eccentricities, would never have been mistaken for Mahatma Gandhi.

Compared to the Internet marketplace, the AI industry is like bird watching. (I say that as a compliment; I'm an avid observer of hawks, larks, towhees, hummingbirds, house sparrows, and crows, all regular visitors to our trees and bird feeders.) For a considerable time to come, AI will be ruled by colorful birds with names like Hinton, LeCun, Hassabis, and Ng—pioneering scientists who have built powerful AIs and made them work, with values and personalities quite different from web titans like Gates, Jobs, Zuckerberg, and Schmidt.[4]

AI is not an industry where you can overcome technical deficiencies with a cool story, a clever interface, or a brutal competitive streak. It takes extremely smart, well-educated people working together creatively and efficiently, building precise systems. It takes lots of such people to build an AI that advances the art in some way. It also takes prodigious compute and data resources and well-thought-out, rigorously tested hypotheses. As a JPL scientist once told me, "AI isn't rocket science. It's not nearly that simple."

Unless and until intelligent machines themselves take over, AIs will be controlled by the humans who have a decent understanding of how they actually work. AI scientists, of course, will be in this number, but so will many nonscientists and nonengineers, including ethicists, doctors, federal officials, teachers, lawyers, and perhaps even a few forward-learning politicians. In the decade ahead, smart people of all kinds will be needed to build sustainable AI ecosystems. On the Manhattan Project, physicists supplied the formulas, but the military provided security; GE, Union Carbide, and other companies provided the means of production; and the US federal government supplied the funding. For the United States to retain its AI leadership, something similar will be required with AI. At this moment in American history, proposing a government-led AI Manhattan Project is just silly. Our body politic is in ICU, and our federal government has become a forty-ring circus whose ringmaster has chosen to star in his own White House reality TV show.

And yet, America's tech businesses are doing extremely well. Apple in 2018 hit the trillion-dollar valuation mark. Amazon, Microsoft, and Google were not far behind. Each of these companies and dozens more like them are hiring aggressively to strengthen their AI hands. Even though AI breakthroughs will not come in start-up garages littered with pizza boxes and Diet Coke cans, AIs can and will be used by a next generation of AI-aware entrepreneurs, who will create substantial new value for their companies.

Through 2025, it is hard to imagine a scenario in which the big tech giants do not continue to produce the world's most sophisticated AI. They will continue to be the high rollers at the AI casino, but they'll hardly be the only ones at the tables. The best and brightest from all walks of life are now streaming in to take their spin of the AI wheel, including one CEO whose last big spin of the wheel of fortune was in outer space.

An Astronaut in the Casino

Scott Parazynski is an energetic CEO whose latest quest is building a hardware device company. He's a former astronaut who conducted one of the most epic space walks of all time and is the only spaceman ever to have summited Mount Everest. He missed making the 1988 US Olympic luge team, so he went to the Olympics as the coach of the Philippines' squad. Oh, and he graduated with honors from Stanford Med School, your basic California slacker dude.

It was a beautiful spring day up and down the West Coast. Scott was driving from Los Angeles to San Diego. He'd generously given me thirty minutes of his time. We're Bluetoothing—Scott cruising I-5, me pacing the upstairs deck outside my home office near chirping sparrow nests. If you were a bird on my shoulder that morning as Scott and I talked on the phone and knew nothing of Scott's background, you'd swear he's just another smart, hungry entrepreneur from Silicon Valley: friendlier than most, definitely strong in the passion department, but extremely down to earth (for a Stanford grad).[5]

We discussed Scott's company, Fluidity Technologies, which makes "single-handed input devices."[6] After hearing Scott's description, I envisioned his product as a kind of falconer's glove for controlling things in three-dimensional space. These joysticks on steroids have smart controls for flying drones (today) and conducting remote open-heart surgeries (day after tomorrow). Scott's controllers are in the process of becoming serious AI learners, continually getting better at reducing the cognitive workload whenever we humans want to execute intricate control tasks remotely. With Fluidity gear, a five-year-old can fly a drone just like an F-16 pilot—at least until the OODA loops start. And the day when kids can do even that may be coming. Fluidity is very cool tech.

As Scott and I talked, what struck me was his effortless balancing of the light and dark sides of AI. His attitude was, *Hell yes, we need to be careful about AI safety, but wow, think of the possibilities!* Scott was an All-American boy who grew up everywhere but in America. His last four schools before graduating from high school were in Dakar (Senegal), Beirut (Lebanon), Tehran (Iran), and Athens (Greece). Now he was excited about how AI can bring ultra-high-quality health care to third world peoples. He believed AI would warn of diseases earlier, further extend medical expertise into the field, and increase life expectancies around the planet. He was enthusiastic that ordinary people can experience the joy of flying while still on terra firma. He was absolutely convinced AIs will deliver a crucial competitive advantage in all sorts of fields in the decades ahead, yet he also had an astronaut's (and mountain climber's) respect for *safety first.*

He'd read parts of an early draft of this book. We discussed China's role in AI and the nature of the Sino–American AI relationship. He pointed out that, in the area of space exploration, China and the United States have enormous potential to become great partners, although NASA isn't currently working with China because of their militarily focused program: "We've worked really well with our other international partners (Russia, Europe, Japan, Canada, and others). Maybe this international collaborative approach we've used in space programs can provide a positive model for AI." Indeed. An astronaut's life—Chinese, Russian, or American—literally depends on rigorous safety standards. Scott said he'd like to see safety and security systems "designed into" AIs from the beginning and then given high priority ever after, the way they are at NASA.

I told Scott a bit about my background in Internet security, how in the 1990s I watched our Internet industry move fast, get rich, and take security shortcuts every step of the way. Software was an inflatable innertube in those days, and security consisted largely of a set of patches you brought along to plug the inevitable leaks. As a software industry CEO, I confess I have fallen into this trap myself. There is such pressure to get your latest application out the door and into the marketplace that getting all the security features coded and tested properly was always a major challenge. I imagine the big pharma firms would also slam drug products out the door before being fully tested and safe were it not for their need to get FDA approval. But there never has been an FDA for software.

I described to Scott how the "safety last" ethic of the dot-com era had come home to roost about fifteen years later with huge breaches of Internet systems. (Lest we forget, in one giant 2013 hack, *three billion* identity records were stolen—*stolen*—from Yahoo, essentially anyone who had ever registered for a Yahoo service.[7]) "We've got to start designing-in security controls," I said to Scott, "or AI will be déjà vu all over again. Only worse this time." Scott didn't disagree.

Like all good astronauts, Scott is completely signed up for safety and security protocols. He'll support them, execute them in AI, just as he did in space. But Scott's focus now was on the positive potential of AI, not its risks. He was eager to see AI-assisted medicine extend to the base camps of mountain climbers, the ships of world sailors, and the triage tents at natural disasters. The way he envisioned it, top-notch medical care eventually will become a global service, helping humans everywhere live a longer, healthier life. That's his big-picture vision. In the meantime, he also sees major changes coming to the American home.

"We're going to see *health care at home* built into new residences. Members of your family will be able to check themselves for skin diseases, collect urine and blood samples, do routine retinal exams, et cetera," said Scott. A "med room," I learned, is space in the home dedicated to family health. Here, families in the near future manage their personal health needs: collecting biometric data, performing various quick self-care checks, and Skyping via big screens to a friendly gaggle of human providers. I use the phrase *friendly gaggle* advisedly. A decade or two in the future, with med rooms in every modern home, health-care providers will all be very upbeat and friendly because the human practice of medicine and related arts will be increasingly about empathy, good communication, decision support, and a sense of humor. Machines will do most everything else.

Families with med rooms (or with wired med huts in sub-Saharan Africa) will have a new first line of defense against illness. AIs will be capturing data and watching bodily functions. Whenever a physical anomaly pops up—a worrisome skin lesion, an eye infection, a spike in blood pressure—a red-flag alert is sent to the appropriate health-care provider. Prevention of disease becomes, in part, a data analytics business, guided, of course, by human MDs. Scott suggested that prodigious amounts of personal health data will be collected once med rooms and AI-empowered remote clinics get traction—and these (properly anonymized) data will be used in everything from clinical trials to family medicine.

I mentioned the remarkable Deep Patient AI in use at New York's Mount Sinai Hospital. Deep Patient has been working alongside physicians for several years now, helping to diagnose various forms of disease. After absorbing health data from 700,000 patients, Deep Patient began to get very good at predicting certain forms of cancer, notably liver cancer. Then it began to predict schizophrenia.[8] This was a true *hel-lo!* moment because there are no medical protocols for predicting schizophrenia. This insidious disease runs in my mother's family, and the idea of preschizophrenics taking prophylactic meds is, for me, jump-up-and-down exciting. And in yet another case of AIs working mysteriously inside their little black boxes, neither the physicians working with Deep Patient nor the computer engineers who built it can explain exactly how Deep Patient does it.

Former astronaut and current CEO Dr. Scott Parazynski is now tackling the task of starting and running a hardware-enabled software company, a company that aspires to produce technology that learns at lightspeed and that, if wildly successful, will enable medical teams in Los Angeles to assist with brain surgeries in Addis Ababa. Launching an AI-savvy start-up like Fluidity can seem like climbing Everest, but Scott's already done that, so this entrepreneurial mountain doesn't appear to faze him. After my interview with him, I jotted in my notebook, "Scott intuitively has the perfect positive/negative balance re: AI." Good balance is one of the ancillary benefits, I suppose, of all that mountain climbing and space walking. Did I mention Scott has summited all of Colorado's fifty-nine mountains above 14,000 feet?

The Best and Brightest

The most intriguing aspect of AI, to me, is the people you run into. Scott Parazynski is one great example, but there are many other overachievers wandering into the AI casino these days. It's as if someone reached out to all the "smartest kid in the class" types from high schools everywhere and gave them all tickets. Step right up, all ye scholars with the ability to master AI! You, and only you, can now bend AI to your purpose!

Sometimes these purposes are downright geeky. The father of deep learning, Geoff Hinton, described himself at a 2015 conference as being in the "camp that is hopeless" about AI because he believes governments will use it "to terrorize people." He was then asked why he continued to work in the field. Hinton's answer: "I could give you the usual arguments, but the truth is that the prospect of discovery is too *sweet*."[9]

AI is closer to quantum physics than to Internet commerce. Today's AI pioneers, I find, are smarter than the tech innovators I grew up with in the early days of the World Wide Web, so perhaps they will not make the same mistakes we did. They definitely strike me as more high-minded. However, the early WWW crowd definitely threw better parties and generally speaking were better looking. (Just kidding, my AI friends. You are good-looking, too, but in a Thomas Middleditch sense, who is Canadian, by the way, which takes us to story number 2 of the best and brightest coming to the AI Casino.)

Dmitry Tuzoff "fell in love with deep learning" the night he drank wine with Yann LeCun in Moscow in 2013. LeCun, you'll recall, is Hinton's deep-learning coinventor who gets my vote for the best AI vision expert on the planet. Tuzoff at the time was a thirty-four-year-old Russian gold-medal scholar who had been programming computers since he was fifteen and had launched several companies in Russia—mostly in high tech but one in wine distribution. He was a definite up-and-comer, though hardly an emerging tech celebrity like LeCun. But Tuzoff was a certified sommelier, LeCun was French, and they made a solid connection tasting and talking wine and discussing deep learning.

Before long, Tuzoff was traveling to Toronto to get a PhD in the mathematics of machine learning, and then he launched a new AI dentistry company in Toronto's famed Creative Destruction Lab. This AI business incubator is arguably the best in the world. He chose dentistry as the field in which to apply his machine-learning expertise because it was still relatively wide open when it came to AI applications and because, due to his personal experience in Russia, he knew how much damage poor dentistry could do. Applying AI to dentistry was a chance to do well by doing good.

Meanwhile, five hundred miles south in Chicago, Dr. Eric Pulver, oral surgeon, son and nephew of famous dentists, academic mentor at Northwestern University and other institutions, was musing about starting a dental-related AI company every day on his drive to work. Sure, he had this stand-up comedy thing he was doing in his early fifties, growing out of his Second City improv training, a fiftieth birthday gift from his wife. He was a leading Chicago oral surgeon who reconstructed whole faces after car accidents, but until recently, the biggest challenge of his life was performing live stand-up on stages in Chicago. (Question: How many dentists does it take to screw in a light bulb? Answer: Dentists don't screw in light bulbs. *Hot tubs*. That's my stupid joke, not Dr. Pulver's, dusted off from those days of the early World Wide Web. For some reason back then, there was always an association in my mind between dentists and hot tubs.) Dr. Pulver's worldview is much more serious and ambitious than my image of the average dentist. Now, his biggest challenges were learning AI and building an emerging new AI company call Denti.ai with his new technology partner, Dmitry Tuzoff.

Through a common affiliation with the University of Toronto, these two met and decided to work together to build Denti.ai. Pulver provided deep domain expertise in dentistry and oral pathology; Tuzoff provided deep-learning skills. Although Tuzoff was then in St. Petersburg and Pulver in Chicago, they launched their company in Canada, in part because of the immigration challenges Tuzoff faced when he considered coming to the United States.

During a wide-ranging phone interview with Dmitry, he and I discussed which country might win the big global AI race. His bet is China, and this is after having worked with a Chinese company for three years. One reason he cited for this belief was the United States' current "visa and immigration policies," which he felt were already hampering AI development in America. (For more on this issue, see the final chapter of this book, "The Way Forward.")

As an entrepreneur, it struck me as odd that a math whiz/computer programmer living in Russia would team up with an oral surgeon from Chicago to launch an AI company in Canada. There is a logic to it: Tuzoff can't easily gain residence in the United States, and Pulver has dual US–Canadian citizenship. But the fact that Denti.ai was launched in Canada is telling. These two men each had impressive careers and interesting lives before entering the AI casino. They found each other because of a common desire to put AI to work to improve dental health. Each man, I discovered in separate interviews, has a real passion for their common mission, and I fully expect that they will indeed soon be making important contributions to the field of dentistry around the world.

"Deep learning is best at imagery," Tuzoff said, "so it made sense to begin with X-rays and see if we can use AI image recognition to advance the recognition of dental pathologies." Pulver suggested that using AIs to recognize oral pathologies can, over time and with ongoing learning, create a kind of objective truth that will build trust about the oral health of individual patients in ways that can improve the entire dental ecosystem—from preventive health care to more efficient dental insurance systems. "This is our attempt to make the world a better place," said Pulver. "Who could pass that up?"

Investing in AI

There are other Parazynskis, Tuzoffs, and Pulvers—the best and brightest, top .1 percent of talent—who are just now rolling into the big AI casino. They are not just scientists, engineers, and doctors; they are Go masters in Seoul, young business execs in Bangalore, hedge fund managers in London, every Fortune 200 CEO worth her salt. All are coming to play the AI tables, yet the casino still has many open seats. There are still careers to be made, lives to be improved, fortunes to be built. When all this career building and fortune will hit the mainstream marketplace is still an unanswered question. As the old Silicon Valley adage goes, it's not hard to see where the tech is going, but it is damned near impossible to predict when it will arrive. And as we in the high-tech business world know all too well, timing is everything.

That said, as a former high-tech entrepreneur, I could not be more bullish on AI: bullish both in the Wall Street sense and in the China-shop sense. I agree with Mark Cuban that AI could produce the world's first high-tech trillionaire, and I agree with Stephen Hawking that AI could be humanity's biggest mistake. As Emerson famously said, "Consistency is the hobgoblin of little minds." Here's what's important: We need to bring AIs onto center stage in Western society, especially in American media, politics, and government. We need smart people in all walks of life starting to learn how AIs work and how they will transform society.

I've always been a glass-90-percent-full guy (What entrepreneur isn't?), so call me a ridiculous optimist, but I still believe there are many, many good-hearted, honest people in America who can join together as citizens and, metaphorically speaking, put an AI on the moon. To me, this means both retaining America's lead in AI and developing these new machines based on humanitarian, democratic values. To do this, we need citizens to get smart about AI—not MIT quantum-physics smart, just reasonably well informed, with an understanding of the big issues in AI—because like it or not, as US citizens, some crucial decisions will be made in our name: decisions about management of an AI economy, AI in the military, AI's role in education, and much more. Individual citizens will not be making these decisions directly, but collectively they will determine America's will to excel in AI.

What's the best way to increase our collective national AI IQ? Easy: Turn America into a nation of AI investors. One thing I learned conclusively in the high-tech industry is that that, if you want people to care about your technology, get them to put a little skin in the game—which brings us back to the casino.

When I speak at professional conferences, one question I'm always asked in the wings is, "What are your favorite AI stock picks?" My short answer usually goes something like this: "Amazon, Baidu, Intel, Microsoft, and Salesforce, in alphabetical order." I do no equity investing any more, not even in NASDAQ stocks. My wife does a bit through a financial advisor, who makes very conservative investments: mostly bonds (or so I hear). I have no visibility into any individual investments, other than our annual top-line returns, and that's the way I like it at this stage of my life. This gives me the freedom to discuss AI investment strategies unencumbered by any known financial conflicts of interest.

Aside from my fairly obvious blue-chip stock choices, there are other investments in AI you might want to consider. You'll be investing in AI, of course, every time you log onto Facebook, order a meal from Amazon, or put your Cadillac on cruise control. But you might also want to consider making direct financial investments in AI companies. If you do, here are a few things to consider:

1. **Saying it's AI don't make it so.** The hype cycle for AI is peaking. Not to have an AI strategy for any tech company is the kiss of death, so some companies are slapping "AI" stickers on everything. Ask these crucial questions when evaluating a specific AI:
   a. Does the company publish detailed statistical analytics of its AI products' performance?
   b. Does its AI learn continually learn or just execute previously trained behavior? If it does learn continually, how fast does it learn?
   c. What are the backgrounds of the company's three smartest AI people? The number of math PhDs, computer scientists, and software engineers who can drive fast-lane AI is quite small.[10] Diligent study of the credentials of the people building and growing an AI is one of the best ways to determine if the system will thrive. If none of the architects and engineers have worked previously at Google, IBM, Stanford, MIT, Cambridge, Caltech, Facebook, Amazon, Baidu, Apple, Microsoft, DARPA, NASA, or University of Toronto, it's probably best to pass.[11]
2. **Look for more Salesforce-type opportunities.** You might wonder why Salesforce.com, the software-as-a-service pioneer, made my top five AI stock pick list. While the company is certainly well known as software innovator, few would describe it as an AI leader. Yet Salesforce is nonetheless putting AI to work in powerful and important ways. Here's a quote from Salesforce's most recent analysts conference call (emphasis added): "[O]ur innovation in artificial intelligence is delivering incredible value to our customers. Salesforce Einstein *now delivers nearly 2 billion predictions every day*, and that's a doubling of our daily predictions [over] just last quarter."[12] What kind of predictions? Customer churn rates, best upsell yields, most effective SEO strategies, and dozens of other practical pieces of business and sales management. Leveraging AI, Salesforce is able to offer its business customers their own personal Einstein, which helps them become a "sales genius" for

only fifty dollars a month. Einstein AI is a huge success. When investing in individual companies, look for vertical-market leaders like Salesforce who are committed to AI and embrace it with sufficient resources to make an immediate impact. Land O'Lakes, an integrated milk-products company specializing in high-quality butter, is another example. It has partnered with Microsoft to put AIs into pastures, dairies, distribution warehouses, and grocery-store shelves. For at least the next five years and probably longer, there will be many great opportunities like Salesforce and Land O'Lakes—vertical-market companies with an solid AI plan and a good head start. I learned recently of a very interesting company that is bringing AI to baking.[13] These sorts of companies can make great long-term investments.

3. **Meet Ms. AI, your new wealth manager.** Since around 2010, AIs have been outperforming human investment managers in hedge funds, currency- and commodity-trading desks, and big stock brokerages. Human judgment is needed in financial investing as much as in medicine, but when it comes to number-crunching predictions, no one does it better today than an AI. If your financial advisor does not have an AI component to her services, get a new advisor.
4. **Learning about AI provides the best ROI.** Read books, attend conferences, watch YouTube videos, bring AI into casual conversations, read blogs, and ignore most of the trumped-up political noise that is keeping the United States from focusing on serious science and technology issues, including, most pressingly, the loss of our scientific and market leadership in AI. We Americans have a job to do. We need to understand and ultimately learn to control AI. This is the era where it not only pays to get smart about AI; it's also a requirement of good citizenship.
5. **Is the AI attempting to solve a math problem or take an essay test?** AIs are really good at math. They can learn rules based on math formulas, and they are extraordinary game players. If the utility (or "reward") function of a particular AI involves solving a problem that is essentially mathematical—crunching huge amounts of data to make precise predictions—it is tackling the right kind of problem. If, on the other hand, the problem is fuzzy, emotional, creative, sensitive, multidisciplinary, or highly nuanced, an AI trying to solve it may well spin its wheels.
6. **Is the AI likely to be regulated?** Will it be able to grow quickly in an open, unregulated field, or will it be tightly controlled? Commercial AI drones are highly regulated, a situation unlikely to change quickly. AIs

in medical devices face the same certification challenges all health-care products face. AIs in domains that are tightly regulated will proceed slowly. AIs for back-office administration (a.k.a., robotic process automation), image filtering, and data storage and retrieval (including, say, for X-rays in a dental clinic) face no such barriers and are likely to produce economic value much faster.

7. **Does the AI have access to high-quality data?** Question AI vendors about the training data they use: Are their data proprietary, open source, or (best case) both? What are the size of their data sets? How are they curated? What biases have they found, and how were they able to correct them? A vendor that does not have a strong, clear data story almost certainly does not have an AI product that can grow quickly.
8. **Is the AI self-learning?** If it is merely trained once and installed, it will certainly not be moving in the fast lane and in my view is not even AI (regardless of marketing-department claims). However, even relatively simple applications using convolution neural networks or recursive learning or both can grow very quickly if coevolving with their specific environment.

For the majority of Americans, the most sensible AI stock market investments will be AI index funds (AI managed, of course). Given the amazing AI market growth curves predicted by nearly every credible financial analyst firm, it probably makes sense to include AI prominently in any long-term personal investment strategy.[14] For anyone under forty who can afford to do so, it is hard for me to see how you could get hurt even with an AI dartboard approach—provided you have enough darts.

Still, the most important AI investments you'll make are likely to be of your time and attention, so the more you understand about this new force—this new intelligence-as-a-service—the better you'll do across the board as a citizen of the twenty-first century. You'll also have more to say at dinner parties and will become more efficient—and valuable—in business. From dentists to auto mechanics, from soybean farmers to sound editors, people who learn to put this new utility to use will have a powerful competitive advantage.

But with all the utilization of AI that is going on in specialty fields today (there are AI products for everyone from lawyers to landscape architects), it bothers me that no one has yet shown up at the AI casino with a business plan to support one particularly important group of business specialists: *entrepreneurs*.

I once was on a high-tech panel in a large hotel meeting room with plenty of stale croissants, fresh coffee, and eager attendees. They had come to hear a number of us discuss entrepreneurialism and innovation. With me on the panel was my late, great friend Wyatt Starnes. Wyatt was founder and CEO of Tripwire, an important cybersecurity company. He was also chair of the industry tech council at the National Institute of Science and Technology (NIST).[15] His NIST chairmanship was a big deal. When Wyatt resigned this role, he was replaced by Vint Cerf (a.k.a., "father of the Internet").

Wyatt and I had migrated from San Francisco to Portland in the 1970s. We both started high-tech companies in Oregon and had served on each other's boards. We knew each other well enough to fire off a few friendly zingers that day on the panel stage. I recall refuting Wyatt's claim that he had fewer college credits than either Bill Gates or Steve Jobs. (It's hard to have fewer credits than Jobs, who mostly just audited classes, barefoot.) Wyatt and I had fun answering a question from the audience about how many companies he and I had started. Wyatt's quick answer: "Charles has started more companies in the last twenty years than the entire state of South Dakota."[16] (Not true.) He made it clear we hadn't enough time to go into either of our entrepreneurial careers in detail. (Wink.)

In the break after our panel, a fortyish woman, bright, tightly wound, definitely a corporate type, came up to the two of us and asked, "How can you do it? Go off on your own, take all these big risks? I'd be scared to death." My impression was that she probably worked in a cube, analyzing earnings before interest, taxing, depreciation, and amortization (EBITDA) or proofing product briefs. She seemed truly mystified that entrepreneurs could put everything on the line to start a company (in Wyatt's and my cases, a series of companies: successful ones and failures).

Wyatt took the hand of the woman asking the question like a preacher giving aid and comfort. "Charles and I became entrepreneurs," he said, "because the only companies that would hire us were those we started ourselves. We had no choice." Wyatt was applying his signature charm and exaggerating, as he often did, but never by too much. Basically, he was saying good entrepreneurs do not make the best employees, and he was right.

When Wyatt and I were growing up in California in the 1960s and '70s, there were no schools of entrepreneurialism. You got into the field by starting and running things, by taking risks. You scrambled to get dollars from family and friends, worked long stretches with no paychecks, and sold dreams with financial pro forma attached. Some dreams worked, some didn't, but you kept moving forward. If you were lucky, winnings from the good dreams outweighed losses from the bad. We were on our own in our entrepreneurial endeavors, making it up as we went. Yet any American economist or politician proclaims, "What our economy needs most are more entrepreneurs! More tech innovators! More job creators! Hallelujah, hallelujah, amen!" But here's how we support young entrepreneurs in America: We tell 'em to jump into the big muddy and start swimming. This is an effective filter, I admit. Make a business work, or drown trying. But it is not the most effective way to grow a new generation of entrepreneurs, particularly in the age of AI.

I have spent most of my life as an entrepreneur. The last job I had at an organization I did not start was with the US Department of Commerce in 1970, when I was a "census enumerator" in the Haight-Asbury District of San Francisco. I was "a long-haired, long-form enumerator," as I described myself at the time. I did US Census Bureau data-collection interviews for a living, full-time, on a one-year contract. Certain randomly selected lucky citizens were forced under law to sit down with me for a forty-five-minute interview as part of the 1970 census. Being a census enumerator was not a bad job, to be sure, and it paid quite well I thought, but the red tape was unbelievable. That fact and something about walking around with a clipboard in hand all day made me not want to apply for another job when the sun set on this one. What I wanted to do was start my own business, and that's what I have been doing ever since.

I've seen great new software tools become available for my friends who are doctors, architects, film producers, lawyers, accountants, photographers, sound editors, yoga instructors, teachers, sales execs, CFOs, project managers, and software testers. But no one, to my knowledge, has developed a tech platform for early-stage entrepreneurs, so it would be amazingly awesome if next-gen AI could deliver such tools as:

Entrepreneur's Apprentice. The best human assistants for entrepreneurs are always entrepreneurs-in-waiting themselves. They are dedicated, loyal, hard-working, and have a little *something-something* on the side. To support an entrepreneur, you've got to think like an entrepreneur. The Entrepreneur's Apprentice would be a niche version of Alexa, Siri, or (my favorite) Cortana, designed for young business risk-takers. This AI would "think" like an entrepreneur, be able to provide start-up legal advice, help whip up high-quality slide decks, book travel, and remind the rising young entrepreneur (pointedly) that she hasn't spoken to her lead investor in more than three weeks. And then, at the end of the workday, it would network with other Entrepreneur's Apprentice AIs to scheme up new businesses of their own.

Monte Carlo. Monte Carlo simulations are tools for projecting various scenarios when multiple variables are in play. They enable entrepreneurs to experiment with different business elements (product price, number of employees, number of offices, etc.) and then spin the big spreadsheet wheel to see how various potential scenarios might play out. I have found them to be useful financial tools for start-ups, where virtually every component of the business has a constantly changing numerical value. Until now, it has taken an expert to set up one of these Monte Carlo models properly, but because Monte Carlo simulations always involve iteration, they are a natural application for neural networks. With an AI Monte Carlo simulator, the entrepreneur would express various business options to this AI and watch as Monte Carlo's resulting predictions played out in front of him, thus helping both to develop long-term financial pro forma and making crucial short-term decisions.

Virtual Angel. Your personal AI investor, without human form. This "qualified" investor would be able to provide loans, buy stock, and trade in cryptocurrency. Virtual Angel monitors your business activities 24/7, and not unlike precision irrigation systems, which use AI to deliver just the right amount of water when crops need it most, Virtual Angel will have the ability to supply money whenever the growth and momentum of your business warrant. Virtual Angels will probably be both proprietary (owned and controlled by hedge funds and VCs) and open source, leveraging crowdfunding. These AIs will definitely be lightspeed learners, so they would continually get smarter about the metrics of successful early-stage entrepreneurialism, thereby delivering better investment returns over time. The best thing for entrepreneurs: no time wasted explaining tech and tech markets to human angels who don't get it.

K Street. Innovative, disruptive companies often run afoul of government regulators. Plus, the US government is one of the world's biggest tech customers. Big companies can afford to hire K Street humans with two-tone shirts and White House cuff links and text links with White House staffers, so why shouldn't start-ups have AI lobbyists as well? With K Street, the AI lobbyist, entrepreneurs can obtain the best congressional staffer briefs on any subject, get agency leaders on the phone (at least occasionally), and (when physically in DC) book a prime lunch table at Founding Farmers.

When I worked in Hollywood, the inside joke was that the most creative people in town were the accountants. Just try parsing the meaning of "adjusted gross profits" in a 1980s-era film or music deal. Talk about convolution layers! When I switched careers from film and TV to the Internet in the early 1990s, I quickly learned the most creative people in Silicon Valley were the ones who designed the business models. Imagine the first Google investment pitch: "We're going to build one of the world's most valuable companies by providing a massively expensive global Internet search service, which we will give away for free. We'll make our money on ad clicks, charging advertisers a rate of less than one-thousandth of a penny for every click on one of their ads." Google's was a wonderfully creative and ultimately massively disruptive business model—the Silicon Valley version of writing *Being John Malkovich*, if infinitely more lucrative.

It's still too early to say exactly where AI business models are headed. There are not yet any AI start-up pure plays, at least none as powerful as Google's in Internet search or Amazon in retail, but they're coming. Mark Cuban's first high-tech trillionaire could well be the creator of one of them. In the field of AI, as in the field of electricity, not everyone can be a Ben Franklin, capturing a lightning strike, or a Thomas Edison, cranking out a series of revolutionary inventions, but the AI revolution also needs plenty of ordinary people from all walks of life.

Most day-to-day AI progress is meted out in small, boring, incremental steps that can indeed add up to huge value-creation over time. Amazon, by leveraging AI, cloud computing, and lots of warehouse robots, drove its stock price up 35 percent in the first six months of 2018, above its 2017 already-dizzying high. Inside Amazon, as well as the most prosaic, lumbering large enterprises, AIs either are now or soon will be managing profits and losses, tax returns, most contracts, and a growing amount of human resource services. A 2017 study by the Human Resources Professionals Association (HRPA) found that 84 percent of its members believe "AI is a useful tool for HR."[17] The biggest HR use of AI is in recruiting, but HR pros also believe AIs can help them manage administrative tasks and help employees design better career paths, thereby increasing retention. If AI is destined to become a big part of HR, of *human* resources, then there's "nothing left to stop the whole green world from burning," as Arthur Miller put it.* AIs will be everywhere in business.

This brings us back to our virtual Bellagio's, our AI casino, the size of which has increased by 3.6 percent since you've been reading this chapter. Regardless if the average person understands AI, they need to understand this: AI is where all the money in the world is going, straight down the funnel into Amazon, Google, Baidu, Microsoft, Alibaba, and the other high rollers in the AI casino. There are plenty of other, smaller players at this casino and room enough for many bright people willing to learn about AI, but in terms of financial opportunity, AI is now the runaway world leader. Increasing your knowledge about AI is a smart investment of time and resources, on financial grounds alone. But AI isn't just about making money, or even just about saving democracy or reducing global warming. AI will also play a major role in entertainment and creativity generally. After all, if the AIs take over most of the means of production Earth, we humans will have to find something to do, right?

*From his 1953 play, *The Crucible*. The full line is, "If Rebecca Nurse be tainted, then nothing's left to stop the whole green world from burning."

CHAPTER ELEVEN

~

Of Poetry, Poodles, and Crows

> "You insist that there is something a machine cannot do. If you tell me precisely what it is a machine cannot do, then I can always make a machine which will do just that."
>
> —John von Neumann

Consider the following two poems. Each was written in 2018: one by a human, the other by a computer. See if you can tell which one was written by a computer. The first poem:

the sun is a beautiful thing
in silence is drawn
between the trees
only the beginning of light

The second:

Oh, what a world it will be
when kitchen bots
chop charcuterie
when you and I, in a rolling bar,
drink Martinis
in our self-driving car.
Yes, what wonderous visions
we shall see
when we all start dancin'
the Singularity.

Which of these was written by a computer? Obvious, right? Even though AI was the subject of the second poem, the first was the one written by a machine. It looks and sounds like poetry, but it's really just juvenile crap—the work product of an AI poet developed by Microsoft and Kyoto University.[1] "The silence is drawn / between the trees" is somewhat interesting but would be so much better without the two *thes*. And it means nothing. "The sun is a beautiful thing" as an opening line isn't even a cliché; it's a joke. This computer-generated poem made it into the finals of a literary competition in Japan, to the judges' ultimate embarrassment.

The second poem clearly has been composed by a human. It may be mere doggerel, yet who but a human poet would think to rhyme *will be* with *charcuterie*? And would an AI poet think to "dance the Singularity"? Unlikely.

I know the second poem was composed by a human because I wrote it. I've been writing and reading poetry all my life, as a hobby. My hero poet is Wallace Stevens, one of America's twentieth-century greats. His poetry is not for everyone, but "Sunday Morning," for my money, is the best poem ever written on religion. And who can forget "The Man with the Blue Guitar"? (Wink.) Obscure or not, certain critics regard it as one of the essential twentieth-century poems. Stevens was a lifelong executive at an insurance company. He'd write poetry in his head as he walked to work in Hartford, Connecticut. Businessman first, writer second, he nonetheless became one of the most influential poets of his era.

I'm no Wallace Stevens, to be sure, but I have long been a businessman who writes poetry. Like Stevens, I use poetry occasionally to blow off a little steam and reduce the stress of marketplace battles. Unlike Stevens's, my poetry will never be the subject of three-credit English classes at top universities. But I've been known to get a laugh or two at wedding receptions, retirement parties, and shows with my acoustic band friends, Trashcan Joe.[2]

This chapter is about AIs and creativity, which is why I am taking such a roundabout route to the subject, a right-brain path, as it were. Our subject is how AIs will affect poetry, music, film, and art of all kinds and how they might also, as a consequence of becoming more creative, change the nature of business innovation, scientific theory, technology patents, filmmaking, and other creative human endeavors.

If you selected my silly "Singularity" poem as the one written by a human, it was probably because it's just too goofy (or singsongy) to have been written by a machine. AIs today have a hard time with irony, play, humor, context, intuition, originality, and a variety of other illogical, nonmathematical capabilities, which raises a number of intriguing questions:

- Are there subtle adaptations in human intelligence that have evolved over the 500,000 years of *Homo sapiens*' time on Earth that have nothing to do with mathematical calculations, scientific theories, and repetitious cognition? "Right-brain" adaptations that AIs will not be able to replicate anytime soon (say, over the next century or two)?
- If there are (which to me seems quite likely), what role will these uniquely human types of intelligence play when humans and AIs start living and working together?
- Just how creative might AIs get? Not right now, but a decade out? And longer?
- What should we make of the role of serendipity, randomness, and luck in the development of great insights?[3]

All open questions, as far as I'm concerned.

A Pack of Poodles, a Murder of Crows

Let's approach the question of AI creativity through the lens of two separate imaginary species, whom we'll call poodles and crows. These are not zoological creatures but AI subspecies who have some of the characteristics of their animal namesakes. The poodles are loyal, physical, human-loving, and on the android AI road. The crows are flighty, independent, quick, and on the road to superintelligence.

These two types of AI are diverging as AI gets smarter and becomes the twenty-first-century's intelligence utility. Twentieth-century electric utilities gave rise to light bulbs, dishwashers, and the Internet. Who knows how many undreamed-of innovations the new AI utility will spawn? However many, I believe that, for the next several decades at least, all of these new AIs will be one of these two types: a poodle or a crow. In the AI poodle group:

- AIs trained under human supervision (supervised learning)
- Human body AI implants and other forms of transhumanism (e.g., Elon Musk's NeuralLink)
- AIs whose entire motivation is to replicate human body functions (e.g., robots on assembly lines)
- AIs who seek to emulate human roles and replace human workers (e.g., Volvo self-driving trucks)
- All AIs whose motivation is to directly serve humans in some way, with humans clearly in control (e.g., Alexa, Siri, etc.)

This admittedly is a loose grouping. What ties these AIs together is the fact they are all tethered to humans. They live and grow, in other words, on a human, carbon substrate, either literally or metaphorically.[4] AI poodles can be highly intelligent, perhaps someday even generally intelligent, but they are always irrevocably tied to humans. They are programmed to love us and serve us. They are our high-end tools, our friendly, tail-wagging pets.

AI crows, on the other hand, are smart but cantankerous. Animal crows are incredibly intelligent but not overly fond of humans.[5] They are strong, mobile, highly adaptative creatures who communicate actively. Some crows use tools, most can recognize individual humans (and squawk at the "bad" ones), and all are omnivores. They'll eat anything from ripe garbage to small live birds. The proper term of venery for them is a *murder of crows*. AI crows have their namesake's feisty independence, mobility, and ability to swarm. They are not necessarily enemies of humans but absolutely learn and act on their own. AIs in the crow group include:

- AIs trained via unsupervised learning, without human direction.
- Reinforcement-learning AIs, which continually make autonomous decisions based on their last actions performed. This type of AI is driven by Pavlovian, goal/reward behavioral feedback. Sometimes they are supervised by humans; sometimes not.
- Fully autonomous AIs that can pursue their unique reward functions almost completely on their own. These are crows that can leap up and fly away and swarm together to accomplish collective goals.

I can envision one future scenario with AI poodles filling every nook and cranny on Earth. In this scenario, with various forms of transhumanism in play, AIs become "learning implants" in human brains.[6] Cameras positioned atop our heads (controlled by our brains) enhance our vision. Tiny chemical sensors up our nose make us, well, poodle-like when it comes to smell. Real-time, health-status dashboards for each human body are projected onto whatever core device each body happens to be wearing. In this AI-poodle-dominated world, human biological evolution continues unabated, albeit somewhat accelerated. AI poodles will be embedded everywhere, but they will remain our friendly, tail-wagging servants. I'd rate this scenario at about 20 percent probability. There would be AI crows in this scenario, just not many of them and none in positions of real power.

There is also a 20 percent chance, by my reckoning, that a murder of AI crows could put humans on their omnivore menu. Not that they would attack and eat us, Alfred Hitchcock style, but their utter (crow-like) indifference to the fate of humanity could result in what an AI might term "involuntary human reduction." Mass murder, from one perspective; repurposing carbon atoms for greater efficiency, from another.

As we move inexorably along the twenty-first-century AI runway, the AI crows deserve our utmost attention, not just because they are designed from day 1 to learn and operate on their own, but because they are likely to be much more creative than the poodles.

The ability to surprise is central to creative intelligence. The ah-ha moment of a physicist, sweet rhyme of a songwriter, third-act complication of a great film, and go-to-market plan of an inspired entrepreneur are all surprise-driven, in a good way.

Like all the best art, good poems surprise. As former US poet laureate (and my favorite living versifier) Billy Collins once said, "A poem should begin in Kansas and end in Oz."[7] The ability to surprise is central to creative intelligence. The ah-ha moment of a physicist, sweet rhyme of a songwriter, third-act complication of a great film, and go-to-market plan of an inspired entrepreneur are all surprise-driven, in a good way. How good will AIs be at generating surprises, at responding and adapting to unanticipated situations in interesting and unusual ways, at coming up with genuinely innovative ideas? The research is, well, *surprising*.

Peter Haas, robotics researcher at Brown University, cites an image recognition experiment in which an ordinary pet dog is mistaken for a wolf by an AI image-recognition algorithm.[8] This recognition error was consistent and baffling to the engineers who built the system, so they rewrote the algorithm specifically to find out why their algorithm was making this mistake. When they did this, they discovered that the "region of interest" extracted from the dog's image for pattern-recognition purposes was not the pet's eyes, ears, or snout. It was the snow in the background. It turns out, virtually all the photos of wolves this AI had been trained on were shots of wolves in snow in winter. In its training, the AI was "taught" that *snow* equals *wolf*. No human would mistake a pet dog for a wolf just because it was standing in snow, but an otherwise very smart AI did, and that surprised everybody in the research program. This is a simple surprise, one a sharp grad student might even anticipate, but as AIs learn faster, their mistakes (a.k.a., surprises) accelerate, as well. The fresh perspectives and new options created by a surprise fuel creativity and originality, yet surprises also pose the greatest safety and security threats.

AIs do surprise consistently but in many different ways. Recall Andrej Szenasy's story in chapter 2, when a face recognition AI linked him with his son with Down syndrome; AlphaZero surpassing computer chess-playing progress of the last forty years in its first sixteen hours; the surprising creativity of digital evolution research paper from chapter 3 and all the unexpected results it documents. AIs are absolutely full of surprises.

Of course, AIs themselves have no idea their results are sometimes shocking to us humans. I know of no instance where an AI attempted on its own to be surprising in pursuit of creativity. Still, it would be the height of *Homo sapiens* hubris to suggest that AIs will never learn how to surprise us artistically and even philosophically. I can't wait to discuss Yeats's *Sailing to Byzantium* with a crow (i.e., independently minded AI) who has studied all serious scholarship on Yeats. We will have good AI poetry critics, I suspect, before good AI poets. Yet someday AIs will write good—really good—verse. As no less an authority than T. S. Eliot said about writing poetry, "There is no method but to be very intelligent."[9] If that's the sole criteria, then AIs may eventually write very good poetry indeed.

The day that an AI writes a truly great, subtle, ironic poem is generations away, IMHO. For one thing, human poetry has what neural network engineers might call a nonoptimal reward function. The reasons people write poetry are fuzzy and diffuse. No one writes poetry for the money in today's world, and even political protest poems are few. Poetry for whatever reason has become quite subjective. There are no absolute standards or forms. Your poems either connect with people, or they don't, so AIs seem ill-suited to the writing of modern poetry, although I'm sure, goaded by software engineers with little ear for it, they will keep trying.

Humans write poems because they love the process of writing them. For me, poetry is opening your mind to the widest possible aperture, letting language stream in, and then chipping away at it. As I once jokingly put it, in a poem,

Word Carving

Writing a poem isn't hard to do.
No reason for trepidation or doubt.
Simply write down the words flowing through you,
Then cut nearly all of them out.

Famously, poetry is what's lost in translation: but it's also what's lost on machines. In all creative endeavors whose goal is to appeal to humans, we carbon lifeforms will be the only ones to pick winners and losers for a long time to come.

A famous record producer—and there are only three or four in America—once said to me, "No way anyone can pick a hit pop song. You get a feeling, yes, people start coming onboard, but you really never know. Not the producer, not the artist, not the suits, not the managers or agents." When it comes to picking hits—in music, in film, in poetry, probably in video games (but just guessing)—nobody knows anything—*except the crowd.* It is the crowd, the *audience*, who ultimately picks creative winners and losers.

This has long been absolute Hollywood gospel. But what if AIs, because of deep connections with the audience, could indeed pick winners and losers? What if movie execs and record producers could sample the great global marketplace before making green-light production decisions? The beginnings of this kind of "AI market research" is already here, but mass polling about creative products is a far cry from actually creating the art that will move the crowd to buy it. Writing a song, or a poem, or a novel is not like playing Go. When you sit down to write, there is no clear binary outcome, the creative equivalent of winning or losing in Go. Absent that kind of clear binary target, training AIs to achieve artist greatness will be quite difficult. In all forms of art, one of the most devastating criticisms is to call a work "derivative," meaning the work is not original but based too much on something else. Derivative works do not surprise us; they do not inspire us. They bore us.

This brings us back, circuitously, to our poodles and crows. AI poodles will have a difficult time creating meaningful art precisely because they are so closely tied to, and are supervised by, humans. Their work will tend to be derivative in the way the computer's poem at the beginning of this chapter was. The form is fine, but there is nothing inspiring or even all that interesting inside it. Freedom of mind—an untethered intelligence, if you will—is required to create real art.

In the realm of AI, it is the unsupervised crows who will have this kind of independence. They will be the AIs creating the most interesting art. Realistic paintings—no problem. Abstract paintings—they'll get the hang of it quickly and will produce great works. Coming up with pop music melodies will also be relatively easy, as will coming up with simple pop lyrics ("My my, baby baby"). I have a hard time believing even the most intelligent and independent crow could ever write a masterpiece like *Adventures of Huckleberry Finn.* But as John von Neumann, a key architect of both the modern computer and the atomic bomb and former atomic energy commissioner suggested in the epigraph of this chapter, never say never when it comes to what a computer can do.

Still, I believe (or perhaps choose to believe) that the ability to write real poems will be one of the last bastions of human intelligence superiority (along with infant care and horse whispering). Poetry has centuries of rhythm, rhyme, and nuance that no AI should ever be expected to understand or even absorb. AIs, at the end of the day, are mathsects: formulas inside algorithms. Humans will continue to train them to write poetry, songs, essays, short stories, and novels—or try to. During my lifetime, my expectation is that the product of most of these efforts—with the possible exception of music compositions, which can have an element of math in them—will be dreck.

There are parts of our humanness we should never even consider farming out to AIs. Religion and spiritual experience are one. If ever someone tries to sell you on a spiritual AI connection, log off. Poetry is another sacrosanct realm of human activity, in my opinion. In fact, I would say that poetry is the art that is most closely linked to our innate humanness and that the ability to recognize human poetry will be a key indicator of humanness for centuries to come. If AIs want to write poems, let them write them for each other.

During my years in business, I spent much time on the road. Often, I would retreat to a hotel room, pour a glass of wine, and write poetry. Writing verse in a hotel room at the end of a day's action on Sand Hill Road or New York City often kept me (somewhat) sane. I'll end this chapter with a piece of light verse I wrote after attending a conference on social networks about a half-dozen years ago. This is not a great poem, but it does, I think, reflect the difficulty machines will have in capturing the social subtleties of creative, ironic language.

Social Love

It began with me following you
all aTwitter,
Tracking you Foursquare
With Pinterest.
We shared Face space,
Floated together on iClouds,
Thumbed each other with abandon
Across nosy-fingered dawns.
Then you unfriended me.

Me, who never invaded your meat space,
Me, who never confronted you with real identity.
Yet you vanished, became disconnected.
We were no longer LinkedIn.
I am left with little more than your sweet smile
Captured on Skype, without guile.
I wish you well, my sweet lamb.
Click here to see your sexting posts on Instagram.

CHAPTER TWELVE

The Way Forward

"We can only see a short distance ahead, but we can see plenty there that needs to be done."

Alan Turing

While researching this book, I kept hearing versions of the same refrain arising from within AI circles: *Hey, we need help here!* AI leaders aren't seeking engineering help or, Lord knows, money. Never has any technology been better funded. No, these leaders are appealing for *social* help in figuring out the economic and humanitarian ramifications of having lightspeed learners in our midst; *political* help in creating smart, coherent national policies; and *moral* help so that AIs have a humanistic, ethical, and therefore sustainable foundation.

Assisting the AI industry in these ways is a job for all of us, especially we citizens of the United States. For better or worse in the decade ahead, the government of the United States will have a huge impact on the growth—and safety—of AI worldwide. American citizens who are at least somewhat AI aware need to do what they can to keep the art and science of AI moving forward in our industries and in our communities.

AI industry leaders also need to make contributions as citizens. This starts with acknowledging their debt to the rest of us—to the American taxpayers who kept AI research and development alive for seventy years. The Apollo space program drove demand for, and funded, the miniaturization of transistors, which fueled the entire Moore's Law hardware revolution. For decades, the only significant neural net research in the world was funded by Uncle Sam—at Bell Labs, the Jet Propulsion Laboratory (JPL), and a handful of universities. For all practical purposes, DARPA invented the self-driving car. Were it not for Uncle Sugar, AI today would still be a gooey chocolate mess.

This is not to suggest that AI is the property of the United States. Far from it. Toronto and Cambridge have been the second- and third-leading AI research centers in the world, and Canada and the United Kingdom have made enormous contributions to AI. What I am saying is that we hear far too little acknowledgment of the role government dollars and scientific leadership played in the development of AI in the United States, the United Kingdom, and Canada. All three governments have had their problems (well, maybe not Canada), but for decades, they have guided and funded the early research and development of nuclear fusion, information networking, and artificial intelligence. Western governments get a lot of shade these days. Let's give credit where credit is due. Western democratic governments of the twentieth and early twenty-first centuries—supported and funded by *we the people*—incubated and successfully developed the three most powerful technologies in history. And, oh, by the way, put the first man on the moon and a Rover on Mars.

We citizens, therefore, must get over the notion that we are somehow encroaching on pristine entrepreneurial pastures when we discuss government regulation of AI. Taxpayers have had skin in the AI game since day 1. Hell, when it comes to the AI casino, we poured the foundation. So when some Stanford grad student rubs two machine-learning sticks together, acts like he's invented fire, and regards the slightest government intrusion into his world as the height of effrontery, I call bullshit. We citizens have *every* right to take our place at the AI table. If we want to make sure our investment in AI actually does some good for the *majority* of our citizens, that's our prerogative. If we want to set up a federal agency charged with regulating AI safety the way the FDA does medical devices and drugs, we can. I wouldn't advise it in the current political climate in Washington (industry self-regulation efforts are probably the best option at the moment), but down the road, we could indeed build the AI expertise inside a government agency necessary to guide and regulate AIs. *Machina sapiens* will affect human society more than pharmacists and should get an even higher level of scrutiny—once the government has the proper national AI policy expertise, and sufficient political will.

The attitude of many in Silicon Valley, on Wall Street, and in Congress (especially on the *R* side of the aisle) is that the most important role for government in AI is to stay out of the way. This is a naïve and ultimately self-defeating position. AI is a big disruption to the entire social fabric of the country and the world. Government *is* involved, like it or not, so government agencies might as well get smart about it.

My former colleague Esther Dyson said in the 1990s in response to a reporter's question about who controlled the Internet, "The Internet is controlled by those who understand it." AI is, as well. With this book, I hope to provide a modest contribution to the growing public understanding of AI under the theory that (1) the more citizens know about AI, the smarter our government will be, and (2) getting government moving on AI is an urgent national priority. In the 1990s, I was a big advocate of Internet industry self-regulation instead of government regulation. I joined and gave a little money to the Electronic Freedom Foundation; even spoke a couple of times at the Cato Institute (on technology, not politics). In hindsight, my earlier techno-libertarianism was a mistake. Avoiding any semblance of regulatory action on data protection and trusted systems led to safety, security, and privacy shortcuts. These shortcuts created serious vulnerabilities. The result today is an Internet where cyberattacks are rampant; data loss, significant; and crimes, easily aided and abetted.[1]

We need a coherent national AI policy as soon as possible, for economic development and maintenance of a strong high-tech engine; for national and homeland security; for the education of our children and economic competitiveness of our schools; for the health and prosperity of our citizens; and for citizen interfaces and information access, for Pete's sake! Maybe we should start there: using AIs make government easier to use. Ultimately, a new, coherent American AI strategy must emerge. If there is no such policy, the United States will continue to lose ground to China and others in the field of AI, and technology risk to American citizens will grow. This technology risk will affect military, scientific, economic and political sectors. We need a national plan with the potential to reduce this risk dramatically.

AI Immigration Policy

What should go into a new plan with the purpose of helping the United States to both grow and control AI? Let's start with immigration policy. As the story of Dmitry Tuzoff in chapter 10 makes clear, immigration barriers thrown up by the Trump administration have had the unintended (at least I hope it's unintended) effect of making Toronto the mecca of AI talent for the world. A young Sergey Brin today would not migrate to the United States and invent the Internet search engine that became Google. He'd be working in Toronto's Creative Destruction Lab.

To compete with China and other AI powers, we absolutely *need more* AI human talent. There are far from enough AI scientists, engineers, and math whizzes in America right now. China is producing many more AI scientists and engineers than the United States, and the only way we can keep pace is by importing new talent. Yet, unless we start sending different immigration messages, all the bright, young AI experts will keep going to Toronto, London, Paris, or Shanghai instead of San Jose, Boston, or Seattle. ICE and other US immigration officials might argue that the goal of immigration policy in the late 2010s in American is to keep the riffraff out and prioritize immigration for the best and brightest. As the grandson of Irish riffraff, I resent the very notion of this policy. But even if that intention were true, I can tell you as a former software entrepreneur, it ain't working. The best and brightest aren't coming to America anymore, this, at a time when we face a critical shortage of the kind of math experts and computer scientists who drive the development of AI, the hottest tech sector on the planet. Ms. Liberty's message lately has been "Stay away! We don't want you!" I fear this cold-hearted, unenlightened attitude will hurt our country for a long time to come.

Uncle Sam [can wave] his AI magic wand and [create] new jobs for millions of Americans: high-value jobs; jobs with a future; jobs for young farmers in Iowa, housewives in New Hampshire, geologists in Louisiana, fishermen on Whidbey Island, and dental assistants in Duluth.

A Crucial Role for States and Cities

Earlier I suggested we Americans shouldn't hesitate to jump in and regulate AI. Indeed, some grand design for the control of AI in this country—complete with nuclear-industry-style inspections—should be under serious consideration. But there's a problem. Asking the federal government of the United States, in its current muddled state, to regulate AI would be like asking the Marx Brothers to undertake a planetary probe of Uranus, which leaves us no choice. Practically speaking, the government jurisdictions that must now save America are (drumroll please) its states and cities.

State governments, I believe, are in an ideal position to kick-start a national AI policy engine. The feds aren't going to do anything meaningful for a while, and at this point, every lost year is a year China is gaining on us. But a handful of the right states and perhaps a few select big cities could really get things moving.

How? All states need to do is start revving up their trusty economic development engines, this time tuned to the AI market. State economic development agencies and networks are like rocket boosters for favored industries in each state. In my experience—eating crab cakes in Baltimore or shrimp platters in New Orleans or drinking Pinot Noir in Oregon—these economic-development folks not only party well, but they also get things done. They're the ones with the most political juice inside many a state government and most big cities, as well. There is nothing economic development groups appreciate more than a hot new industry bringing lots of new jobs. *Well, Madame Governor and Mr. Mayor, have I got a new industry for you.*

> *Red Alert! AI will create more jobs in greater magnitudes than any number of data centers or even Amazon warehouses. . . . [C]ities and states with just a modicum of vision can still grab more than their fair share of these new jobs.*

A little over a decade ago, my home state of Oregon began recruiting data centers to eastern Oregon. There were no data centers in eastern Oregon at the time, not one, but Bonneville Dam's hydropower was cheap and green, and the ski slopes of Mount Bachelor not far away. Today, Amazon alone has nine data centers in eastern Oregon. Facebook and Google have big centers, as well, along with a dozen other companies. All this economic activity in a region struggling with a declining natural-resources economy came about because of an enlightened economic-development initiative for the state of Oregon, with much local support on the ground in rural regions of the state.

Michigan, New York, California, Delaware, and other states also know how to play this high-tech recruiting game. Frankly, all states are good at it. So, to all of you state public- and private-sector leaders in the "econ dev" field: Red alert! AI will create many more jobs in greater magnitudes than any number of data centers or even Amazon warehouses (which themselves contain high numbers of AIs). From Kenai, Alaska, to Jacksonville, Florida, cities and states with just a modicum of vision can still grab more than their fair share of these new jobs, high-paying jobs for smart folks with common sense, for new kinds of workers valued not so much for their cognition skills but for their EQ, empathy, creativity, and common sense, the areas in which machines are most deficient.

Across America and around the world, humans and machines are learning to work together. As you read this, a long-haul trucker is cruising past

Bakersfield with his self-driving software buddy; an oncologist in New York is consulting with her Deep-Patient colleague; film producers everywhere are working with AI animation tools. All this activity is proving a powerful new equation:

1 human +1 AI = 3+ units of value

Cities and states that understand and implement this formula will be the economic leaders in the decade ahead. A full-spectrum, AI-savvy workforce—with everyone from math PhDs to truck drivers—will be a tremendous competitive asset. AI is now an industry where nonengineer humans work side by side with smart machines, as if it's the most natural thing in the world. Not everywhere and far from in every sector, but the trend lines are already clear.

AI in the end will not be about engineers. Auto mechanics seldom make the best race-car drivers. The human winners in the AI casino will be the hotshots who, like Formula One drivers, can drive fast and safe at the same time, with AIs by their side. *Augmented intelligence* is the official term for the new field where humans learn to work closely with AIs. It's one of the hottest career paths on the planet. You know who I'd be signing up and training if I wanted to start promoting the world's first AI-ready workforce in my city or state? Every massage therapist, pet-shelter manager, kindergarten teacher, theater performer, and hospice worker who could create a new website on their phone in seven minutes and pass a white-hat phishing test. I'd teach them the basics about AIs and provide them with hands-on training, working with various kinds of AIs. In addition, I'd start compiling directories of qualified data collectors, data curators, robotics supervisors, and AI safety inspectors. I'd build an AI-business-recruiting campaign tied to the development of a certified, AI-ready workforce in my region. And then, as my Irish grandfather used to say, Katie bar the door.

To affect income inequality, state and city governments must develop AI programs that extend to all levels of society. The emergence of an AI-ready workforce operating at multiple pay grades will not happen magically overnight anywhere, but it is not too late to start the kind of initiative in AI that Oregon took with data centers, though recruiting AI will definitely require a greater investment in human training.

The biggest opportunity, however, lies not in sponsoring generalized AI instruction. It is in training young farmers in the use of AI in precision agriculture in Iowa, training nurses in Minneapolis to use AI radiology scanners, training animators in Marin county to create new virtual worlds with their

AI friends, training supervisors of self-driving shuttle buses in Vegas and South Beach, and training shift managers of fast food restaurants with an all-machine staff in small towns everywhere.

Feed a Chicken, Catch a Monkey

If states starting cranking up their local AI economic development engines, the impact will be felt immediately in Congress, as well. Someday we may even be able to pass federally funded training programs again, the kind that help us to remain economically competitive the old-fashioned way: by having talented, well-trained workers who know how to use the latest tools. But ideally, having states actively engaged in AI economic development could even shame the feds into getting their national-AI-policy act together.

The strategy here is what the Chinese might call Feed a Chicken to Catch a Monkey. Get states and cities fat with AI so they get the feds' attention. The feds swoop in, and Uncle Sam waves his AI magic wand and funds training for millions of potential AI industry workers, leading to new jobs for millions of Americans: high-value jobs; jobs with a future; jobs for Americans who have been left behind; jobs for young farmers in Iowa, housewives in New Hampshire, geologists in Louisiana, fishermen on Whidbey Island, and dental assistants in Duluth. To keep AI on the fast track in America, to have any hope of staying ahead of China, it will take serious federal funding and an army of smart, energetic, compassionate *humans*. Humans *and* AIs, BFF.

There is the still-open question of whether this augmented-intelligence army of human workers will make mostly minimum wage or high-end consultant fees. I predict pretty solid salaries, actually, because anyone with AI knowledge is in demand these days. The more citizen involvement and cohesive national support of AI, the higher the wage scale is likely to be.

Truth be told, there will be economic and personal growth opportunities across all pay grades, industrial sectors, and economic zip codes. As the old gospel-influenced Curtis Mayfield tune puts it, there's a train a-coming; time to get onboard.

Dark Side of the Moon

All the new jobs AI creates will, of course, be offset by the many more that will disappear. Robert Reich, former US Secretary of Labor under President Obama, writing in a Sunday *New York Times* book review in summer 2018, quipped that, if you don't have enough to worry about with global warming, North Korea, and Trump in the White House, there's always AI. The point of his review (nominally of two books on universal basic income) was to consider what AI might do to our economy in the next ten years. Near the end of this piece, he made an interesting aside to the effect of, Unless we fix our gross economic inequalities, who is going to buy all the new robots? Setting aside his conflagration of robots with AI, Reich makes an excellent point: Extreme income inequality is not in anyone's interest, not even billionaires'. There is no reason we the people can't use AIs to level the economic playing field, at least a little; maybe a lot. In this context, funneling big money to states and cities for various forms of AI education and training makes good economic and political sense.

This book's central focus is to explore the social, economic, and political dimensions of AI and to suggest ways the "rest of us" can participate in this technology revolution. Today, the torch of safe and "friendly" AI is being carried by groups such as the Future of Life Institute, which I discuss later. I hope all high-minded AI groups keep going and growing in pursuit of a world with friendly, ethical AIs. But sooner rather than later, government must get involved, and at the federal level, that begins by electing at least a few AI-savvy members of Congress.

I am fairly certain the big AI companies in both the West and China will voluntarily adopt new ethical AI self-governance policies, as most have to some extent already, and that they will continue to build a global AI ecosystem, or noosphere, where core human values endure. I'm confident even Putin and Xi are on the side of we Homo sapiens. What's most important is that *nations* get AI right. For reasons spelled out in this book and others that are not, there simply is no other option. The current generation of international leaders still has a chance to overcome all other diplomatic friction and say, "Yes, as other great leaders have done before us with nuclear, biological, and chemical weapons, we now will work together to contain and control AI, and at the same time use it for the greater good."

This is an enormous challenge, getting the world's heads of state to sanction cooperation in AI, especially given the widespread proliferation of AI weapon systems, not to mention the current state of international affairs, which, as I write in early 2019, looks like a Risk gameboard tossed in drunken petulance at 3 a.m. So, I'll forgive you if you think the goal of international agreement on AI safety, security, and ethics is a Pollyanna pipe dream, yet we must start down this path. A simple, friendly mutual inspection agreement between the United States and China would be a great place to start.

I did not begin writing this book with an AI strategy for America in mind, much less any notions of grand global treaties. My plan was to look around for stories and key AI issues and see if my background in high tech and journalism could enable me to shed a little light on a significant new technology. But after reading, talking, and thinking deeply about AI, it all seemed to boil down to a single tag line: AI is real, and real important.

Yes, AI is complicated; so is my Comcast cable box, so is laser brain surgery, and so is Formula One racing. The fact that we can't personally do brain surgery, deliver video-on-demand, or tweak a race engine's high-caliber combustion doesn't mean we can't have an opinion about brains, cars, or cable. I hope this book has convinced you, if nothing else, that you not only can have an opinion about AI but that *you must*.

I have friends, smart friends, who think AI is overrated. It's partly the cry-wolf syndrome: after too many Napsters, Segways, and Google Glasses, AIs can seem just the latest tech hype, but the evidence is now in: They are not. In my short time in the AI industry, I learned that AIs are something altogether new in intelligence on Earth. Numerous AIs are already performing "narrow" cognitive functions at superhuman levels. AI is the biggest news in intelligence since *Homo sapiens* showed up in East Africa 200,000 years ago, and we're just getting started. If AI were a train traveling from Oakland to Boston, so far, we'd have made it to Sacramento.

Perhaps this book has convinced you that AI matters in business and finance; in health care; in education; in government; and, most of all, coming soon, in your everyday life. Trust me on this much: By 2030, AIs will be swarming all around you. Let's just hope they're all *friendlies*.

An AI Declaration of Principles

If AI is indeed to become our new global operating system, the indispensable "electricity" of the twenty-first century, and if it is in fact the most powerfully disruptive technology ever unleashed on Earth, then, as I've said perhaps ad nauseum, we need to be taking steps now to make sure that this powerful tech stays friendly to humans and makes beneficial contributions to human life. In January 2017, more than two hundred of the world's top AI experts attended a conference at Asilomar, a beautiful seaside conference grounds. Among the attendees were AI researchers, economists, psychologists, and authors. Among other things, this group produced a remarkable series of panel discussions, which you can view on YouTube.[2] But most impressive was the AI principles document they wrote and cosigned. This statement of principles has now been signed by more than 1,200 AI and robotics researchers, including Dennis Hassabis of Google, Yann LeCun of Facebook, Yoshua Bengio of the Montreal Institute of Learning Algorithms, and many other

AI leading lights. Conference attendees agreed on twenty-three principles to guide the development of safe and beneficial AI. Getting such a broad, heterogenous group to achieve an effective consensus on these principles was an amazing achievement. I close this main portion of this book now, by printing these principles in their entirety, in hopes that they can take root around the world.

The Asilomar AI Principles

Research Issues

1. **Research Goal:** The goal of AI research should be to create, not undirected intelligence, but beneficial intelligence.
2. **Research Funding:** Investments in AI should be accompanied by funding for research on ensuring its beneficial use, including thorny questions in computer science, economics, law, ethics, and social studies, such as:
   How can we make future AI systems highly robust so that they do what we want without malfunctioning or getting hacked?
   How can we grow our prosperity through automation while maintaining people's resources and purpose?
   How can we update our legal systems to be more fair and efficient, to keep pace with AI, and to manage the risks associated with AI?
   What set of values should AI be aligned with, and what legal and ethical status should it have?
3. **Science-Policy Link:** There should be constructive and healthy exchange between AI researchers and policy makers.
4. **Research Culture:** A culture of cooperation, trust, and transparency should be fostered among researchers and developers of AI.
5. **Race Avoidance:** Teams developing AI systems should actively cooperate to avoid corner cutting on safety standards.

Ethics and Values

6. **Safety:** AI systems should be safe and secure throughout their operational lifetime and verifiably so where applicable and feasible.
7. **Failure Transparency:** If an AI system causes harm, it should be possible to ascertain why.
8. **Judicial Transparency:** Any involvement by an autonomous system in judicial decision making should provide a satisfactory explanation auditable by a competent human authority.

9. **Responsibility:** Designers and builders of advanced AI systems are stakeholders in the moral implications of their use, misuse, and actions, with a responsibility and opportunity to shape those implications.
10. **Value Alignment:** Highly autonomous AI systems should be designed so that their goals and behaviors can be assured to align with human values throughout their operation.
11. **Human Values:** AI systems should be designed and operated so as to be compatible with ideals of human dignity, rights, freedoms, and cultural diversity.
12. **Personal Privacy:** People should have the right to access, manage, and control the data they generate, given AI systems' power to analyze and utilize that data.
13. **Liberty and Privacy:** The application of AI to personal data must not unreasonably curtail people's real or perceived liberty.
14. **Shared Benefit:** AI technologies should benefit and empower as many people as possible.
15. **Shared Prosperity:** The economic prosperity created by AI should be shared broadly to benefit all of humanity.
16. **Human Control:** Humans should choose how and whether to delegate decisions to AI systems to accomplish human-chosen objectives.
17. **Nonsubversion:** The power conferred by control of highly advanced AI systems should respect and improve, rather than subvert, the social and civic processes on which the health of society depends.
18. **AI Arms Race:** An arms race in lethal autonomous weapons should be avoided.

Longer-Term Issues

19. **Capability Caution:** There being no consensus, we should avoid strong assumptions regarding upper limits on future AI capabilities.
20. **Importance:** Advanced AI could represent a profound change in the history of life on Earth and should be planned for and managed with commensurate care and resources.
21. **Risks:** Risks posed by AI systems, especially catastrophic or existential risks, must be subject to planning and mitigation efforts commensurate with their expected impact.
22. **Recursive Self-Improvement:** AI systems designed to recursively self-improve or self-replicate in a manner that could lead to rapidly increasing quality or quantity must be subject to strict safety and control measures.

23. **Common Good:** Superintelligence should only be developed in the service of widely shared ethical ideals and for the benefit of all humanity rather than one state or organization.

APPENDIX

~

Personal AI Strategies

In this final section, I list several personal and business strategies for taking advantage of the power of AIs in your life. I am now collecting and blogging such strategies at www.lightspeedlearners.com. Please stop by to learn the latest strategies I have discovered.

Strategy 1: Create Value with Data

A chief purpose of any enterprise is to create value for stakeholders. At small start-ups, global multinationals, and government agencies, management continually tries to identify key value creators: factors that increase stock price, make a start-up more attractive for acquisition, or get an agency a bigger budget. For the last several decades, information technology (IT) has been the world's largest and most potent value creator. Amazon and Google in twenty years have created more than $1.5 trillion in market value (combined) by leveraging innovative IT. That's *trillion*, with a *T*.

But it's not just West Coast techie companies who are profiting. In the first decade of the twenty-first century, Walmart used a competitive advantage in supply-chain IT to become the world's dominant retail company. UPS and FedEx invested heavily in logistics IT and became global shipping leaders. iRobot used IT to become the world's most valuable vacuum cleaner company. Clearly, infotech has been the big kid on the block for the first part the twenty-first century, and it will continue to be the chief value creator in the enterprise for the foreseeable future. But the success formula underlying IT is changing dramatically.

One of the pillars of value creation with IT has been the notion that proprietary intellectual property (IP) is key to a defensible technology-based business. This has been especially true in the enterprise software business, where IP has been a powerful value creator. For several decades now, enterprises of all sizes and sectors have been developing and acquiring software IP to become more competitive and more valuable, with patents, nondisclosure agreements, and IP lawyers playing a vital role.

Writing code for elegant AI software is no trivial task, and optimizing AI performance in training processes is a rare art. But owning proprietary code is no longer a key differentiator nor a big value creator. The two big value creators in AI are (1) data—massive amounts of it organized well—and (2) human AI experts who are available to feed the AIs and train them properly. Excellent underlying algorithms that enable recursive learning are freely available. For any enterprise (other than one with a huge AI R&D commitment), launching an AI project with either open-source or commercial third-party software is the only sensible strategy.

In AI, data, not software, is the real value creator. The story told most often in AI circles to illustrate this point is that of Blue River. I have heard several versions. Two Stanford graduate students take an AI class in the early 2010s. One has a background in business and agriculture; the other, in computer science. They decide to work together on their class project. Unlike others in the class, they choose to spend time not writing algorithms but collecting data. They head south to Salinas and personally photograph thousands of heads of lettuce, or they go east to Modesto and with the help of Stanford undergrads build a huge image database of cabbages in various stages of growth. They start a small AI company whose business plan is to use AI to help farmers pick which specific green plants to pull during thinning and which to let grow. They build an AI app for this purpose, and it works well, or it doesn't. What is indisputable is that Blue River built the world's largest image database for the growing of greens and other crops, and in 2017, John Deere, the ag-industry giant, acquired the company for approximately $300 million.

Using data collection and cultivation as a first step in entering the AI field is a strategy not limited to lettuce farming. It can and is being applied today in hospitals, banks, schools, and manufacturing. Bringing AI into an existing business does not require an internal R&D department doing AI experimentation. There is plenty of good AI software being produced and made available by the big tech companies and by the open-source software community. Even with relatively small teams and modest investments, data can start being collected in meaningful new ways and used to train and grow open-source AIs. At the turn of the twentieth century, a company that viewed itself as in the horse-drawn-carriage business was probably in big trouble, but forward-thinking carriage makers who viewed themselves as *transportation companies* were poised for greatness. The same is true today for companies in a variety of business sectors.

Leveraging your data for AI is a relatively simple strategy but one that holds tremendous promise for the incumbent companies in a position to collect it. For such companies, it's time to get started. Chances are some of your competitors already have.

Strategy 2: Launch an AI Start-up

Entrepreneurialism drives innovation and sometimes creates great wealth. There are many start-up failures but also a surprising number of modest successes—new, small, profitable companies that find a niche. These companies create millionaire founders, not billionaires.

Scott Galloway, brand expert, NYU professor, and author of *The Four* (about the GAFA giants), claims it's now easier to become a billionaire than a millionaire. Statistically this is not even close to being accurate, but it rings true rhetorically because income disparity is accelerating. The rich-get-richer-poor-get-poorer cycle is in overdrive, and AI will only intensify it.

What Galloway is getting at (and he discusses this at length in *The Four*) is the issue of scale. To win in technology-driven businesses (and which aren't these days?), the crucial success questions are, How big is your network? How much data do you have? How many data streams? How much compute power? How many connected customers? How much high-value stock that can be used as currency? To move the AI needle technologically, companies need strong answers to all of the above.

In the world of AI, big is beautiful. The more data, compute power, active customers, strong partners, the better. Challenging the giant tech companies with respect to fundamental AI innovations is folly. When I founded an AI start-up in 2014, our image-recognition technology was roughly akin to what Google had (or at least what Google was showing publicly). In the following eighteen months, Google passed us like an F-16 buzzing a truck convoy.

Occasionally, a group of extraordinarily talented AI engineers find each other, raise a little capital, experiment with a new platform, and then quickly get acquired (e.g., Nervana and Mobileye).[1] But the odds of some geek hacking a clever AI breakthrough in her start-up garage, something that will shake AI to its foundations, are remote in the extreme. AI start-up opportunities—and there are many—are not on the "write a brilliant algorithm and build a platform around it" end of the spectrum. They are on the "get an AI license, then build a specialized business on it" side.

Imagine the year is 1905, and you've done your homework. You know electricity is a powerful, disruptive force and that its business value is under-appreciated. You know—*know*—that electrification is coming, first to cities, obviously, but then to rural areas, as well. Urban electrification will be fueled by private investment; rural areas, by government aid. That much is fairly clear. At this point, you can't know that it will take twenty years to electrify the homes, offices, and factories in the cities of America and another fifty years to get electricity to all of rural America. In 1905, you can't know precisely when and where future electrification business opportunities will appear, but you know it's coming and that it will affect everything.

High-tech entrepreneurs and tech-savvy investors are in similar position today with respect to AI. They realize the only business sectors that will *not* need AI in the decades to come are the same ones who didn't need electricity one hundred years ago (an extremely short list: Sherpa hiking tours, survivalist training camps, hot-air-balloon rides, etc.). Figuring out the when and where of AI opportunities and matching the right AI with the right problem will be the trick with AI start-ups. That, and keeping an extremely narrow focus.

The biggest challenge for any AI start-up is recruiting a competent technical staff. True AI talent is in critically short supply. But it does not take an army of AI engineers to launch a start-up that has a niche mission and that leverages existing AI platforms (either open-source or proprietary). One or two real experts is enough, surrounded by some of the many career techies anxious to acquire AI skills.

James Barrat calls AI "our final invention," the technology that will "end the human era." If he's right, entrepreneurs and investors will want to look closely for opportunities to launch new AI companies because we may not get another chance.

Strategy 3: Score High on EQ

"It is easier to manufacture seven facts . . . than a single emotion."

Mark Twain

One thing we can say for certain about *Machina sapiens* is that emotional intelligence and creative insight are not its strong suits. AI systems today are nowhere near human-level competence in such areas as empathy, intuition, and imagination. They may never get there. Therefore, it's a good bet these distinctive "soft" human capabilities will become ever more valuable in an AI-enabled world. It makes sense to cultivate them.

Say you are a Hollywood studio executive, ten minutes into the future. You own massive data about moviegoers' tastes and preferences and have the algorithms to slice and dice these data in order to predict box-office success. Your new AI box-office prediction systems are proving to be pretty effective, yet you soon discover that, while they can select the correct story formula for *Fast and Furious 17*, they are relatively useless in creating the next *Downton Abbey*. For producing a hit that is both new and unexpected, you still need literate, creative humans. An AI-powered world will need humans who have cultivated soft skills of the heart, who understand brainstorming and leap-frogging, and who know how to tell (and get) a joke. Humans who have honed these skills will be in great demand.

One career field certain to grow in the AI era is that of the "AI whisperer": humans who support and augment AIs in various ways. These human AI caretakers must manage various situations and relationships. These humans will bring empathy, creativity, and context to AI problem solving. Already, this job category is growing. For job applicants in this field, emotional quotient (EQ) will be more valuable than intelligence quotient (IQ).

The primary definition of EQ in the Free Dictionary is a "measure of a person's adequacy in such areas as self-awareness, empathy, and dealing sensitively with other people." To which I would add, a "measure of a person's adequacy or excellence in such areas . . ." Become excellent at empathy, self-awareness, creativity, and sensitivity with others. Take that new undergraduate class in human–machine relationships. Get really good at innately human skills, and you'll gain a killer competitive advantage in the new AI-driven job market.

Notes

Chapter One

1. "Robotic Colorectal Program Named an Epicenter," George Washington University Hospital, 2018, https://www.gwhospital.com/conditions-services/robotic-surgery/robotic-colorectal-surgery.

2. Larry Greenemeier, "How NASA's Search for ET Relies on Advanced AI," *Scientific American*, December 28, 2017, https://www.scientificamerican.com/article/how-nasas-search-for-et-relies-on-advanced-ai/.

3. Alex Hern, "'Partnership on AI' formed by Google, Facebook, Amazon, IBM and Microsoft," *Guardian*, September 28, 2016, https://www.theguardian.com/technology/2016/sep/28/google-facebook-amazon-ibm-microsoft-partnership-on-ai-tech-firms.

4. Aaron Mak, "Google Taught AI How to Program More AI," Slate, October 16, 2017, http://www.slate.com/blogs/future_tense/2017/10/16/google_created_machine_learning_software_that_can_program_machine_learning.html.

5. I've coined the term *mathsect* to give AIs a degree of speciosity. *Mathsect* is a nod to their mathematical nature and suggests the swarming metaphor that is used heavily in this book.

6. See DeepMind, https://deepmind.com/research/, for a complete review of AlphaZero's history and much more. This website is continually one of the most important sources of information on AIs in the world.

7. Richard Gall, "Five Polarizing Quotes from Stephen Hawking on Artificial Intelligence," Packt Hub, March 15, 2018, https://hub.packtpub.com/stephen-hawking-artificial-intelligence-quotes/.

8. David Faggella, "(All) Elon Musk Artificial Intelligence Quotes—A Catalogue of His Statements," techemergence, June 18, 2017, https://www.techemergence.com/elon-musk-on-the-dangers-of-ai-a-catalogue-of-his-statements/.

9. Sam Shead, "Google Billionaire Sergey Brin Urges Caution on AI Development," *Forbes*, April 28, 2018, https://www.forbes.com/sites/samshead/2018/04/28/google-billionaire-sergey-brin-urges-caution-on-ai-development/2/#28b99b2a2258.

10. Jargon alert: AIs are individual instances of artificial intelligence. For example, "The twelve AIs in the back of the room—the drones, robots, and sensors—all need a power source." Or, "The AIs in the data center are starting to learn really quickly now."

11. This may be apocryphal. It is certainly subjective. The world's top one hundred AI experts, says who? But I have heard this "fact" cited multiple times in AI circles, which does give it some credibility. And it is close to being true, if not precisely accurate.

12. OODA loop refers to the decision cycle of observe, orient, decide, and act, developed by military strategist and USAF Colonel John Boyd for the purpose of winning fighter plane dogfights. It is now used as a model in many commercial operations and learning processes.

13. David Ellis, *Deus Ex Machina Sapiens: The Emergence of Machine Intelligence* (Detroit: Elysian Detroit, 2011).

14. *Noosphere*, coined by French Jesuit priest and mystic Teilhard de Chardin, refers to a growing cloud of knowledge covering the Earth.

15. For example, Boston Dynamics' new Atlas robot, "the world's most dynamic humanoid." To learn more, go to: https://www.bostondynamics.com/atlas.

16. Andy Kiersz, "A Seemingly Benign Viral Game about Paperclips Reveals Why AI Could Be a Huge Danger to Humanity," Business Insider, October 11, 2017, https://www.businessinsider.com/paper-clip-game-superintelligence-theory.

17. Dave Gershgorn, "Human-Like: Facebook Is Using Our Data to Build 'The World's Best' Artificial Intelligence Lab," *Popular Science*, August 20, 2016.

18. FPGAs are graphically oriented computer chips originally designed for the video game industry, but they have been found to be quite useful in various types of AI processing (notably AI image and speech recognition).

19. Charles Jennings and Lori Fena, *The Hundredth Window: Protecting Your Privacy and Security on the Internet* (New York: Free Press, 2000).

20. As I was writing this paragraph, an alerting service I subscribe to reported that Boeing had been hit hard by a WannaCry ransomware hack and Under Amour suffered a data breach resulting in the loss of 150 million personal records. In other words, just another day at the office in the world of cybersecurity.

21. To cite just one example, the Internet lacks a true human identity layer in its computing stack. Today, 65 to 80 percent of all data breaches are caused by stolen or forged identities. In my humble opinion, focus on identity verification twenty years ago would have greatly reduced the number of identity-related hacks today.

22. Mike Allen, "'Deepfake' Danger," Axios AM, accessed April 26, 2018, https://www.axios.com/newsletters/axios-am-491bfbad-ca22-47f1-93c7-e6ad5d96157d.html?chunk=5#story5.

Chapter Two

1. George Dyson, *Darwin among the Machines: The Evolution of Global Intelligence* (New York: Basic Books, 2012).

2. Yann LeCun, *Unsupervised Learning* (New York: New York University, March 8, 2016), https://cilvr.nyu.edu/lib/exe/fetch.php?media=deeplearning:2016:lecun-20160308-unssupervised-learning-nyu.pdf.

3. Also known as overfitting. When analysis of data overfits, it conforms too rigidly to the specific pattern of the data at hand, rendering the analysis less likely to process new data sets effectively. When analysis of data underfits, little if any underlying pattern within the data is discovered.

4. Robin, "History of Artificial Intelligence," Artificial Intelligence, November 24, 2009, http://intelligence.worldofcomputing.net/ai-introduction/history-of-artificial-intelligence.html#.WsLMiExFw2w.

5. James Kennedy, Russel Eberhart, and Yuhui Shi, *Swarm Intelligence* (San Francisco: Kaufmann, 2001).

6. Murray Shanahan, *The Technology Singularity* (Cambridge, MA: MIT Books, 2015), 210–12. This book, one of my personal favorites in the AI field, has a fascinating description of the paper clip maximizer problem.

7. James Barrat, *Our Final Invention: Artificial Intelligence and the End of the Human Era* (New York: Thomas Dunne Books, 2013), 60.

8. Catherine Clifford, "Google CEO: A.I. Is More Important than Fire or Electricity," CNBC, February 1, 2018, https://www.cnbc.com/2018/02/01/google-ceo-sundar-pichai-ai-is-more-important-than-fire-electricity.html.

Chapter Three

1. Christianna Reedy, "Kurzweil Claims That the Singularity Will Happen by 2045," *Futurism*, October 5, 2017, https://futurism.com/kurzweil-claims-that-the-singularity-will-happen-by-2045/.

2. L. Mastin, "Singularities," Physics of the Universe, October 2009, https://www.physicsoftheuniverse.com/topics_blackholes_singularities.html.

3. Socrates, "When Vernor Vinge Coined the Technological Singularity," *Singularity* (blog), May 14, 2012, https://www.singularityweblog.com/when-vernor-vinge-coined-the-technological-singularity/.

4. April 24, 2018.

5. "Kevin Kelly Quotes," AZ Quotes, accessed October 25, 2018, https://www.azquotes.com/author/7863-Kevin_Kelly.

6. Upton Sinclair, in his book *I, Candidate for Governor: And How I Got Licked*, 1935.

7. Tony Bradley, "Facebook AI Creates Its Own Language in Creepy Preview of Our Potential Future," *Forbes*, July 31, 2017, https://www.forbes.com/sites/tonybradley/2017/07/31/facebook-ai-creates-its-own-language-in-creepy-preview-of-our-potential-future/#2462f3f3292c.

8. Joel Lehman, et al., "The Surprising Creativity of Digital Evolution: A Collection of Anecdotes from the Evolutionary Computation and Artificial Life Research Communities," arXiv, March 29, 2018.

9. *Fitness* in cognitive science is the degree to which an AI fits into its problem and solution set. It is the chief performance metric of algorithms and neural networks.

10. Paul, "The Singularity Is Near: How Kurzweil's Predictions Are Faring," Antropy: Ecommerce Experts, January 29, 2017, https://www.antropy.co.uk/blog/the-singularity-is-near-how-kurzweils-predictions-are-faring/.

11. One example of real-world inertia: The first title I proposed for this book was @ *Lightspeed*. A nonstarter, my publisher explained, because various online systems can't handle the ampersand in a book title. Maybe it's just me, but I took this as an omen. Yes, the world of technology is racing ahead at warp speed. Yes, machine systems are getting super smart. But ampersands can still foul up online retail systems? Integrating new technology into the real world is always harder and slower than you think.

12. The show was *Cycling through China*, which aired on the Disney Channel in the United States and on CCTV in China.

13. Emil Protalinski, "Microsoft Reports $23.6 Billion in Q3 2017 Revenue: Azure up 93%, Surface Down 26%, and Windows Up 5%," Venture Beat, April 27, 2017, https://venturebeat.com/2017/04/27/microsoft-reports-23-6-billion-in-q3-2017-revenue-azure-up-93-surface-down-26-and-windows-up-5/.

14. Garson, "The Creator Has an Inordinate Fondness for Beetles," Quote Investigator, June 23, 2010, https://quoteinvestigator.com/2010/06/23/beetles/.

15. Chris Williams, *The Register*, March 19, 2015. See https://www.theregister.co.uk/2015/03/19/andrew_ng_baidu_ai/.

16. Catherine Clifford, "Mark Cuban: The World's First Trillionaire Will Be an Artificial Intelligence Entrepreneur," CNBC, March 13, 2017, https://www.cnbc.com/2017/03/13/mark-cuban-the-worlds-first-trillionaire-will-be-an-ai-entrepreneur.html.

17. Bloomberg, "This Chinese Facial Recognition Surveillance Company Is Now the World's Most Valuable AI Startup," *Fortune*, April 9, 2018, http://fortune.com/2018/04/09/sensetime-alibaba-ai-startup-600-million/.

18. I regard entrepreneur and Stanford professor Andrew Ng as the best AI teacher in the world. I believe he is still a bit trapped deep in the forest, but his views are always smart and insightful. I strongly recommend watching his lectures, starting with his "Introduction to O2O," YouTube, September 23, 2015, 2:40, https://www.youtube.com/watch?v=ZFnj2HMnHW0, which focuses on the issue of the impact of AI on various industries.

Chapter Four

1. Laura Tyson and Lenny Mendonca, "No Worker Left Behind," *Gulf Times*, April 17, 2018, http://www.gulf-times.com/story/589418/No-worker-left-behind.

2. Matt McFarland, "Uber Self-Driving Trucks Are Now Hauling Freight," CNN Tech, March 7, 2018, https://money.cnn.com/2018/03/07/technology/uber-trucks-autonomous/index.html.

3. David H. Freedman, "Self-Driving Trucks," *MIT Technology Review*, March/April 2017, https://www.technologyreview.com/s/603493/10-breakthrough-technologies-2017-self-driving-trucks/.

4. Alan Ohnsman, "Quanergy Ramps Up Low-Cost LiDAR Production as Laser Vision Battle Intensifies," *Forbes*, December 20, 2017, https://www.forbes.com/sites/alanohnsman/2017/12/20/quanergy-ramps-up-low-cost-lidar-production-as-laser-vision-battle-intensifies/#55bf1d59459b.

5. Other potential canaries: body-scanning systems in health care, legal research for law firms, robotic night watchmen in factories, and quite a number of others. The trucking industry is just one of many in AI's cross-hairs.

6. The Jubitz (jubitz.com) Truck Stop on North Vancouver Ave. in Portland, some truckers say, is the best truck stop in America. There is only one Jubitz truck stop, operating at the same site for more than sixty years.

7. "Truck Driver Salaries in the United States," Indeed, last updated September 2, 2018, https://www.indeed.com/salaries/Truck-Driver-Salaries.

8. Anita Balakrishnan, "Self-Driving Cars Could Cost America's Professional Drivers Up to 25,000 Jobs a Month, Goldman Sachs Says," CNBC, May 22, 2017, https://www.cnbc.com/2017/05/22/goldman-sachs-analysis-of-autonomous-vehicle-job-loss.html.

9. Nanette Byrnes, "Goldman Sachs Embraces Automation, Leaving Many Behind," *MIT Technology Review*, May/June 2017.

10. *Goldisox* is a slightly irreverent term for the large investment firm known as Goldman Sachs.

11. Steven Sheer, Reuters, May 16, 2018. See https://www.reuters.com/article/us-israel-tech-intel-mobileye-exclusive/exclusive-intels-mobileye-gets-self-driving-tech-deal-for-8-million-cars-idUSKCN1II0K7.

Chapter Five

1. Disclosure: I served as Northwest Academy's chair of the board of trustees for four years, 2000–2004. I currently have no affiliation with the school, other than being a supporter.

2. This quote has been classified by the Library of Congress as "unverified," but was first attributed to Franklin by the *Daily Evening Transcript* (Boston, MA) on February 16, 1849, and has been attributed to Franklin many times since.

3. Deviant Threads, Facebook, accessed October 26, 2018, https://www.face book.com/deviantthreads/.

4. Mohammad Hassan Falakmasir, et al., "Spectral Bayesian Knowledge Tracing," *Proceedings of the Eighth International Conference on Educational Data Mining* (June 2015): 360–63.

5. Chris Piech, et al., "Deep Knowledge Tracing," *Proceedings of the Twenty-ninth Conference on Neural Information Processing Systems*, Montreal, Canada, 2015, https:// stanford.edu/~cpiech/bio/papers/deepKnowledgeTracing.pdf.

6. iTalk2Learn, accessed August 14, 2018, http://www.italk2learn.eu/.

7. "Synaptic Plasticity," Wikipedia, last updated June 20, 2018, https:// en.wikipedia.org/wiki/Synaptic_plasticity.

8. See https://enterprise.microsoft.com/en-us/customer-story/industries/process -manufacturing-and-resources/land-o-lakes/.

9. See "V-Model," Wikipedia, last updated October 12, 2018, https:// en.wikipedia.org/wiki/V-Model. The V-Model is a data-management method that weights user ideas and preferences heavily. It supports (human) product manager efforts designed to answer two questions: Are we building the right thing? and, Are we building it right?

10. William Pang, "The Common High-School Tool That's Banned in College," *Atlantic*, December 22, 2016, https://www.theatlantic.com/education/ar chive/2016/12/the-conundrum-of-calculators-in-the-classroom/493961/.

11. For an exploration of both sides of the debate in educational circles about the role and value of technology, see Aaron Mak, "Facebook Suspends 200 Apps for Suspicious Data Use," Slate, May 13, 2018, https://slate.com/technology/2018/05/ facebook-suspends-200-apps-suspicious-data-use-cambridge-analytica-scandal.html.

Chapter Six

1. In my humble opinion. IMHO is one of the most venerable social net-speak acronyms, dating back to the early 1990s.

2. Google, transitive verb; in this book, to use a search engine to find information on the Internet, whether the engine is Google or, what I nearly always use, Microsoft's Bing.

3. David E. Lilienthal, *The Journals of David E. Lilienthal*, vol. 2, *The Atomic Energy Years 1945–1950* (New York City: Harper & Row, 1964).

4. David Meyer, "Robots May Steal as Many as 800 Million Jobs in the Next 13 Years," *Fortune*, November 29, 2017, http://fortune.com/2017/11/29/robots-automa tion-replace-jobs-mckinsey-report-800-million/.

5. See Mark Weinberger, *Business Insider*, March 25, 2018: https://www.busines sinsider.com/steve-mnuchin-automation-ai-2017-3/.

6. See Peter S. Goodman, "Capitalism Has a Problem. Is Free Money the Answer?" *New York Times*, November 15, 2017, https://www.nytimes.com/2017/11/15/

business/dealbook/universal-basic-income.html, for a report on the worldwide movement toward a guaranteed income for everyone.

7. In this context, two interesting and opposing worldviews are emerging: the AI utopians and the AI dystopians.

Chapter Seven

1. *Old Men* is a colloquial Chinese term for the leaders of the PRC. It dates back to the late twentieth century, when the leaders of the PRC were all literally old men, veterans of the Long March and other epic battles of the Chinese Communist Party prior to the 1949 revolution.

2. These military experts include, notably, David O. Work, former secretary of defense under Obama and a thought leader in AI systems for military defense. See also the whole roster of experts at the Center for a New American Security (CNAS).

3. David O. Work is careful to clarify that, at this time, China is only a "potential AI adversary." He and other top military AI experts believe it is too early to say for certain whether China will be friend or foe in AI, but he also advocates planning and acting as if China were an AI enemy. "It is like a political campaign," Work has been known to say. "You should always run as if you are losing."

4. Elsa Kania, "Technological Entanglement? Artificial Intelligence in the U.S.–China Relationship," Jamestown Foundation, December 22, 2017, https://jamestown.org/program/technological-entanglement-artificial-intelligence-u-s-china-relationship/.

5. "China's New Generation of Artificial Intelligence Development Plan," Foundation for Law and International Affairs, July 30, 2017, https://flia.org/notice-state-council-issuing-new-generation-artificial-intelligence-development-plan/.

6. "President Xi Jinping's Top 10 Quotes from Davos 2017," *Telegraph*, January 24, 2017, https://www.telegraph.co.uk/news/world/china-watch/business/president-xi-davos-top-quotes/.

7. Alex W. Palmer, "The Case of Hong Kong's Missing Booksellers," *New York Times Magazine*, April 3, 2018, https://www.nytimes.com/2018/04/03/magazine/the-case-of-hong-kongs-missing-booksellers.html.

8. Tyler Durden, "Google Employees Revolt, Refuse to Work on Clandestine AI Drone Project for the Pentagon," Zero Hedge, May 14, 2018, https://www.zerohedge.com/news/2018-05-14/google-employees-revolt-refuse-work-clandestine-ai-drone-project-pentagon.

Chapter Eight

1. Many cybersecurity writers would use the term *insecure* in this sentence, and while it now might begin to make sense in the context of the feelings of robots and other devices, I have always preferred *nonsecure* or *unsecure*.

2. Charles Jennings, "From Armadillos to Monkeys: Charles Jennings at TEDx-Bend," June 15, 2012, Bend, OR, TED video, 16:16, https://www.youtube.com/watch?v=RJJUtLJRfgY.

3. I am not referring here to the "stateful vs. stateless" API debate, just to the overall status of a device, at the off/on level.

4. Full disclosure: I've worked with both these companies for several decades. I have never had a job at either one, but I have partnered with both. One was an investor in two of my start-ups; the other was the most important customer for a company I started. One of them was directly responsible for the biggest payday of my life; the other, for my biggest financial loss. I've crossed swords with them many a time, but I trust them to play fair—mostly.

5. Catherine Clifford, "Mark Cuban: The World's First Trillionaire Will Be an Artificial Intelligence Entrepreneur," CNBC, March 13, 2017, https://www.cnbc.com/2017/03/13/mark-cuban-the-worlds-first-trillionaire-will-be-an-ai-entrepreneur.html.

6. The moment I finished typing this paragraph, I could visualize the troll arrows flying in from people who've been in the cybersecurity field maybe twenty minutes. *How dare you let Intel off the hook for its huge security flaws?* That's fine. One of the better things about getting old is that, when it comes to speaking and writing your own subjective truth, you no longer give a damn if it rattles the cages of morons.

7. PYMNTS, "Banks and the Blockchain Scramble," PYMNTS.com, August 29, 2018, https://www.pymnts.com/news/b2b-payments/2018/blockchain-distributed-ledger-international-regulations/.

8. Sean Williams, "20 Real-World Uses for Blockchain Technology," Motley Fool, April 11, 2018, https://www.fool.com/investing/2018/04/11/20-real-world-uses-for-blockchain-technology.aspx.

9. I say this with my cyberpunk cap on, sideways.

10. Nakamoto may have been a lone hacker from Japan, a team of crypto nerds from Berkeley, or any number of other guesses. Nakamoto, whoever they are, has chosen to remain fully and completely anonymous.

11. "The Eight Most Common Causes of Data Breaches," Dark Reading, May 22, 2013, https://www.darkreading.com/attacks-breaches/the-eight-most-common-causes-of-data-breaches/d/d-id/1139795.

12. *Verizon's 2017 Data Breach Investigations Report: Executive Summary* (New York: Verizon, 2017), http://www.verizonenterprise.com/resources/reports/rp_DBIR_2017_Report_en_xg.pdf; FIDO stat.

13. United States of America v. Viktor Borisovich Netyksho, et al. (2018), 18 U.S.C. §§ 2, 371, 1030,1028A, 1956, and 3551 et seq.

14. Tor is an open network designed to provide full anonymity when browsing through the use of circuitous routing protocols. It is used often in deep web and dark web networking.

15. See Swan Island Networks, www.swanisland.net

16. "Welcome to UL," UL, 2018, https://www.ul.com/aboutul/history/.

17. "Welcome to UL."

Chapter Nine

1. European Union press release, April 25, 2018, http://europa.eu/rapid/press-release_IP-18-3362_en.htm.

2. "About," Vector Institute, accessed August 5, 2018, https://vectorinstitute.ai/.

3. Mark Minevich, "These Seven Countries Are in a Race to Rule the World with AI," *Forbes*, December 5, 2017, https://www.forbes.com/sites/forbestechcouncil/2017/12/05/these-seven-countries-are-in-a-race-to-rule-the-world-with-ai/#52e516234c24.

4. Jon Thompson, Jennifer Sun, Richard Möller, Mathias Sintorn, and Geoff Huston, *Akamai's State of the Internet Q1 2017 Report*, vol. 10, no. 1, ed. David Belson (Cambridge, MA: Akamai, 2017), https://content.akamai.com/gl-en-pg9135-q1-soti-connectivity.html.

5. This DoD agency funded all early autonomous-vehicle research, which in turn funded many AI projects in computer vision and other AI-driven technologies.

6. Officially, on DC maps, the Lombardy is on I Street, but locally it is most often known as Eye Street, in part because of the row of optometrist clinics between the Lombardy and the White House.

7. Software delivered over the web and sold as a subscription.

8. The ODNI under George W. Bush led a thirty-agency "sensitive-information-sharing" project, Last Mile Intelligence Technologies (LMIT). Swan Island Networks provided the information-sharing platform for this program.

9. "2005 Fed 100: E to L," Federal Computing Weekly, March 21, 2005, https://fcw.com/Articles/2005/03/21/2005-Fed-100-E-to-L.aspx?Page=2.

10. After working with DC govie types, this deep-state nonsense that is creating such a buzz these days strikes me as laughable. My biggest takeaway after switching from Silicon Valley to DC: Behind its Oz curtains, our federal government is mostly string, duct tape, and bubblegum.

11. IMHO, the most honest and scientifically grounded federal contractor is Lockheed Martin. This opinion is 100 percent anecdotal, but in my dealings with a dozen or so big-name federal contractors, Lockheed Martin was the best in terms of both honest dealings and respect for what Internet experts could bring to their efforts.

12. I have edited this statement a bit for cleaner English but have not changed the AISG's core message.

13. *60 Minutes*, season 50, episode 39, "Singapore Stakes/Secret Weapon/JR," aired June 10, 2018, on CBS.

14. See my book with Lori Fena, *The Hundredth Window: Protecting Your Privacy and Security on the Internet* (New York: Free Press, 2000).

15. KYC systems are an upgrade of earlier identity-management systems and are a vital part of contemporary cybersecurity design.

16. This line is a paraphrase of Bob Dylan's "A Hard Rain's a-Gonna Fall" from *Freewheelin' Bob Dylan*, released in 1962.

Chapter Ten

1. Louis Columbus, "Roundup of Machine Learning Forecast and Market Estimates, 2018," *Forbes*, February 18, 2018, https://www.forbes.com/sites/louiscolumbus/2018/02/18/roundup-of-machine-learning-forecasts-and-market-estimates-2018/#e6fd2e52225c.

2. James McCormick, "Predictions 2017: Artificial Intelligence Will Drive the Insights Revolution," Forrester, November 2, 2016, https://go.forrester.com/wp-content/uploads/Forrester_Predictions_2017_-Artificial_Intelligence_Will_Drive_The_Insights_Revolution.pdf.

3. Daniel Faggella, "Valuing the Artificial Intelligence Market, Graphs and Predictions," TechEmergence, September 16, 2018, https://www.techemergence.com/valuing-the-artificial-intelligence-market-graphs-and-predictions/.

4. Eric Schmidt, former CEO of Google and architect of Alphabet.

5. Disclosure: I attended UC Berkeley.

6. The description of Fluidity's product came from Scott Parzynski during an interview with the author. For more information about this innovative company, see https://fluidity.tech/.

7. Selena Larson, "Every Single Yahoo Account Was Hacked—3 Billion in All," CNN, October 4, 2017, https://money.cnn.com/2017/10/03/technology/business/yahoo-breach-3-billion-accounts/index.html.

8. For a good technical introduction to Deep Patient and a very interesting read overall, see Will Knight, "The Dark Secret at the Heart of AI," MIT Technology Review, April 11, 2017, https://www.technologyreview.com/s/604087/the-dark-secret-at-the-heart-of-ai/.

9. Raffi Khatchadourian, "The Doomsday Invention," *New Yorker*, November 23, 2015, https://www.newyorker.com/magazine/2015/11/23/doomsday-invention-artificial-intelligence-nick-bostrom.

10. Abhi Arunachalam, "How Deep Is Your Learning?" *Forbes*, March 29, 2016, https://www.forbes.com/sites/valleyvoices/2016/03/29/how-deep-is-your-learning/#5ae39b162e6e.

11. In my humble, 100 percent subjective opinion.

12. "Salesforce.com, Inc. (CRM) CEO Marc Benioff on Q1 2019 Results—Earnings Call Transcript," Seeking Alpha, May 29, 2018, https://seekingalpha.com/article/4177957-salesforce-com-inc-crm-ceo-marc-benioff-q1-2019-results-earnings-call-transcript?page=2.

13. PreciBake, 2018, http://www.precibake.com/index.html.

14. For a summary of recent AI market growth predictions, see Faggella, "Valuing the Artificial Intelligence Market."

15. NIST all technology and scientific standards in the United States.

16. My "companies started" numbers are skewed significantly because I worked in the film industry as an independent producer for a decade, and each film, by tradition, was always a new company. As a line producer, I was often the person who started them.

17. This white paper from the HRPA is entitled *A New Age of Opportunities—What Does Artificial Intelligence Mean for HR Professionals*. It is available to HRPA members.

Chapter Eleven

1. Dan Robitzski, "Artificial Intelligence Writes Bad Poems Just Like an Angsty Teen," *Futurism*, April 26, 2018, https://futurism.com/artificial-intelligence-bad-poems/.

2. Trashcan Joe, https://www.facebook.com/Trashcan-Joe-174119859271348/.

3. The question of AI randomness was raised by Octavo at NWA (see chapter 5). I've been struggling with it ever since he brought it up. At a minimum, it is a most elegant question.

4. A substrate in both biology and computer science is the surface on which an organism grows.

5. See the groundbreaking research by Professor John Marzluff at "Environmental and Forest Sciences, John Marzluff, Professor," College of the Environment, University of Washington, 2018, https://environment.uw.edu/faculty/john-marzluff/.

6. There are many strains of the transhumanism movement, which advocates for combining human biology with advanced technology as the next step in human evolution. If you are interested in this aspect of AI, I recommend the following Boolean search: "Gary Wolf + Kevin Kelly + transhumanism."

7. Billy Collins, *Aimless Love*, Random House, 2013. http://www.randomhouse.com/highschool/catalog/display.pperl?isbn=9780679644057&view=print.

8. Peter Haas, "The Real Reason to Be Afraid of Artificial Intelligence," December 15, 2017, at Portland, ME, TED video, 12:37, https://www.youtube.com/watch?v=TRzBk_KuIaM.

9. For more on the context of this quote and other thoughts of Eliot on writing poetry, see this excellent essay on Eliot on the Poetry Foundation website: https://www.poetryfoundation.org/poets/t-s-eliot.

Chapter Twelve

1. You contemporary cybersecurity pros who scoff at the claim that systems could today be much safer than they are if proper measures had been taken in the early 1990s, consider this: The Internet has no trusted identity layer. Had one been deployed years ago with a common set of "roots of trust," many of today's problems would be solved. And think how much stronger security would be if whole ecosystems had dynamic hardware and software white listing as a matter of course. These are just two specific measures we could have taken, but there could have been many more, had we the will.

I've had this debate before, so sorry to the rest of you who are not cybersecurity professionals. But let me just say: Don't let anyone tell you that safety, security, and privacy protection designed into technology from day 1 would not make a huge difference.

2. See Vika Krakovna, "Highlights from Asilomar Workshop on Beneficial AI," filmed January 6–8, 2017, Future of Life Institute, Asilomar, CA, 14:22, https://www.youtube.com/watch?v=EIx3BbwPl_g, or just search YouTube for "Asilomar AI conference."

Appendix

1. Nervana was a company of forty some employees acquired by Intel for approximately four hundred million dollars, basically because its innovative, low-level AI architecture worked in the lab. Mobileye was an Israeli company.

Bibliography

60 Minutes. Season 50, episode 39, "Singapore Stakes/Secret Weapon/JR." Aired June 10, 2018, on CBS.

"2005 Fed 100: E to L." Federal Computing Weekly. March 21, 2005. https://fcw.com/Articles/2005/03/21/2005-Fed-100-E-to-L.aspx?Page=2.

"About." Vector Institute. Accessed August 5, 2018. https://vectorinstitute.ai/.

Allen, Mike. "'Deepfake' Danger." Axios AM. Accessed April 26, 2018. https://www.axios.com/newsletters/axios-am-491bfbad-ca22-47f1-93c7-e6ad5d96157d.html?chunk=5#story5.

Aoun, Joseph E. *Robot-Proof: Higher Education in the Age of Artificial Intelligence*. Cambridge, MA: MIT Press, 2017.

Arunachalam, Abhi. "How Deep Is Your Learning?" *Forbes*. March 29, 2016. https://www.forbes.com/sites/valleyvoices/2016/03/29/how-deep-is-your-learning/#5ae39b162e6e.

Balakrishnan, Anita. "Self-Driving Cars Could Cost America's Professional Drivers Up to 25,000 Jobs a Month, Goldman Sachs Says." CNBC. May 22, 2017. https://www.cnbc.com/2017/05/22/goldman-sachs-analysis-of-autonomous-vehicle-job-loss.html.

Barrat, James. *Our Final Invention: Artificial Intelligence and the End of the Human Era*. New York: Thomas Dunne Books, 2013.

Biltz, Michael. "'Citizen AI': Teaching Artificial Intelligence to Act Responsibly." Venture Beat. March 31, 2018. https://venturebeat.com/2018/03/31/citizen-ai-teaching-artificial-intelligence-to-act-responsibly/.

Bloomberg. "This Chinese Facial Recognition Surveillance Company Is Now the World's Most Valuable AI Startup." *Fortune*. April 9, 2018. http://fortune.com/2018/04/09/sensetime-alibaba-ai-startup-600-million/.

Bolstrum, Nick. *Superintelligence: Paths, Dangers, Strategies*. Oxford: Oxford University Press, 2017.

Bradley, Tony. "Facebook AI Creates Its Own Language in Creepy Preview of Our Potential Future." *Forbes*. July 31, 2017. https://www.forbes.com/sites/tonybradley/2017/07/31/facebook-ai-creates-its-own-language-in-creepy-preview-of-our-potential-future/#2462f3f3292c.

Buckley, Tim, and Simon Nicholas. *China's Global Renewable Energy Expansion*. Cleveland, OH: Institute for Energy Economics and Financial Analysis, January 2017. http://ieefa.org/wp-content/uploads/2017/01/Chinas-Global-Renewable-Energy-Expansion_January-2017.pdf.

Byrnes, Nanette. "Goldman Sachs Embraces Automation, Leaving Many Behind." *MIT Technology Review*. May/June 2017.

Chardin, Pierre Teilhard de. *The Phenomenon of Man*. London: Wm. Collins Sons, 1955.

"China's New Generation of Artificial Intelligence Development Plan." Foundation for Law and International Affairs. July 30, 2017. https://flia.org/notice-state-council-issuing-new-generation-artificial-intelligence-development-plan/.

Christian, Brian, and Tom Griffiths. *Algorithms to Live By: The Computer Science of Human Decisions*. New York: Henry Holt, 2016.

Clifford, Catherine. "Google CEO: A.I. Is More Important than Fire or Electricity." CNBC. February 1, 2018. https://www.cnbc.com/2018/02/01/google-ceo-sundar-pichai-ai-is-more-important-than-fire-electricity.html.

———. "Mark Cuban: The World's First Trillionaire Will Be an Artificial Intelligence Entrepreneur." CNBC. March 13, 2017. https://www.cnbc.com/2017/03/13/mark-cuban-the-worlds-first-trillionaire-will-be-an-ai-entrepreneur.html.

Columbus, Louis. "Roundup of Machine Learning Forecast and Market Estimates, 2018." *Forbes*. February 18, 2018. https://www.forbes.com/sites/louiscolumbus/2018/02/18/roundup-of-machine-learning-forecasts-and-market-estimates-2018/#1f2c7a442225.

Crumpton, Henry A. *The Art of Intelligence: Lessons from a Life in the CIA's Clandestine Service*. New York: Penguin Books, 2012.

Deviant Threads. Facebook. Accessed October 26, 2018. https://www.facebook.com/deviantthreads/.

Domingos, Pedro. *The Master Algorithm: How the Quest for the Ultimate Learning Machine Will Remake Our World*. New York: Penguin Books, 2015.

Durden, Tyler. "Google Employees Revolt, Refuse to Work on Clandestine AI Drone Project for the Pentagon." Zero Hedge. May 14, 2018. https://www.zerohedge.com/news/2018-05-14/google-employees-revolt-refuse-work-clandestine-ai-drone-project-pentagon.

Dyson, George. *Darwin among the Machines: The Evolution of Global Intelligence*. New York: Basic Books, 2012.

"The Eight Most Common Causes of Data Breaches." Dark Reading. May 22, 2013. https://www.darkreading.com/attacks-breaches/the-eight-most-common-causes-of-data-breaches/d/d-id/1139795.

Ellis, David. *Deus Ex Machina Sapiens: The Emergence of Machine Intelligence*. Detroit, MI: Elysian Detroit, 2011.

"Environmental and Forest Sciences, John Marzluff, Professor." College of the Environment, University of Washington. 2018. https://environment.uw.edu/faculty/john-marzluff/.

Faggella, David. "(All) Elon Musk Artificial Intelligence Quotes—A Catalogue of His Statements." TechEmergence. June 18, 2017. https://www.techemergence.com/elon-musk-on-the-dangers-of-ai-a-catalogue-of-his-statements/.

———. "Valuing the Artificial Intelligence Market, Graphs and Predictions." TechEmergence. September 16, 2018. https://www.techemergence.com/valuing-the-artificial-intelligence-market-graphs-and-predictions/.

Falakmasir, Mohammad Hassan, Michael Yudelson, Steve Ritter, and Ken Koedinger. "Spectral Bayesian Knowledge Tracing." *Proceedings of the Eighth International Conference on Educational Data Mining* (June 2015): 360–63.

Freedman, David H. "Self-Driving Trucks." *MIT Technology Review*. March/April 2017. https://www.technologyreview.com/s/603493/10-breakthrough-technologies-2017-self-driving-trucks/.

The Future of Life Institute. https://futureoflife.org/.

Gall, Richard. "Five Polarizing Quotes from Stephen Hawking on Artificial Intelligence." Packt Hub. March 15, 2018. https://hub.packtpub.com/stephen-hawking-artificial-intelligence-quotes/.

Galloway, Scott. *The Four: The Hidden DNA of Amazon, Apple, Facebook, and Google*. New York: Portfolio/Penguin, 2018.

Garson. "The Creator Has an Inordinate Fondness for Beetles." Quote Investigator. June 23, 2010. https://quoteinvestigator.com/2010/06/23/beetles/.

George Washington University Hospital. "Robotic Colorectal Program Named an Epicenter." 2018. https://www.gwhospital.com/conditions-services/robotic-surgery/robotic-colorectal-surgery.

Gershgorn, Dave. "Human-Like: Facebook Is Using Our Data to Build 'The World's Best' Artificial Intelligence Lab." *Popular Science*. August 20, 2016.

Goodman, Peter S. "Capitalism Has a Problem. Is Free Money the Answer?" *New York Times*, November 15, 2017. https://www.nytimes.com/2017/11/15/business/dealbook/universal-basic-income.html.

Greenemeier, Larry. "How NASA's Search for ET Relies on Advanced AI." *Scientific American*. December 18, 2017. https://www.scientificamerican.com/article/how-nasas-search-for-et-relies-on-advanced-ai/.

Haas, Peter. "The Real Reason to Be Afraid of Artificial Intelligence." December 15, 2017, Portland, ME. TED video, 12:37. https://www.youtube.com/watch?v=TRzBk_KuIaM.

Hern, Alex. "'Partnership on AI' Formed by Google, Facebook, Amazon, IBM and Microsoft." *Guardian*, September 28, 2016. https://www.theguardian.com/technology/2016/sep/28/google-facebook-amazon-ibm-microsoft-partnership-on-ai-tech-firms.

Husain, Amir. *The Sentient Machine: Coming Age of Artificial Intelligence*. New York: Scribner, 2017.

iTalk2Learn. Accessed August 14, 2018. http://www.italk2learn.eu/.

Jennings, Charles. "From Armadillos to Monkeys: Charles Jennings at TEDx-Bend." June 15, 2012, Bend, OR. TED video, 16:16. https://www.youtube.com/watch?v=RJJUtLJRfgY.

Jennings, Charles, and Lori Fena. *The Hundredth Window: Protecting Your Privacy and Security on the Internet*. New York: Free Press, 2000.

Kania, Elsa. "Technological Entanglement? Artificial Intelligence in the U.S.–China Relationship." Jamestown Foundation. December 22, 2017. https://jamestown.org/program/technological-entanglement-artificial-intelligence-u-s-china-relationship/.

Kasparov, Gary. *Deep Thinking: Where Machine Intelligence Ends and Human Creativity Begins*. New York: Public Affairs, 2017.

Kelly, Kevin. *The Inevitable: Understanding the 12 Technological Forces That Will Shape Our Future*. New York: Viking, 2016.

———. *Out of Control: The New Biology of Machines, Social Systems and the Economic World*. New York: Addison-Wesley, 1994.

Kennedy, James, Russell C. Eberhart, and Yuhui Shi. *Swarm Intelligence*. San Francisco: Kaufmann, 2001.

"Kevin Kelly Quotes." AZ Quotes. Accessed October 25, 2018. https://www.azquotes.com/author/7863-Kevin_Kelly.

Khatchadourian, Raffi. "The Doomsday Invention." *New Yorker*. November 23, 2015. https://www.newyorker.com/magazine/2015/11/23/doomsday-invention-artificial-intelligence-nick-bostrom.

Kiersz, Andy. "A Seemingly Benign Viral Game about Paperclips Reveals Why AI Could Be a Huge Danger to Humanity." *Business Insider*. October 11, 2017. https://www.businessinsider.com/paper-clip-game-superintelligence-theory.

Knight, Will. "The Dark Secret at the Heart of AI." *MIT Technology Review*. April 11, 2017. https://www.technologyreview.com/s/604087/the-dark-secret-at-the-heart-of-ai/.

Krakovna, Vika. "Highlights from Asilomar Workshop on Beneficial AI." Filmed January 6–8, 2017, Future of Life Institute, Asilomar, CA, 14:22. https://www.youtube.com/watch?v=EIx3BbwPl_g.

Larson, Selena. "Every Single Yahoo Account Was Hacked—3 Billion in All." CNN. October 4, 2017. http://money.cnn.com/2017/10/03/technology/business/yahoo-breach-3-billion-accounts/index.html.

LeCun, Yann. *Unsupervised Learning*. New York: New York University, March 2016. https://cilvr.nyu.edu/lib/exe/fetch.php?media=deeplearning:2016:lecun-20160308-unssupervised-learning-nyu.pdf.

Lee, Edward Ashford. *Plato and the Nerd: The Creative Partnership of Humans and Technology*. Cambridge, MA: MIT Press, 2017.

Lehman, Joel, et al. "The Surprising Creativity of Digital Evolution: A Collection of Anecdotes from the Evolutionary Computation and Artificial Life Research Communities." arXiv. March 29, 2018.

Lilienthal, David E. *The Journals of David E. Lilienthal*, vol. 2: *The Atomic Energy Years 1945–1950*. New York City: Harper & Row, 1964.

Mak, Aaron. "Facebook Suspends 200 Apps for Suspicious Data Use." Slate. May 13, 2018. https://slate.com/technology/2018/05/facebook-suspends-200-apps-suspicious-data-use-cambridge-analytica-scandal.html.

———. "Google Taught AI How to Program More AI." Slate. October 16, 2017. http://www.slate.com/blogs/future_tense/2017/10/16/google_created_machine_learning_software_that_can_program_machine_learning.html.

Mastin, L. "Singularities." Physics of the Universe. October 2009. https://www.physicsoftheuniverse.com/topics_blackholes_singularities.html.

McCormick, James. "Predictions 2017: Artificial Intelligence Will Drive the Insights Revolution." Forrester. November 2, 2016. https://go.forrester.com/wp-content/uploads/Forrester_Predictions_2017_-Artificial_Intelligence_Will_Drive_The_Insights_Revolution.pdf.

McFarland, Matt. "Uber Self-Driving Trucks Are Now Hauling Freight." CNN Tech. March 7, 2018. https://money.cnn.com/2018/03/07/technology/uber-trucks-autonomous/index.html.

Meyer, David. "Robots May Steal as Many as 800 Million Jobs in the Next 13 Years." *Fortune*. November 29, 2017. http://fortune.com/2017/11/29/robots-automation-replace-jobs-mckinsey-report-800-million/.

Minevich, Mark. "These Seven Countries Are in a Race to Rule the World with AI." *Forbes*. December 5, 2017. https://www.forbes.com/sites/forbestechcouncil/2017/12/05/these-seven-countries-are-in-a-race-to-rule-the-world-with-ai/#52e516234c24.

Mlodinow, Leonard. *Elastic: Flexible Thinking in a Time of Change*. New York: Pantheon Books, 2018.

Ng, Andrew. "Introduction to O2O." YouTube, September 23, 2015, 2:40. https://www.youtube.com/watch?v=ZFnj2HMnHW0.

Ohnsman, Alan. "Quanergy Ramps Up Low-Cost LiDAR Production as Laser Vision Battle Intensifies." *Forbes*. December 20, 2017. https://www.forbes.com/sites/alanohnsman/2017/12/20/quanergy-ramps-up-low-cost-lidar-production-as-laser-vision-battle-intensifies/#55bf1d59459b.

Palmer, Alex W. "The Case of Hong Kong's Missing Booksellers." *New York Times Magazine*. April 3, 2018. https://www.nytimes.com/2018/04/03/magazine/the-case-of-hong-kongs-missing-booksellers.html.

Paul. "The Singularity Is Near: How Kurzweil's Predictions Are Faring." Antropy: Ecommerce Experts. January 29, 2017. https://www.antropy.co.uk/blog/the-singularity-is-near-how-kurzweils-predictions-are-faring/.

Piech, Chris, Jonathan Bassen, Jonathan Huang, Surya Ganguli, Mehran Sahami, Leonidas Guibas, and Jascha Sohl-Dickstein. *Proceedings of the Twenty-ninth Conference on Neural Information Processing Systems*. Montreal, Canada, 2015. https://stanford.edu/~cpiech/bio/papers/deepKnowledgeTracing.pdf.

PreciBake. 2018. http://www.precibake.com/index.html.

"President Xi Jinping's Top 10 Quotes from Davos 2017." *Telegraph*. January 24, 2017. https://www.telegraph.co.uk/news/world/china-watch/business/president-xi-davos-top-quotes/.

Protalinski, Emil. "Microsoft Reports $23.6 Billion in Q3 2017 Revenue: Azure up 93%, Surface Down 26%, and Windows Up 5%." Venture Beat. April 27, 2017. https://venturebeat.com/2017/04/27/microsoft-reports-23-6-billion-in-q3-2017-revenue-azure-up-93-surface-down-26-and-windows-up-5/.

PYMNTS. "Banks and the Blockchain Scramble." PYMNTS.com. August 29, 2018. https://www.pymnts.com/news/b2b-payments/2018/blockchain-distributed-ledger-international-regulations/.

Reedy, Christianna. "Kurzweil Claims That the Singularity Will Happen by 2045." *Futurism*. October 5, 2017. https://futurism.com/kurzweil-claims-that-the-singularity-will-happen-by-2045/.

Reese, Byron. *The Fourth Age: Smart Robots, Conscious Computers, and the Future of Humanity*. New York: Atria Books, 2018.

Robin. "History of Artificial Intelligence." Artificial Intelligence. November 24, 2009. http://intelligence.worldofcomputing.net/ai-introduction/history-of-artificial-intelligence.html#.WsLMiExFw2w.

Robitzski, Dan. "Artificial Intelligence Writes Bad Poems Just Like an Angsty Teen." *Futurism*. April 26, 2018. https://futurism.com/artificial-intelligence-bad-poems/.

"Salesforce.com, Inc. (CRM) CEO Marc Benioff on Q1 2019 Results—Earnings Call Transcript." Seeking Alpha. May 29, 2018. https://seekingalpha.com/article/4177957-salesforce-com-inc-crm-ceo-marc-benioff-q1-2019-results-earnings-call-transcript?page=2.

Shanahan, Murray. *The Technological Singularity*. Cambridge, MA: MIT Press, 2015.

Shead, Sam. "Google Billionaire Sergey Brin Urges Caution on AI Development." *Forbes*. April 28, 2018. https://www.forbes.com/sites/samshead/2018/04/28/google-billionaire-sergey-brin-urges-caution-on-ai-development/2/#28b99b2a2258.

Snooks, Graeme Donald. *The Dynamic Society: Exploring the Sources of Global Change*. London: Routledge, 1996.

Socrates. "When Vernor Vinge Coined the Technological Singularity." *Singularity* (blog). May 14, 2012. https://www.singularityweblog.com/when-vernor-vinge-coined-the-technological-singularity/.

"Synaptic Plasticity." Wikipedia. Last updated June 20, 2018. https://en.wikipedia.org/wiki/Synaptic_plasticity.

Tegmark, Max. *Life 3.0: Being Human in the Age of Artificial Intelligence*. New York: Alfred A. Knopf, 2017.

Thompson, Jon, Jennifer Sun, Richard Möller, Mathias Sintorn, and Geoff Huston. *Akamai's State of the Internet Q1 2017 Report*, vol. 10, no. 1. Edited by David Belson. Cambridge, MA: Akamai, 2017. https://content.akamai.com/gl-en-pg9135-q1-soti-connectivity.html.

Trashcan Joe. Accessed November 11, 2018. https://www.facebook.com/Trashcan-Joe-174119859271348/.

"Truck Driver Salaries in the United States." Indeed. Last updated September 2, 2018. https://www.indeed.com/salaries/Truck-Driver-Salaries.

Tyson, Laura, and Lenny Mendonca. "No Worker Left Behind." *Gulf Times*. April 17, 2018. http://www.gulf-times.com/story/589418/No-worker-left-behind.

United States of America v. Viktor Borisovich Netyksho, et al. 18 U.S.C. §§ 2, 371, 1030,1028A, 1956, and 3551 et seq., 2018.

Verizon's 2017 Data Breach Investigations Report: Executive Summary. New York: Verizon, 2017. http://www.verizonenterprise.com/resources/reports/rp_DBIR_2017_Report_en_xg.pdf.

"V-Model." Wikipedia. Last updated October 12, 2018. https://en.wikipedia.org/wiki/V-Model.

"Welcome to UL." UL. 2018. https://www.ul.com/aboutul/history/.

Williams, Sean. "20 Real-World Uses for Blockchain Technology." Motley Fool. April 11, 2018. https://www.fool.com/investing/2018/04/11/20-real-world-uses-for-blockchain-technology.aspx.

Index

~

About the Author

Charles Jennings is a serial entrepreneur, writer, and speaker who has been starting and running growth organizations for over 40 years. He was founder or CEO of three successful Internet companies launched in the 1990s. Jennings has written several books on technology, including the seminal work, *The Hundredth Window: Protecting Your Privacy and Security in the Age of the Internet* (2000), which was translated into five languages. Jennings has been a regular newspaper columnist (for the *Seattle Times* and others); from 2014–2017, Jennings served as CEO of NeuralEye—an AI company set up to transfer technology from Caltech/JPL to the commercial market. Jennings is an experienced and entertaining public speaker whose credits range from his TEDx talk, "From Armadillos to Monkeys," to a keynote at the UN 50th Anniversary Conference on the Declaration of Human Rights in Toulouse, France. Jennings is still an active keynoter on AI at conferences around the world. Jennings has long been a thought leader in Internet trust and security. He was a delegate to the Nobel Technology Summit in Oslo, and named by Federal Computing Week as one of the 100 Most Influential People in Government technology. He's a recipient of the prestigious lifetime achievement award of the Oregon Entrepreneurs Network, and was also the subject of a major feature story in *Wired* magazine (December 2005 issue).